Spirit of the Siskiyous

Substantial gifts from the following donors
helped make publication of this book possible.
The Oregon State University Press is grateful for their support.

❀ ❀ ❀

Crater Lake Natural History Association
Evergreen Federal Savings and Loan Association
Headwaters
Siskiyou Audubon Society
Siskiyou Regional Education Project

Spirit
of the
Siskiyous

❀❀❀

The Journals of a Mountain Naturalist

by
Mary Paetzel

❀❀❀

Edited by
Jacqueline Elliott and Lee Webb

Oregon State University Press
Corvallis

To Lee Webb and Jackie Elliott,

my good friends,
without whose untiring efforts
this book never would have been published

Cover photos by Lee Webb

The paper in this book meets the guidelines for permanence and durability
of the Committee on Production Guidelines for Book Longevity of the
Council on Library Resources and the minimum requirements of the
American National Standard for Permanence of Paper for Printed Library
Materials Z39.48-1984.

Library of Congress Cataloging-in-Publication Data
Paetzel, Mary.
   Spirit of the Siskiyous : the journals of a mountain naturalist / by Mary
  Paetzel : edited by Jacqueline Elliott and Lee Webb.
    p. cm.
  ISBN 0-87071-449-X (alk. paper)
  1. Natural history—Siskiyou Mountains (Calif. and Or.) 2. Paetzel, Mary.
  I. Elliott, Jacqueline. II. Webb, Lee. III. Title.
  QH105.5.S54P24 1998
  508.795'2—dc21   98-36704
                                            CIP

Oregon State University Press
101 Waldo Hall
Corvallis OR 97331-6407
541-737-3166 •fax 541-737-3170
www.osu.orst.edu/dept/press

Contents

❀ ❀ ❀

Foreword

⚘ ⚘ ⚘

Much of my life has followed roads unknown until I turned the next page in the atlas. By chance, I found a job as a wildlife biologist with the Siskiyou National Forest in 1975 and moved to Oregon from West Virginia. Shortly after my arrival in Grants Pass, an interesting thing happened which helped make the journey worthwhile and rewarding. I met Mary Paetzel: unique, independent, doing things her way, on her schedule (and the rest of the world can do as they please!).

Mary came into my life in 1975. An acquaintance of Mary's who worked for the Forest Service thought I would be interested in meeting a lady who was conducting independent botanical field work at various special places on the Siskiyou National Forest. I was interested, of course, and thus began our friendship. In the beginning of our relationship, I did sense Mary was a little wary; after all, I was one of those "damn government bureaucrats." Mary has never been the least bit shy about telling "bureaucrats" what's on her mind (and as public servants, we need to hear it, good or otherwise). She has told me how she felt about the Forest Service more times than I can remember.

Mary has two sides. The stories in this book display her quiet and sensitive side. Her outspoken and assertive side is featured in this foreword. Both aspects of Mary's personality spring from the same source—her love for the natural world.

I recall a day in 1980 when our Forest Supervisor came in from the field and related an unusual incident. He and the Galice District Ranger had been touring the district looking things over (both these folks had strong personalities and were used to giving "orders" to subordinates). On this trip they had met an older lady on Chrome Ridge, driving an old Volkswagen bus, and she had done all the talking. This lady had told them in colorful terms how she felt about the Forest Service's management and mismanagement of "her" national forest. These two "bureaucrats" had been impressed with the lady's spunk and willingness to let them know how she felt about her public lands. I saw an unspoken question on the supervisor's face. I said two words to him: Mary Paetzel.

I had always enjoyed reading Mary's reports about her explorations of the Siskiyous. Several years ago when we were discussing her work, she told me about the extensive journals she had kept for several decades. I copied and read them, and realized her work should be available to a wider audience. Jackie Elliott, of the Siskiyou Audubon Society and a Forest Service volunteer, felt the same way. Thanks principally to Jackie's typing, organizational skills, *and* prodding, this book finally has come to fruition. We persuaded Mary to let us build a book from selected journal entries. Mary's intimate daily stories about the land and its plants, butterflies, and wasps take you with her to the field to share her experiences.

At the time she was engaged in writing her daily journal, Mary also began work on a monograph she titled "Spirit of the Siskiyous." This monograph provided an objective history of the geologic and climatic forces that created the unique plant communities of the Siskiyou Mountains. To give the reader a context for Mary's daily journal entries, parts of her draft monograph were used to introduce this book and each chapter. Mary relied heavily on a paper by R. H. Whittaker ("Vegetation of the Siskiyou Mountains, Oregon and California," *Ecological Monographs,* Vol. 30, No. 3, July 1960) to write her monograph. Jackie and I realized that Mary herself is the real "Spirit of the Siskiyous," and thus arose the title of this book.

Many businesses, organizations, and individuals contributed funds to help OSU Press with the cost of publishing this book. Businesses include Evergreen Federal Savings and Loan Association, and Roe Motors Inc. Organizations include Crater Lake Natural History Association, Headwaters, Rogue Valley Audubon Society, Siskiyou Audubon Society, Siskiyou Chapter of the Oregon Native Plant Society, and Siskiyou Regional Education Project. Individuals include Marie Anaker, Mariana Bornholdt, Rex and Jackie Elliott, Charlotte Escott, Linda Heinze, Pat Kellogg, Mike and Kathy Klem, Conny Lindley, Esther Marple, Linda Mullens, Bonnie Brunkow Olson, Helen Pratt, Eleanor and Bob Pugh (Lichen Co-op), Maggie Purves, John and Lorraine Roach, Anita Seda, Jim Skibby, Veva Stansell, Sue Thomas, Maria Ulloa, Dennis Vroman, Lee, Pat, Jes and Nathan Webb, Louise Webb, and Margaret Wiese.

Mary's Chronicle

I interviewed Mary several times as we worked together editing this book, and compiled this brief life history. Words in quotations are Mary's.

Margaret Mary Ann Paetzel was born to Mae and Charley Paetzel on September 21, 1919, in Peru, Indiana. When Mary was one or two years old, the family left Indiana and headed west. Mary's first memory is of a train ride through snow-covered mountains near Dolores, Colorado; she was three or four years old. From 1924 through 1942, Mary and her family spent a total of six or seven years living "off and on" in Dolores; the rest of the time the family lived in California, near Mae's relatives in Santa Monica. The Paetzels preferred the mountains and climate around Dolores, but jobs were scarce in Colorado and available in California. "Once Ma saw the mountains in Colorado she never really wanted to live anywhere else." Charley, a barber, moved alone to Arizona in 1927; after that it was just Mary and Mae. Mary received most of her formal education in a Catholic parochial school near Santa Monica, California. She spent many hours searching for wildflowers in Elysian and Griffith Parks: "they were wild then." Mary completed the ninth grade in 1935, and looked forward to focusing on science courses in high school. However, school administrators insisted she concentrate on domestic science (cooking and sewing). She quit school.

By 1936 the years of traveling back and forth between Colorado and California had been enough. Mary and Mae came back to Dolores for an extended stay, and Mary worked on several farms upriver from Dolores. Mary was happy to be back in the area she loved. She had "imprinted" on southwest Colorado's high mountains, with their snow-covered peaks of winter and wildflower-covered slopes of summer. "Out in the open" work suited her. She labored on a potato farm at Line Camp for several years. She lived with the farm owners during the week and dug potatoes by hand for fifty cents a day plus room and board. She spent weekends with Mae in Dolores, and rode the "Galloping Goose" narrow gauge railroad to the farm and back. On days off, Mary climbed nearby rimrock and marveled at the profusion of wildflowers. She fondly remembers Mesa Verde and multitudes of sunflowers growing right up to the base of the cliffs (an illustration of this scene is in the epilogue, "Journey Into Memory").

Charley wrote Mary and Mae occasionally, and in 1938 Mary left to visit her father in Clifton, Arizona, where he operated a barbershop. But Charley had died the week before Mary arrived. Instead of renewing a relationship, she spent a month settling her father's estate.

After the Pearl Harbor attack, Mary attempted to enlist in the Army; because Mary had sight in only one eye, her request was rejected. That did not stop her. In March 1942, she traveled to Durango and took the Civil Service exams for stenographer and mechanic. In August, the War Department sent her a letter of acceptance: she was to be an airplane mechanic (and not a stenographer, thank goodness). Later that year she reported to aircraft mechanic school in Eugene, Oregon (her first look at the state). She was sent briefly to Geiger Air Base in Spokane, and then in February 1943, Mary transferred to Hill Air Base near Salt Lake City, to be closer to Dolores and mother Mae. Mary specialized in the repair of generators and starters for B-17 and B-24 bombers. She loved her work. While at Hill, she worked on the Swoose (a bomber named after a combination swan and goose) and a number of other inventively named planes. By the end of 1943, the war effort was slowing down, and the War Department released her in the spring of 1944. She briefly considered taking a job with Douglas Aircraft Company in California, but didn't want to live in a city.

Mary briefly returned to live with mother Mae in Dolores, but jobs were scarce—potato digging was no longer alluring. Servicemen hadn't yet come home from the war. In June 1944, Mary moved to Westwood, California, and ran a Standard Oil Service Station (sold gas, gave lubes, changed tires and batteries). Mary stayed with the service station about a year—"When I worked for Standard Oil it was at a service station, not a garage. In those days, 'service' meant just that, and no one pumped their own gas or checked their own tires!" In October 1945, a few months after the end of World War II, Mary decided to leave California for good and move to Oregon, where the winters weren't as severe as Colorado's.

In 1945, Lillian Terrill, a friend from the Paetzels' California days, retired from her job as a Western Union phone operator. Lillian had vacationed

frequently in the Grants Pass, Oregon area. In October 1945, Mary and Lillian moved to Josephine County. In 1946, they pooled their funds and bought twenty acres of land on Donaldson Road in the Louse Creek drainage, just north of Grants Pass, at $32 an acre. Mary and Lillian built a small house on the property and finally began living there in September 1947. With all this land, they could have ducks, geese, chickens, guinea hens, peacocks, vegetables, and flowers! A few years later, an uncle and cousin built another small house for Mae. Off and on Mae worked between California and Oregon, until she came to Grants Pass to stay in 1959. The trio thought of themselves as the first environmentally conscious people in the area. Loggers tried more than once to buy their trees, but they wouldn't sell.

Within a few years, the three friends started a three-quarter-acre iris nursery and sold rootstocks. In 1957 Lillian died, and Mary's friend Charlotte Matthews began helping in the nursery. By 1959, Mary tired of the "government inspectors and their rules" and sold all the iris stock to Charlotte, who moved the plants to her home near Winston (later the location of Wildlife Safari).

Mary found other outdoor work. In the 1950s and '60s, she worked in local hops and gladiolus fields for seventy-five cents an hour. She plucked goose down from her geese at two dollars per ounce. She still has scars on her ribs to prove it; evidently, the geese didn't look forward to the weekly plucking sessions. Mary left the goose down business when "government regulations" became too onerous for her.

About 1950, Mary realized their property didn't have enough water to grow vegetables for sale, and they needed to generate some income. She had heard herbs could be grown for profit in Oregon, so she contacted sixteen companies that dealt with these commodities. No luck—but one company was looking for pollen collectors in the Pacific Northwest. In 1951, Mary began collecting pollen for the Greer Pharmaceutical Company in North Carolina, for use with allergy tests conducted by doctors and hospitals. She liked working with Greer because "they never cheated on the weight." She collected pollen from more than thirty wild and cultivated plants during each year's six-month flowering season. Bigleaf maple was the best income producer. One year she collected enough pollen from this species to earn a $2,500 check! In 1962, Pacific Power wrote about Mary's unusual occupation in their customer newsletter. She stopped collecting pollen after 1981 because of "too many government regulations" (OSHA safety and sanitation rules).

Mary's pollen collecting reactivated her lifelong interest in the insect world, particularly butterflies and wasps (some of Mary's adventures with these creatures are included in this book). Ever curious, Mary became fascinated with the myriad insects attracted to the blossoms of the plants she visited for their pollen. She became especially intrigued with wasps—Mary described this fascination in an unpublished manuscript on her wasp studies:

> *Pollen gathering keeps the collector out in the field from early morning to late afternoon every sunny day of the blooming season, and it is during these most favorable hours that a vast aggregation of flying insects parade among the blossoms. In the beginning I paid the lively crowd little attention, dismissing them as just a lot of "flying bugs." But more and more they intruded on my work, and I became so bewitched by their antics I spent more time watching the insects than collecting pollen.*
>
> *At first they seemed a bewildering multitude of flying, darting creatures—a few butterflies were the only familiar ones among them. But gradually I sorted them out into families and species; there were flies, beetles, butterflies, moths, bees and wasps. Out of all that dazzling crowd, the wasps fascinated me most of all. They visited the flowers briefly, quietly sipping nectar, then departed on other business. But what business? What sort of life did they live? What kinds of nests did they build? Were they members of a group, or did they work alone? They raised a thousand questions, for it was impossible to observe them without wanting to know more.*

Mary began exploring the Siskiyou Mountains and Siskiyou National Forest when she started her pollen-collecting enterprise. She started gathering information in earnest on some of the Siskiyous' wild sites in 1972; she did sketches and plant surveys, and looked up the plants she didn't know. In 1975 I began accepting the written information she had gathered, on behalf of the Siskiyou National Forest. In 1984, Mary collected her first paycheck from the Forest Service; she contracted with us to survey several timber sales for the Galice Ranger District. In 1987, the Forest Service hired Mary as a temporary botanist to help gather information to be used in development of a recovery plan for the area burned by the 96,000-acre Silver Fire; this work continued into 1988. Over the next several years, until 1993, she intermittently continued to survey timber sale areas on the Galice District for rare plants, first as a contractor, and later as a volunteer. She also conducted a butterfly survey of the Dutchman Peak area for the Applegate Ranger District of the Rogue River National Forest. Mary found two rare butterflies and was instrumental in encouraging the district to ban butterfly collecting in the area.

In 1989, Mary's mother Mae died; she was ninety-five. Mae had always been interested in nature, just like Mary. Although in earlier years Mae often accompanied Mary on her explorations, Mae never had the opportunity to live her life as close to nature as she would have liked. Mae left school after the eighth grade, and later had subsisted by taking care of invalids and doing domestic work. Though Mary and Mae had lived in different houses, their mother-to-daughter relationship was close. Mary faithfully looked after

Mae in later years. Mae's death left Mary alone, but with the independence to pursue new adventures.

Mary put her acreage up for sale in 1991. She had lived on the Donaldson Road property for forty-four years. Her home site had "provided firewood, been a bird sanctuary, and a good garden had been built up." Mae and Mary certainly had been good land stewards. Mary was proud that their property was now in much better shape than when they arrived in 1947. The land sold in 1992. For Mary, the land "wasn't that hard to leave, because everything was gone: Ma, the geese and dogs." Also, it "was not the same place as in the beginning—not as much bird song, and the Colonial Valley [area had been] built up." Mary said she never dreamed she would stay in Oregon that long; she "couldn't afford to get out until the land prices went up."

Mary always lived on a shoestring budget. She was "lucky to have $200 in the bank" at any given moment. But she earned enough to get by. Mary wanted to be in the field, and always noticed things she wanted to investigate, "and no one pays for that." Once her property sold, she was free to visit new places and follow long-dormant aspirations.

In 1992, Mary bought a small travel trailer and moved to the Merrill, Oregon area (southeast of Klamath Falls—away from the winter fogs of the Rogue Valley). In the summer of 1992, Mary began work as a volunteer for the Klamath Basin National Wildlife Refuges. Until April 1993 she parked her trailer across from refuge headquarters at Tulelake, and catalogued plant species on the various units of the refuge. She also squeezed in a few plant surveys for the nearby Lava Beds National Monument. She straightened out their herbarium and "discovered some rare plants they didn't know they had." In August 1992, while doing her botanical work, Mary raised an alarm about young white pelicans at Clear Lake in Northern California that were perishing for lack of water. The story even made the *Oregonian* and *San Francisco Chronicle* newspapers. She stirred things up and made people think about the conflicts between human and wildlife use of water in the Klamath Basin.

Mary moved her trailer to Summer Lake, Oregon in the summer of 1993, and conducted plant surveys as a volunteer for the Oregon Department of Fish and Wildlife. In September 1993, she moved her trailer to an RV park just outside of Merrill; this is now her home base. She spends plenty of time in the field, living out of her four-wheel-drive pickup; the flue pipe for a small wood stove pokes through the canopy. She loves to watch the waterfowl and other wildlife in winter, and especially likes to "keep track of my swans."

Ever since coming to Oregon in 1945, Mary had been yearning to revisit her Colorado "hills of home"—the mesa and mountain land of southwest Colorado. She especially missed the flowers in high elevation meadows and the frequent summer thunderstorms. In the summer of 1991, Mary finally had her wish. With several friends from Grants Pass she briefly visited her old haunts. That visit whetted her desire, and in 1994 she traveled alone into her long-sought "Journey Into Memory." She spent the entire summer in the San Juan Mountains of southwest Colorado. She kept a diary of the experience. Excerpts are included in the epilogue to this book, to give readers a sense of why Mary's *Spirit of the Siskiyous* contains recurring heartfelt references to the mountains of her youth. I have twice visited Mary during her summer sojourns to Colorado, and the "hills of home" are remarkably beautiful. Now I understand.

Mary also spent the summers of 1995, 1997 and 1998 camping and hiking in her beloved San Juans. In 1994 and 1995, she volunteered to do herbarium work for the San Juan National Forest. In 1996, she didn't feel up to her near-annual trek to Colorado, and instead spent all summer exploring Oregon's Steens Mountains.

Companions Mentioned Frequently in Mary's Journals

Charlotte Matthews appears often in Mary's journals. They met when Charlotte, a retired schoolteacher (born 1894), stopped by to visit the "new" iris nursery. In the 1920s and '30s, Charlotte had been a forward-thinking schoolteacher in Douglas County who stressed conservation issues with her students. Mary found a "very good" companion in Charlotte—a fellow artist, writer, and naturalist—and they shared a deep love of the Siskiyous. Charlotte went on her first "field trip" with Mary in 1959. She accompanied Mary on dozens of trips over the years until 1986. At eighty years of age, Charlotte even climbed Lake Mountain with Mary.

Sally, or "Ding," was Mary's four-legged friend ("Ding" because she would slip away, and Mary had to put a bell on her collar). Sal was six months old when Mary got her in 1964. The dog had belonged to a woman who moved to town from the country. Sal was "not a town dog." She didn't have the disposition of a domestic dog, and Mary thought Sal had some characteristics of coyotes (yellow eyes). "She was loyal, intelligent and aloof, and did her own thing when she wanted to—the best trail dog I ever had." Sal was Mary's constant companion on the many trips to Bigelow Lakes. Sal died in 1978. Eleven years passed before Mary could bring herself to visit the area again. Sal is depicted in several of this book's illustrations.

Mary as an Artist and Writer

Mary has no formal art training—just natural talent. She began sketching plants and birds in 1936 while roaming the rimrock of southwest Colorado. An ardent inner need for self-expression compelled her to record what she saw; she "just had to do it." Her first attempts were so inadequate she became quite discouraged. Through constant trial and error she gradually taught herself to draw well. She experimented with a variety of media and obtained a pleasing effect from colored pencils and watercolors (including watercolor pencils); both media often were applied to the same sketch. She also used charcoal and sketching pencils. She ultimately concluded that a watercolor foreground (main) subject with a pencil background gave her the best results. Oils just couldn't give her the detail she wanted.

Mary exhibited her artwork twice in the lobby of the Siskiyou National Forest headquarters, in 1983 and 1984. In 1997, several volunteers produced 108 custom copies of an art book by Mary: *Butterflies and Plants of the Siskiyou Mountains.* The book contains seventy-seven of Mary's full-page color drawings of scenes from or near the Siskiyou National Forest (several of these drawings are included in *Spirit of the Siskiyous*). Text in Mary's unique style accompanies each picture. Hardbound copies of the book were given to local libraries in Josephine, Jackson, Curry, and Coos counties for their permanent collections. Other copies were placed in local Forest Service offices.

Mary also has natural talent as a writer. In the 1960s, she once gathered "some extra pollen dollars" and subscribed to a correspondence course for writers; it "helped some, but I still preferred my own style." Just as with artwork, an inner need to record her observations compelled her to write. In the 1960s she submitted articles on cultivated plants to various magazines and some were published. *Sunset* published three; *Better Homes and Gardens* accepted several more. *Canadian Audubon* published an article on wasps; *Westways* (published by the American Automobile Association) published several more. In 1973, Mary a scientific article was published in the *Panpacific Entomologist* about a male wasp helping a female stock a nest with prey (she received numerous requests from around the world for reprints of the article—all addressed to "Dr." Paetzel).

Nevertheless, Mary was more interested in publishing articles about nature—the type of stories she wrote daily in her journal. But publishers weren't interested in her nature writings; she collected "two binders of rejections over eighteen years, and eventually it became very discouraging." Some of the topics she wrote about coincided with the environmental movement in America. She "wanted people to know what was out there before it was destroyed." In the 1980s, the Siskiyou Audubon Society discovered Mary's journals and began printing excerpts in their monthly newsletter. Paul Fattig of the Medford, Oregon, *Mail-Tribune* devoted a column to Mary's journals on July 19, 1992 ("From Nature's Beauty, a Writer Is Born"). The positive reception her stories received encouraged Mary to consider publishing her journals in book form. Eventually, a draft of *Spirit of the Siskiyous* was prepared and submitted to OSU Press. This book documents a long journey for Mary, and I am proud of her.

Mary Helped Manage the Siskiyou National Forest

Although Mary has been exploring the Siskiyou Mountains ever since arriving in Oregon, she actually began helping manage the Siskiyous' rare plant resources as a volunteer in 1973; she provided site-specific botanical information that helped Forest Service managers be better land stewards. Mary furnished important sighting information for use in several editions of a comprehensive *Guide to Sensitive Plants of the Siskiyou National Forest.* Mary provided information that led to the designation of Bigelow Lakes and Chrome Ridge/Freeland Mountain as Botanical Areas in the 1989 Land and Resource Management Plan ("Forest Plan") for the Siskiyou National Forest. Several other smaller botanical sites also were protected as a result of Mary's help.

Mary is also a self-taught butterfly expert. In 1986, she discovered the Mariposa copper (*Lycaena mariposa*) butterfly in the Mud Spring area. At that time, only five populations of this rare butterfly were known from the mountain ranges of the Pacific Coast. Based on Mary's information, an in-progress timber sale was modified to protect the butterfly population. The discovery of this butterfly is chronicled at the end of Chapter 3.

In 1988, I persuaded Mary to write a booklet on *The Butterflies of the Siskiyou National Forest*. Complete with anecdotes, this booklet is a gem (to obtain a copy, write the Supervisor's Office of the Siskiyou National Forest in Grants Pass). In 1989, Mary received a special Region 6 (OR/WA) "Caring for the Land" award for her work with rare plants and butterflies on the Siskiyou National Forest.

How do I feel about Mary?

She makes life more interesting for others. Mary is one of a kind—as she puts it, "Thank goodness, one is enough!" Mary and I share a love of the land—the Siskiyous. Mary's journal entries make me want to leave my desk and head for the woods. Her words remind me why I chose a career working for the Forest Service, helping to manage our national forest land. At times, during field trips with other Forest Service folks to places Mary has written about, I have even taken some of her writings with me and read them aloud to the group.

As I read her words, she swiftly transports me to the natural world—she lets me smell the forest, hear the wind in the trees, feel the texture of the crusted snow, and see the delicate beauty of a flower or insect. I have visited many of the places Mary describes, and I often wonder how I missed things she saw. Her words portray the pleasantness of the forest, the real world—the natural world. She paints elegant word pictures of the strength and mystery of an old snag, the pacific quietness of moonlight on a deserted meadow, the stark beauty of a winter snowstorm, and the infinite variety and mystery of Mother Nature's weather patterns and flow of the seasons.

Mary admonishes us:

"There are so many quiet spots here in the Siskiyous where we can retreat from the traffic, noise and confusion of daily life" (Magic of Moonlight, Chapter 4—Briggs Valley and Horse Creek).

"Each little world must be explored exclusively by itself to be understood and appreciated. Every day of each season brings something new and unexpected, and only the one who comes faithfully to watch and learn will be initiated into the secrets of these shy and unknown inhabitants of the wild places of canyon, river, and hillside" (The Bee Wolf, Chapter 2—The River and Hellgate).

You do not have to know Mary's places firsthand to enjoy this book and buttress your appreciation for the land. Her themes are universal and apply to the natural world in general. Her insights and observations heighten our awareness to the natural world surrounding us. Mary and her journals are a treasure of the Siskiyous worth far more than all the gold flakes that still lie in the streambeds of the mountains. This book brings Mary's work to the public, so all who wish to can share in the wonder and beauty of the natural world in the Siskiyou Mountains. Wherever you live, I hope this book encourages you to go to the woods, go out on the land, and get down on your hands and knees.

Other than her home site on Louse Creek (Chapter 1), all of the places Mary wrote about are on public land (map, page xx). The best "field" guide to Mary's special places is a recreation map for the Siskiyou National Forest (sold at all Forest Service offices in southwest Oregon).

Lee Webb
Forest Wildlife Biologist
Siskiyou National Forest
February 9, 1998

Introduction

In 1945, when I first came to southern Oregon, there was little time to explore the wonderful Siskiyou Mountains and their renowned plant communities. But in the 1950s and '60s, I began collecting pollen for a large drug firm and this took me out in quest of numerous tree, shrub, and wild plant pollens. And I discovered the wonderful diversity of these fascinating mountains. My old Volkswagen bus faithfully took me up every logging and skid road in the forest. It was then that I came face to face with the accelerating destruction the chainsaw and bulldozer were bringing upon the last of the ancient forests of the Northwest. Then I knew I must document what I was finding in the hidden places that soon might be destroyed without a trace. But that was for my own records, and I never intended these essays to be published. They are, in reality, more like a personal diary, and diaries usually are not meant for public scrutiny—ask any government official! However, I have been persuaded (reluctantly) that others who love the wild places would enjoy the descriptive narrative style of the journals. In this book my selected journal entries are arranged by earliest to latest date within each chapter.

My Odyssey began at Hellgate Canyon in October 1966, with the tiny flowers, insects, and butterflies of that rugged area above the Rogue River, and progressed to the higher country of Briggs Valley, Chrome Ridge, Freeland Mountain, Bigelow Lakes, and Mount Elijah. Even humble little Louse Creek, across the field north of my twenty acres in Colonial Valley, had its stories to tell of birds and lowland flowers.

In 1979, I wrote a last goodbye to Bigelow Lakes and Lake Mountain. The two most faithful companions of these adventures were Charlotte Matthews, a friend of more than twenty years, and Sal, or old Ding, my half-coyote, half-shepherd dog. Unfortunately, canine companions must depart before their human friends, and the last journal entries from Bigelow Lakes are filled with a recurring theme of fond memories of our adventures together. My last journal entry describes a 1989 visit to Horse Creek on a crisp winter night.

Because I came to the Siskiyous from the high country of southwest Colorado, my narratives also contain a thread of nostalgic memories of snow, high mountain meadows, and lazy summer days, with thunderclouds on the distant horizon.

You who read these journals will be transported to many places that no longer exist. May these writings inspire you to greater efforts to save those still left to enjoy.

I especially want to thank Lee Webb, of the Siskiyou National Forest, and Jackie Elliott, of Siskiyou Audubon Society, for the long hours of painstaking work editing, correcting, and arranging the drafts of these stories into readable book form. John Coulter and Alison Baker reviewed my manuscript. Tom Atzet reviewed the introductory section on the natural history of the Oregon Siskiyous. Without their dedicated efforts, this collection would still be gathering dust in my files.

Mary Paetzel
Merrill, Oregon
January 1998

Lord, How Do I Know Thee?

❀ ❀ ❀

You ask, Lord, how do I know You? And I answer. I see You in the buttercups and bluebells of a high mountain meadow. I hear You in the wind in the willows. I feel Your love in the warm suns and blue skies of June. I speak to You in the shadowed aisles of a mountain trail. I see Your sufferings in the tortured shapes of trees at timberline. I catch a glimpse of Your glory in the avalanche lily blooming at the edge of Your eternal snows in the high places.

You, Lord, gave me this wild nature—made me one with the creatures of Your hills and forests. You set me apart, for a reason I am only now beginning to understand. You turned my feet down a dim and lonely trail and I will follow. But when troubles come and evil lies like evening shadows across my path, bid me not come to You in some great cathedral, down carpeted aisles. Speak not to me from marble altars, through strange rituals. I ask not that You deny these things to others who need and cherish them, but call to me and comfort me in the quiet and beautiful places of earth. There I hear Your voice in the wind. There I sense Your Presence in the rustling grass, and I am at peace. For, Oh Lord, I have loved the beauty of Your house, and the place where Your glory dwells.

July 7, 1974

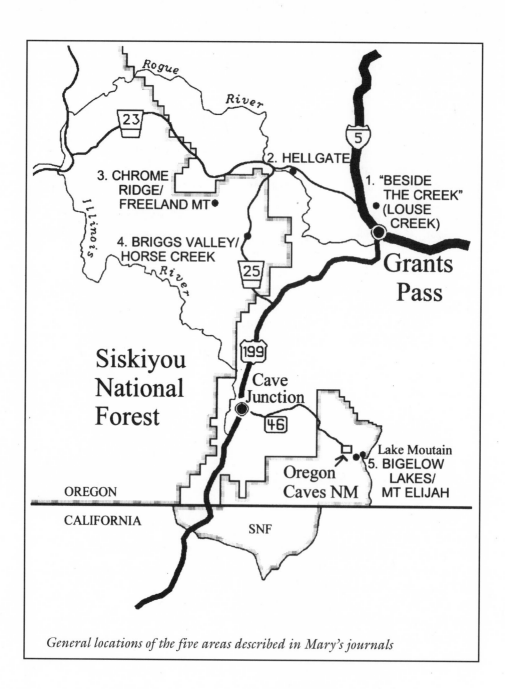

Rogue River

23

3. CHROME
RIDGE/
FREELAND MT •

Illinois

4. BRIGGS VALLEY/
HORSE CREEK

River

25

2. HELLGATE

5

1. "BESIDE
THE CREEK"
(LOUSE
CREEK)

Grants
Pass

Siskiyou
National
Forest

199

Cave
Junction

46

OREGON

Oregon
Caves NM

Lake Moutain
5. BIGELOW
LAKES/
MT ELIJAH

CALIFORNIA

SNF

General locations of the five areas described in Mary's journals

Preface

❀ ❀ ❀

In the mountains of the West lives a small butterfly known as the Mariposa Copper. "Mariposa" means "butterfly" in Spanish, so this species may be thought of as the Butterfly Butterfly. As a young lepidopterist in Colorado, I held out a special fascination for this nickel-sized insect that is the color of an old penny until just the right angle of sunbeam strikes it amethyst. My gospel, F. Martin Brown's *Colorado Butterflies*, reported one old, questionable record of *Lycaena mariposa* for the state. So when a friend came home from a collecting trip with a specimen, I was thrilled and quickly reported the find in the Lepidoptera literature.

As it turned out, the Mariposa had been collected near Yellowstone, where it is common, and accidentally confused with some Fort Collins butterflies. The record had to be suppressed in an embarrassing retraction. So when, years later, I heard from a naturalist in southwest Oregon that she had found a small colony of Mariposa Coppers not far from the coast, I was at first skeptical. True, I had since found a coastal colony on the Olympic Peninsula far from the known population in the Olympic Mountains, but these seemed clearly related to those discovered long ago on the Queen Charlotte Islands—a relict of lower sea levels and boggier times along the post-Pleistocene Northwest Coast. These putative Siskiyou Mariposas would be still more distant from the known Cascadian/Sierran range of the species: a significant range extension. After the Colorado *faux pas*, I wanted to be quite sure before the Northwest Lepidoptera Survey accepted the record. Sure enough, on examination these coppers had the checkered fringe and "Morse code" black-on-gray pattern on the underside that signify *Lycaena mariposa*.

So unusual was this discovery, so unique the bog that supported the coppers, that the United States Forest Service eventually protected the site as a botanical preserve. And the dot designating this distinctive colony of coppers duly appears in *An Atlas of Oregon Butterflies*, edited by John Hinchliff (Oregon State University Bookstore, 1994). Yet this discovery, significant in conservation and biogeographical terms, was not an isolated incident from some itinerant collector's season afield. Rather, it was one expression of a broad and varied life lived in the full context of the out-of-doors. It exemplifies the contribution of the gifted, passionate amateur to the perpetual colloquy between observers and observed that we call "natural history."

The correspondence surrounding her butterfly discovery suggested I was talking with a woman of unusual wit, observational skills, and dedication. I was right. Mary Paetzel long ago chose to make herself a living, moving, interrelating component of the Siskiyous' ecology. Over the years, going out daily, Mary became one with her habitat. But unlike many who go to the country to enjoy its generalized qualities, she learned and addressed its specific features. Seeking out bees and wasps, lichens, special wildflowers, rare and common birds, peak views, sunsets, good lunch spots, and of course butterflies, Mary became a self-trained naturalist of remarkable breadth and depth. She grew to be a creature of these mountains herself, but unlike the other organisms in that she recorded what she saw, both in words and images. The result is this book.

The contribution of the self-trained amateur to our collective knowledge of nature is legion and well known. In a time when few professional academics and museum people are employed to actually go afield and do alpha-level botany and zoology, when "old-time natural history" is out of vogue in the academy, citizen enthusiasts have made up the balance. (The Oregon butterfly atlas, compiled entirely by amateurs, is a fine example.) The Mariposa Copper is scarcely the only increment Mary Paetzel has added to the faunistics and floristics of southwest Oregon. In fact, the Forest Service recognized her expertise by hiring her to conduct plant species surveys on the Siskiyou National Forest, in spite of her frequently acerbic responses to the agency's management plans.

We know these mountains much better for her careful, loving attention to them.

Yet, however much Mary Paetzel has added to Siskiyou natural history, her larger accomplishment may be artistic. Unlike biology, the field of nature writing (or the "literature of place," as it has recently been called) is composed chiefly of amateurs. While we recognize some names as preeminent in the genre and call them "professionals," it is a fact that almost no one really makes a living solely by writing about the natural world. Just as Charles Darwin was an "amateur" biologist, Henry David Thoreau was an "amateur" writer. Each made the largest single contribution to date in his discipline. After all, the word *amateur* means "one who loves." When science and art grow out of sheer love of the subject or the practice, why should we be surprised when the results are marvelous or lasting? Not that personal enthusiasm and affection for topic guarantee excellent treatment of the topic. For every significant achievement, numberless worthy undertakings go unnoted and unremembered. But when keen observation combines with artistic talent and zeal, their offspring can truly shine.

Such is the case with the Siskiyou journals of Mary Paetzel. Her language is a plain, straightforward English in which rich description and poignant detail can stand out. While we always know we are in the company of a careful witness and a true individual, the writer often dwells in the background. It is the land itself, and its denizens, that take center stage most of the time. And of special note, hers is a language backed up by the real stuff of natural history knowledge. I cannot overstate the importance of this distinction. Graceful writing is a fine thing on its own, but when informed by *particular acquaintance* with the intimate, actual details of the countryside, and a questioning sensibility, grace acquires authority. It is what Kim Stafford calls "weaving a rooted companionship with home ground," and it is what Mary Paetzel has done in the Siskiyous.

Many recent books have laid out the love affairs of good writers with their neighborhoods. Far too few of these carry the authority of pure and simple knowledge of natural history. Likewise, lots of books appear that are full of facts but not much fun to read. *Spirit of the Siskiyous* is an unpretentious book written for the writer, to record, validate, and honor her days afield and her thoughts engendered in close contact with other species. Yet, unassumingly, it gathers the elusive qualities of solid natural history and splendid words and blends them into a book both delightful and informative.

Happily, Mary recorded her passion for the Siskiyous in memorable drawings and paintings as well as words. Her pictures have an evanescence, a soft mastery of color that magically captures red admiral, winter willow, manzanita. I put her visual depiction in the same rare in-between-land as her written images: they have the accuracy of close attention and sound understanding of detail, and the personal character that comes from an individually attuned sense of nuance. Or, to turn it around, as Nabokov (another butterfly lover) put it: "the precision of poetry, the art of science."

Spirit of the Siskiyous joins a small but growing raft of recent books in which watchful writers concerned with the nature of their surroundings have come to terms with particular places. Jack Nesbit's *Purple Flat Top*, set in the Pend Oreille; Robert Schnelle's Kittitas chronicle, *Valley Walking*; and Jim Lemonds' *South of Seattle* in the Cowlitz country are some of the titles that follow classics like Betty MacDonald's *The Egg and I*, William Kittredge's *Hole in the Sky*, Shannon Applegate's *Skookum*, and David Rains Wallace's *The Klamath Knot*—the last book that memorably tackled the sense and sensuality of the Siskiyou region. Unlike all of these, Mary did not conceive her book for a broad audience, and she makes no pretensions for its literary consequence. Yet, in its own homely, land-lover's fashion, it makes as sound an appearance as any of these. In her acumen as both naturalist and artist, she brings to mind Ann Zwinger.

In *Spirit of the Siskiyous*, Mary Paetzel demonstrates the way in which the larger literature of the land is built upon the lovingly recorded lifeways of the true, self-trained and self-motivated observer. It is a grand tradition, and this is one of the best of the species. Now, whenever I see the flicker of the Mariposa Copper in a mountain meadow in high summer, I think of Mary, and I take pleasure knowing that I may always visit this remarkable landscape with her as my personal guide in these rich pages.

Robert Michael Pyle

Brief Natural History
of the Oregon Siskiyous

❀ ❀ ❀

The very name "Siskiyou Mountains" conjures up thoughts of mystery, of Indian rituals and ancient times. Even Mt. Shasta with its strange legends and superstitions, while not technically a part of the Siskiyous, is a close neighbor to these fascinating peaks, canyons, and plateaus, and many Siskiyou plants are a part of Shasta's flora as well.

The true essence and spirit of the Siskiyous lies in their unusual and varied plant life, for their ancient soils have been occupied continuously by flowering plants since their advent sixty million years ago. Nowhere else can such a variety of rare and endemic plants be found in so small an area. Running in an east-west direction along both sides of the California-Oregon border, the Siskiyous begin at the edge of the Coast Range and reach to the foothills of the Cascades, forming a bridge between the two. Bounded on the north by the Rogue River and on the south by the Klamath River, this rugged area appears as a jumble of broken mountain ridges and steep, rocky slopes terminating in narrow canyons. Life zones in this area range from Upper Sonoran on the dry south exposures of river canyons in the lowlands, to the Upper Canadian on high peaks on both sides of the state line.

The geological history of these mountains is more complex than any other part of the state, beginning sometime in the Paleozoic, around three hundred million years ago, when a shallow inland sea laid down deep deposits of sediments. Through various epochs and eras since, this region has been lifted, submerged, folded, and faulted at least four times. Upheavals of every imaginable kind have occurred: intrusions of igneous materials, volcanic action, glaciers, erosion by wind and wave, tilting, shifting. These titanic forces laid down such a bewildering complex of rock types and soils that even a geologist has trouble sorting them out.

The sweep of glaciers, flow of lava, lifting, submerging, and tilting episodes left islands of untouched material where ancient communities of plants flourished and new species evolved.

The old monadnocks such as Grayback and Sugarloaf, extrusions of deep underlying material, are especially rich in plant species that have survived those cataclysmic forces.

Glaciers brought plants from their ancestral homes far to the north, from high mountain peaks and sheltered valleys; wind, water, and other natural forces sowed seeds from faraway deserts and the humid coastal region. Some of these travelers from far-off lands found the soil and climate here to their liking, took root and flourished while their kindred in the lands from which they came perished in the great climatic changes taking place elsewhere.

Therefore in the Siskiyous it isn't at all unusual to find species from the desert growing in close association with plants from high mountain meadows or the tundra. Many times I find the little Siberian *Juniper communis* surrounded by *Arenaria* and *Eriogonum*—both desert species from the eastern part of the state. Often it seems that each peak and canyon has its own resident plant communities not found in surrounding areas. Such rarities as Bolander's lily and Kalmiopsis may be found on one particular hillside, and nowhere else for miles around.

The great diversity of rock material exposed by the upheavals of early times produced a wondrous variety of soils as they weathered into compounds that could support plant life. These soils and their parent rock include marble, slate, clay, granite, argillite, quartz, and dozens more. However, three main types of soil seem to support the largest number of rare and unusual native plants in the Siskiyous. These are quartz-diorite, serpentinite, and gabbro. Plant populations on these soils have been studied intensively. A great deal has been learned about the fragile habitat and special requirements of our most rare and endemic species.

Montane and sub-Alpine forests on diorite soils at higher elevations contain flowering plants which migrated from the high country of the Cascades and Sierra Nevada. At elevations of six thousand to seven thousand feet, dense stands of hemlock, noble fir, and Shasta red fir cover the ridges; unusual species occur on some higher slopes, such as quaking aspen on the south side of Mount Ashland.

In many places, stands of these conifers are extremely dense, and the ground beneath them is littered with dead branches, needles, and cones. Very few of the smaller species can grow in such deep shade, with the exception of *Pyrola*, *Arnica*, small colonies of coral root, and a few others. The flowering plants of the high country have claimed the open, gravelly places on steep hillsides and on top of windswept ridges as their own. Here little plants seen only above timberline in other mountain ranges can be found growing with transition-zone species usually at home in lower, more sheltered valleys.

In some places, glacial cirques and fields of rocky aggregates attest to the action of ice-age glaciers. These scoured-out depressions are surrounded by steep, tree-covered slopes whose melting snows produce lush, well-watered meadows where an endless variety of flowers bloom, from the first glacier lily of spring to the last *Helenium* and aster of fall.

By contrast, serpentine soil is barren and arid in the extreme with its sparse tree cover, brushy patches, and rocky open spaces. In spite of its high mineral content and low calcium availability, serpentine produces the greatest number of rare and endemic plants of any soil in the Siskiyous.

Gabbro soils appear to be intermediate between diorite and serpentine, both chemically and in the plants found there. Although vegetation on gabbro looks superficially like vegetation on low elevation diorite, the patterns of growth are quite different. Gabbro soils are much more open, without the heavy tree and brush understory of diorite. Tree stands on gabbro are more open then the dense Montane forests of diorite, but not as arid and scattered as the Jeffrey pine steppes of serpentine.

Gabbro shares plant species in almost equal proportions with diorite and serpentine. Although serpentine has twenty percent more flowering plants, gabbro boasts almost fifty percent more tree species. Usually light tan in color, and of a dense, clay-like hardness when dry, gabbro soil loses its moisture very quickly on exposed south and west slopes. Even in early spring, after a week of sunny weather, all traces of surface moisture may have disappeared. Nevertheless, a number of rare plants have found these conditions to their liking, and flourishing populations of Kalmiopsis, California lady-slipper, myrtle, and others hide away in undisturbed canyons and quiet hillsides.

Serpentine Soils

Of the numerous soils that make up the Siskiyou region, serpentine is the most fascinating, by virtue of the great variety of plant species it supports, many of which are found in very few numbers or not at all on other soils. This soil is dry to the point of being almost a desert habitat; with its rocky, thin topsoil, and high mineral content, it seems impossible that anything could thrive and reproduce there. Serpentine is distinctive in its two-phase growth of open Jeffrey pine woodlands above a scrub understory with scattered open grassy spaces in between. This vegetation pattern produces a visual effect unlike that produced on any other soil type in this region. Essentially a magnesium-iron silicate, formed by metamorphosis from peridotite, serpentine varies greatly in its mineral content; some areas contain a large proportion of heavy metals such as nickel, chromium, molybdenum, and iron. The soils from these rocks are mostly a rusty-reddish in color and can be surprisingly loamy and friable under certain conditions. But under the fierce sun and lack of moisture in summer, they bake into a hard, impenetrable, clay-like consistency, and few plants bloom after the end of June.

The "serpentine syndrome" (poor plant growth, dwarfism) results from a combination of four factors. First, serpentine soils contain elevated amounts of heavy metals, which at higher levels are toxic to cell metabolism, and this limits plant growth. Because plant growth has a great deal to do with soil development, serpentine soils are typically shallow. Second, the calcium/magnesium ratio in serpentine soils is atypical, and the high level of magnesium interferes with cell processes. Third, serpentine sites dry out quickly, because their clay soils hold water tightly. Fourth, soil structure is not conducive to optimum plant growth—heavy clays result in low water availability, which results in lackluster root penetrability.

But in spite of these harsh conditions, many plant species have developed serpentinicolous, or serpentine-tolerant, varieties. Many of these variants are often miniature editions of their larger relatives growing on "normal" soils: Brewer's oak, chinkapin, tan oak, myrtle, ocean spray—to name but a few.

A number of genera and species are endemic to serpentine, and found only sparingly or not at all on other soils, such as Bolander's lily, California lady-slipper, brook trillium, and the white bog violet. Invariably these plants decline and die in a few years when transplanted from their natural habitat, no matter how skillful the gardener may be.

Many botanists believe that some of the serpentine plants have crossbred with other near relatives on other soils and produced intermediate botanical hybrids.

Not all plants are dwarfed on this soil, for some of the largest old Port-Orford-cedars, Jeffrey pines, and incense-cedars I've found grow on the serpentine outcrops of Chrome Ridge. The large trees, dense shrub understory, and the wealth of flowering plants often represent maximum plant development on serpentine soils. The rich floras of serpentine communities are a product of millions of years of species evolution.

Flowering Plants of the Serpentine

Interspersed among this dense brush and open forest growth are occasional clear spaces, some several acres in extent, others no more than a few yards across. Little grassy meadows, wet in winter and spring, open to the sun, dry and barren in summer—here the flowering plants of the serpentine come into their own. Competition from trees and brush decreases as the soil becomes more xeric and rocky, and the low-growing, unassuming species from desert and canyon, from high mountain meadows and even from the sheltered slopes of the Coast Range, find a haven in these isolated places. Having somehow adapted to the harsh conditions of these exposed ridges, many species grow in thriving colonies that have all but disappeared in other, more "promising" environments. A few examples are serpentine butterweed, shrubby everlasting, rock cress, and fleabane. Like the brushy species, many are endemic variants whose ancestors have occupied these small islands of vegetation for untold aeons of time. Almost every flowering plant family has at least one representative—from lilies to roses, sedum, figworts, sunflowers, ferns, grasses, and sedges—the list is endless and reads like a Who's Who of the plant world!

Some plants seem to prefer sheltered areas at the edge of the brush where the soil is less rocky and more fertile; some grow more in the open, but in the shelter of a bush or larger plant. But as the brush runs together and becomes dense, producing a canopy of leafy branches, these small plants disappear; the competition for sunlight and moisture is too much for them. Some species do equally well in heavy brush or open areas alike; Bolander's lily, *Haplopappus*, pennyroyal, and bear grass are some of these adaptable ones. Even so, the greatest number of species and individuals are found in the bare, unsheltered spots where sunlight and moisture can best be utilized by these lower growing herbs, which are no match for the tough competition of the aggressive shrubs and trees.

Each small plant appears to have found its particular niche—some in the crevice of a boulder, another at the root of a dead stump, a few in the shadow of a rocky outcrop, others in a little patch of deeper soil. Always I have the feeling of much trial and error, and many seedlings must perish before fate places one in the exact right place for it to grow and hold its own against the tremendous odds.

At the lower elevations, serpentine often appears as an outcrop or field of flinty, obsidian-like chips—truly serpentine barrens. In this most forbidding of habitats, the small flowering plants colonize the open spaces; blue gilia, rock cress, godeta, sandwort, a tiny California poppy, sickle-leaved onion, and lewisia are all even more diminutive than their relatives on other serpentine locations.

In these extreme conditions the two-phase growth is much reduced, with scattered incense-cedar, stunted Douglas-fir and Jeffrey pine, dwarf Brewer's oak, and a shrubby form of myrtle representing the trees, while deer brush and manzanita make up the brushy understory.

This is the extreme of plant adaptation, but the most surprising of all are the insects of these serpentine wastelands, who have adapted along with their necessary plant associates. Witness the leaf-cutter bee, who cuts her nest material from the godeta flowers; the digger wasp, who finds her prey on the skimpy bushes; and the strange little grey-green grasshopper so much the color and shape of a serpentine chip he's invisible until he jumps to avoid being stepped on!

It has been said that concentrations of rare endemic plants are related to concentrations of environmental extremes—certainly the serpentine ridges, plateaus, and barrens of the Siskiyous bear this out in a remarkable degree.

1
Beside the Creek

The Setting

This little creek has its headwaters somewhere on Walker mountain, above the old Granite Hill mine. On the early maps it's listed as "Grouse Creek," but through an error in spelling, or just plain carelessness, it was recorded in later documents as Louse Creek, and it's been known by that unlovely name ever since!

Like so many other creeks in these unstable decomposed granite hills, the rushing waters of winter have produced out-washes and benches of loose material along the stream banks, which erode badly when disturbed. The creek has cut its way through the lower flats of mostly decomposed granite—very loose and unstable when disturbed, and dry and unproductive through our Mediterranean summers. But when left in its natural state, the native plants adapted to these xeric conditions can put on a show of color in early spring that rivals the desert displays.

Large patches of trillium throughout the open brush cover and acres of buttercups, California poppies, and meadow foam appear as early as February and March.

In earlier days, several mines operated near the headwaters of Louse Creek, but they seem not to have damaged the downstream environment, as so many of the larger operations did in other areas. For many years after the mines closed, there was no disturbance on the hills nor along the banks of this quiet stream or its tributaries. Sandbar willows and sedges grew thick beside the small pools that persisted in the hottest of summers.

Until the developers found it, this little, unknown waterway with its quiet pools was a haven for wildlife. Water birds such as the herons, spotted sand piper, and killdeer foraged undisturbed in the cool green depths of its willow thickets. And it was here I, too, found a quiet place close enough to home to visit every day—to sketch or write, or just sit and observe the wild creatures.

Now the monotonous green of lawns and modern shrubbery dot the landscape. And many acres of this area that haven't been developed are taken over by cheat grass and other introduced weeds.

Fairy Bells on the Winter Air

White mist has descended to the tops of the trees and a soft grey rain slants across my quiet fields. The hill is a study in muted greys and greens, and beneath last autumn's rotting leaves, spring queens (*Snythyris reniformis*), shooting stars, and lamb's tongues are stirring. Even now, catkins of the hazel brush are inches long and soon will be shedding their pollen on the damp winter breeze.

Somewhere beneath the bark on an old log, a mourning cloak—a kind of tortoise shell butterfly—is waiting patiently for a brief sunny hour, to be on the wing in the first warm moments of the New Year. But for now, the rain streams relentlessly down and the white mist drops lower among the tree tops. Rain will soon turn to snow, for this is the month of cold, ice, freezing fog, and that strange hybrid that is neither rain nor snow, but the worst of both.

Sometimes, though (once in a decade perhaps), snow comes before the rain. White and soft and dry, it dances among the trees and over fields light and gentle as thistledown. Then all the magic of a winter wonderland casts its spell for a brief time over this wet, foggy, rainy country.

There have been a few such times in all the years this place has been mine. If the day is especially blessed and the sun should chance to shine, it creates an experience so memorable it will never be forgotten.

The new snow gleams and sparkles like a thousand, thousand diamonds, and the clearing sky takes on that unbelievable cerulean blue reserved for winter skies of the high mountain meadows.

Once there was a span of days like this, one after another, with clear skies and brilliant sun, followed by frigid arctic nights. Each day the snow melted slightly, then fused in the cold of night into beautiful patterns of long, delicate crystals—crystals that even the slightest breath of air shattered into a million tinkling fragments. It was a never-to-be-repeated experience to stand quietly among the trees on the hillside and see these myriad tiny structures falling in luminescent strands from the branches, and to hear their musical tintinnabulation like so many fairy chimes on the winter air.

Each January, I wait expectantly when the snow begins to fall, but never again have conditions been just right to repeat the experience, and it is with a vague sense of regret that I turn the calendar to the month of February.

January 15, 1969

Bees and Cherry Blossoms

❀ ❀ ❀

Sitting among the cherry blossoms this green and gold morning in spring, I think what a pleasant job I have—I'm taking a "bee census."

The April sun is warm, but a chill wind blows from the north and I think of alpine meadows at timberline. But I'm content—for once—and the buzz of the bees and flash of their myriad tiny wings is all I desire for this spring day.

Each kind of bee fly, and even butterfly, has its own song. Some higher, some lower, and I know who each little worker is by the sound she makes. Even the little crescentspot butterfly tells me who she is as she flutters in the branch behind my ear.

But I think *Bombylus,* the bee fly, has the most pleasant tune of all. As she hovers in the air before a blossom she's hardly audible, but when she revs her tiny propellers to dart away she produces a high-pitched whine that only the bee flies are capable of.

But most of all, I love to hear them in the heat of summer when two (probably a pair) dance in mid-air, and, facing each other a few inches apart, converse by altering the sound of their wings. First a whine almost too high for my ears to catch, then a lower droning hum, then a series of middle notes, sustained like a lingering chord on the violin. All done without changing position in the air in the slightest. But this performance is for later, and usually done best by the small, black-and-white- or yellow-striped *Eristalis* hover flies.

Today the bees work, and I listen, and I know the tiny things are as glad as I that the snows and cold of winter have departed and the warm suns and blue skies and white clouds of spring are here at last.

April 25, 1969

Thirty Days Hath September

❀ ❀ ❀

Thirty golden days washed with sparkling skies and billowing clouds—days without time—when the killdeer calls and little brown birds twitter and scold in the brambles, restless, never still, eager to be gone. Now the sea bird's cry is more plaintive than before, and purple asters beckon from the sea meadows among the dunes.

Thirty days to spend recklessly among the treasures of dying summer, to watch and listen beside the tidal pool, to lie dreaming on a sunlit hill, to feel the first raindrops of autumn. And beyond the horizon, to hear, with the ears of the mind, the first restless honking of the geese, impatient to leave their summer homes for the windswept tulles of autumn and the leaden skies of October.

In September comes the first restless call of the wild to all creatures of earth and sky. The monarch flies with an urgent wing-beat that was lacking only a week before, the sparrow moves with a haste and purpose the lazy days of summer never knew, the scolding of the grey squirrel sounds through the woods with a greater insistence, and the fitful killdeer circle and call the night through.

Now comes the equinox and the wild storms sired in the meeting of summer's heat and winter's cold. Thunder—and clouds piled high, wind—and slashing rain. Then the calm sunny days and once again the bright flowers toss in soft breezes, and purple grapes grow fragrant in the golden light. Once more the cricket sings loud in evening shadows and a yellow harvest moon gently lays its brilliance over woods and field.

The wild goose dreams—and I would dream with it, for I would know what the wild goose knows—I would go where the wild goose goes. Then one day soon, on October's red hill I'll watch the geese and hear their cries. They will go, and I will stay—for I know, as I've always known—autumn's voice is meant for ears other than mine.

September 1, 1972

A Rejoicing of Robins

❀ ❀ ❀

On this dark December day, my hill and the surrounding area are alive with a rejoicing of robins. Two hundred, five hundred, or more—flying, caroling, chirping, scolding, and singing—making the gloomy woods come alive with their invasion. They have come for the annual feast of the madrone berries, and no matter how dark the day, how cold, how miserable, they seem to be in the happiest of moods, a carnival spirit of feasting and good fellowship.

Always the number of birds is in proportion to the amount of the brilliant red berries. This year the trees produced the largest crop of recent years, and the birds are so numerous the din of their chatter can be heard in all surrounding valleys.

I walked up the old logging road to the top of the hill to watch their comings and goings. They ebb and flow like the tide, first on one hillside, then down in a valley, then to a nearby rise, and back again to my trees. For a while I seemed to be in the midst of them, and the round red berries were dropping all about like hail. After the main flock passes on, a few birds remain, and in the quiet after the tumult one or two will begin to sing: a rather hesitant, trial-like song—a sort of practice session for the coming joyous carols of spring.

Often I've seen flocks on the hill above the river where the top of the ridge is covered with madrone. And, a few times, as I've been resting in a long, sloping meadow on the north side of the river, the whole group would alight among the new grass and forage for insects. It's quite a sight to see a hundred or so red-breasted birds dotting the green expanse of an open hillside—and always, the old song comes to mind—"a red, red robin just a-bob-bob-bobbing along."

I had never seen robins in large numbers until we came to Oregon. It seems they winter in all the inland valleys of the state—Willamette, Umpqua, and Rogue. But I've never been able to find out whether these birds go inland to the mountain states in summer, or whether they are more or less resident to the coastal areas.

At home, in Colorado, we never saw more then a few pairs nesting in the orchards or near the river. And if as many as a hundred had ever appeared all at once, I'm sure everyone for miles around would have come to look at them!

The robin: celebrated in song and poetry as the cheerful messenger of spring. Still, to really appreciate just how lilting and uplifting is the song of this red-breasted bird, one should hear it on a dark day in December, while standing on a lonely hill, beneath a lowering sky, with evening shadows gathering in the valleys below.

December 26, 1978

The Tea Party Beside the Creek

The sun is still behind the trees on the hill and the little pool is in deep
shadow, but the air is already warm with promise of another scorching day.
The sky is a pale, cloudless blue so typical of midsummer in this rainless
Oregon country. Somewhere over my hill a young hawk calls, and I hear my
geese gabbling in response. This is the kind of day I never have any
ambition to do anything, but Charlotte and I have come to the creek for
breakfast—and of all things, carrying a huge brown teapot known as
"Brownie," to dispense adequate quantities of our morning tea. Fortunately,
we met no one as we crossed the road, for heaven knows what a sight we
must have been. One carefully holding the teapot, the other loaded down
with cushions, food, sketching materials, etc. All of this at five-thirty in the
morning!

Years ago, before the houses were built on this side of the road, and the
creek was still wild and undisturbed, we did this often in the heat of the
summer when we had no desire to go anywhere else. Actually, the creek is
only six to seven hundred feet across the road and through a field from my
place, a three or four-minute walk at most. And yet it has been ten or more

SUMMER MORNING   JULY 15 '70

years since we've been here in the early morning to sit beside the quiet pools and listen to the birds, to sketch, or just talk.

In the late 60s, the real estate people found this little haven and began subdividing the level spots and building houses. Then sand and gravel were taken from the creek, and the destruction was complete. I walked back to the old haunts several times, but everything we had taken pleasure in was gone, or changed somehow. The houses could be seen from the water's edge, effectively ruining the sense of privacy and contentment we had known there.

But today Charlotte said, "Let's go and see what it looks like, it's been so long." And we were amazed! The willows, poplars, and alders have quietly returned, and their thickets are now tall enough to obscure houses, yards, and TV antennas; sounds of the freeway are muted by the tangled growth. The creek has several channels now, and piles of rock from the gravel operation are everywhere. But we've found several deep pools beneath the alders, and the big poplar still leans over the quiet stretch of water we enjoyed so much years ago.

So we sit beside the still pool, have our breakfast and watch the little fish darting about, and listen to a towhee scratching in the alder leaves.

It was here one morning the big black-and-white Muscovy duck flew in for a bath, and left in disgust when she saw us on the bank. Here too, a beautiful grey-green sandbar willow grew. Symmetrical, and rounded of form, its long, thin leaves a blur of green against the clay bank, it always seemed alive with twittering birds.

One morning, two small birds, one yellow-breasted, the other red, flew out of the dense branches and began bathing in the quiet pool. Neither of us will forget the picture they made as their jewel-like reflections shimmered in the water, and the silvery drops showered about them as they played.

We're glad we decided to come, though it's not the same, nor will it ever be again. But the wild things have returned and reclaimed some of their destroyed territory. We were happy to see numerous little animal tracks in the sand, and hear a covey of quail calling in the underbrush. Breakfast at Tiffany's, or anywhere else, could never offer that kind of entertainment!

July 14, 1979

Sandbar Willows

❀ ❀ ❀

Of all the willow species in the Northwest states, I think the sandbar is the most attractive. In open spaces, with ample sun and room to grow, it expands into a lovely rounded bush that from a distance appears as a soft, grey-green mist. The very narrow leaves are greyish-white beneath and silvery-green on top. However, when growing in crowded conditions, the little bushes become rather scrawny, twiggy trees, but still they have that sage green mistiness to their leaf masses. To an artist, it is a joy to try to capture that graceful airiness, that blending of grey and silver and green.

In autumn, they may turn a pale yellow-orange and keep their colored leaves for some time. But in years of dryness and excessive heat they merely turn brown and lose their leaves almost all at once. After the creek bank has been disturbed, the sandbars are the first to return, sprouting quickly either from seeds or pieces of root lodged among the rocks.

"Sandbar" seems to be a colloquial name for a group of willows no more than fifteen feet high, with slender limbs and branches and very narrow, greenish-grey leaves, pointed at both ends. Lyon's *Trees, Shrubs and Flowers to Know in Washington* lists only three under the category of sandbar: *Salix argophylla*, silverleaf willow; *S. exigua*, coyote willow; *S. caudata*, whiplash willow.

So today, Charlotte and I sketched sandbar willows—big ones, little ones, low bushes, tall bushes—anything that looked like a willow. The little trees are deceptive. To look at them, it would seem easy to draw that soft, rounded form and place those thin branches in graceful symmetry—but it isn't. Their thick, twiggy interiors are alive with all kinds of birds, and what a grand hiding place it is for them. But all that twittering activity and jumping about in there makes concentration on the artwork next to impossible!

July 14, 1979

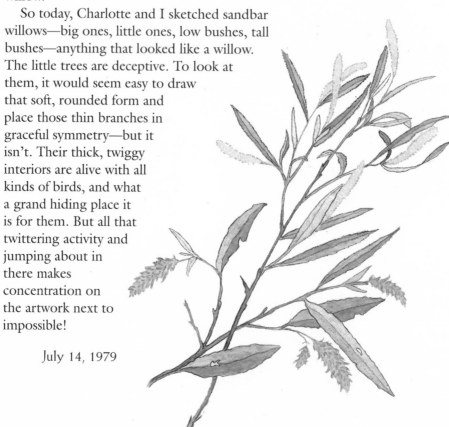

The Heron

This morning I'm back at the little pool among the alders, watching the tiny fish jump and dash about. The first few times we came here last month, I didn't know there were fish in the pool at all, as we never saw any. But for about a week now they have been very active, even flinging themselves several inches out of the water. If I were any kind of entomologist, I'd check and see what is exciting them these past few days. But I'm lazy and really want to stay hidden to see what might come prowling so early in the day.

Then quite suddenly the great blue heron flies low, wheels, alights in a tree, and stares disapprovingly at me. So much for my alder cover! I hardly dare to breathe—hoping it really doesn't see me, and is only resting before it comes in for breakfast.

The rocks get harder, and my right leg is asleep and my neck has a crick in it from watching that bird. But it stands still as a statue. Once it turns its head to watch something downstream, but acts as though it has all morning, and couldn't care less if it has breakfast or not. Then I shift my position a little to keep both legs from becoming paralyzed, and with a loud, disgusted croak it takes off for a less crowded spot.

The great blue heron is something I wasn't familiar with until I began my wasp studies along the Rogue River down by Hellgate Bridge. There I'd often surprise one fishing along the shore.

And once, I startled one out of a low madrone tree beside the trail that runs along the south side of the river. What a flipping, flapping, flopping commotion until that ungainly bird became airborne! To look at one of those long-legged birds, you'd never know they could perch in a tree, much

less build a nest in one. Several times I've seen them landing in their huge nest across the river, and I always say to myself, "It's just impossible, they're not perching birds—how can they keep their balance so high up on those stilt legs?" But they do, and even raise their chicks high above the river. What a sight it must be to see their first efforts when they leave the nest and learn to fly.

But today my heron is unsociable and I pack up my things and leave, as disappointed as he that the day started out so badly.

August 6, 1979

A Surprising Visitor

Again I'm sitting deep among the young alders, hidden from the quiet pool, and hoping something will wander in without seeing me. Then at a distance I hear that strange squawk announce the arrival of my "duck" of last week. Closer it comes—I grab the binoculars, and stop breathing. Then right across from my hiding place, twenty to thirty feet away, a dark, noisy bird lands in the top of a small alder. Through the binoculars it has the head and crest of a merganser, a dark body, and legs of a small heron. It cranes its neck, crest raised, and looks in my direction. Of course it was careful to be partially screened by a thick branch of leaves, so all I see is a dark silhouette with a long neck. But gradually it seems to gain confidence and moves about a little, and I see a glint of green on the wings and maroon on the breast. A little green heron? It's certainly not the big blue—and not my duck of last week. When I get home I'll check in *Peterson's Field Guide to Western Birds*, but I'm almost sure it's a small heron. Yet that strange call was identical to the one I heard when I saw— or thought I saw—a bird with a mottled head and brown duck bill. Now I'm more confused than ever!

In all the years I haunted Hellgate and the river below the canyon, I never saw a green heron. The big blue could always be depended on to be around somewhere, either flying grandly overhead or fishing motionless in the shallows. So why should a green heron, which must be rather uncommon in this area, be fidgeting around a shallow, mostly dried up, minor creek like this when he has the whole long, wide river to revel in?

I wait and dare not move, and still the bird sits in the tree, preens its feathers, looks about, stands first on one leg then the other—but seems to have no intention of coming in to fish or bathe in the pool. Finally, when rigor mortis has set in (for me), it flies off with a derisive croak, leaving me to again wonder what it is I've seen.

August 8, 1979

Reflections

❀ ❀ ❀

There has been rain in the hills, and to my delight when I came for breakfast I found more water in the creek, and some of the smaller pools are much wider and deeper this morning. I'm sitting out in the open across from the Garry's oak and can see the reflections of a clump of scarlet mimulus that I'm sure wasn't blooming a few days ago. The pool is now deep and wide; I can see every rock and tree and bush on the other bank mirrored on the smooth surface.

I'm sitting enchanted by the brilliant red of the flowers when, with just a whisper of sound, a big, fat robin glides in and lands on a rock at the water's edge (his reflection is mirror-perfect too), and the red of his breast almost matches the hue of the mimulus. He is in no hurry to leave, and nothing disturbs the serenity of this little moment in time. I was hoping he would take a dip and send a shower of silvery drops into the early morning sunlight. But he declines—perhaps because he has an audience—and presently flies off, leaving only the red flowers as a reminder of his visit.

In vain these past few days I've tried to win the green heron's confidence by remaining quiet in the same spot, so it could become accustomed to my being there. It flies in, perches in a tree, and watches me. It is a green heron, and really not so rare as I thought. I think it had been fishing in this deepest pool all summer, until I disrupted its routine. Several mornings I've seen crayfish moving slowly about among the rocks in the pool, and also found bleached shells of their claws and tails scattered on the little sand bars along the shore.

It doesn't trust me, and I really don't want it to, so I'll leave the little pool and go elsewhere to eat and sketch. After all, the green heron found it first!

August 15, 1979

Dead Trees

❀ ❀ ❀

All summer I've noticed down here along the creek that the dead trees are
never without their tenants. The four old pines at the entrance where the
road ends, the solitary dead oak downstream, and the old leafless poplars
around the bend always have a varied company of little, medium, and large
birds. The birds don't seem to do much but just sit and survey the world.
The noisy sapsuckers are always chattering among themselves, the jays call
back and forth, but the little birds just rest and look about.

The past week or so I've seen a lone hawk sitting quietly in the big
cottonwood at the edge of the field. It lets me go along the road, but if I
stop it flies off. However, the last day or so I've been able to stop opposite
its perch and watch it through the binoculars. It's nervous when I do this,
but I've had a good look at it, and I'm sure it's a young bird—possibly one
of the nestlings the pair raised on my hill last summer. Every spring, in all
the years we've been here, a pair of old red-tailed hawks have nested back on
my hill, and usually raise two fledglings. The young hawks make nervous
wrecks out of us after their parents give them up, as they cry and cry and
carry on as though they were starving to death. Just when we can't stand it
any more, their mother will come with something for them—and what a
wild scramble! They normally stay around their old territory until late
summer, but the piteous crying gradually diminishes until only occasionally
we hear a rather juvenile hawk-like call back on the hill. I think when the
young birds are learning to catch their own dinner, they come down here to
the creek and sit in the dead trees waiting for something to scramble over
the open piles of rock. When we see the old hawks bringing food home,

they usually come from this direction, frequently with a snake or long-tailed lizard.

I think, for sheer popularity, the dead, bare trees far outdo the green leafy ones. Of course, the birds are more visible in the dead trees, but even so they appear to be a common meeting place where territorial rights are more or less forgotten. Certainly there seems to be very little fighting or bullying of the smaller birds. Since no one builds a nest in such an open place, perhaps they don't feel crowded or threatened. And it always looks to me as though they all like the companionship, because invariably when two or three fly in to rest a minute, after a little while several more will come, and presently a whole flock of various sizes will be sitting quietly watching the rest of the world go by.

September 19, 1979

Cardinal Flowers and a Rufous Hummer

❁ ❁ ❁

This first day of September brings the grey clouds of coming fall. Not so dark and thick as the autumn storm clouds, yet they bring a welcome relief from late summer heat. In the night they quietly overspread the sky, but no rain has fallen yet. So this morning, as it's a little colder than usual, I'm sitting right in the dry creek bed, out of the breeze, looking downstream and enjoying a large clump of red, red mimulus that seems all the brighter because of the grey sky. And as I sketch, a rufous hummer zooms in from upstream and begins exploring the flowers. Since there is no sunlight, its little jeweled bib appears almost black, but occasionally it turns at the right angle and I see a flash of dull red. It's not at all worried at my being here and proceeds to visit every flower in a systematic circle about the plant. Then, after it's dipped into all of them, it begins again —just in case it might have missed one.

Several rufous hummingbirds have been attracted to the mimulus in the past week or so, but none have come as close as this in their nectar hunting. Since it's a little cooler this morning, the hummer is a slight bit slower, so I get a better look at it. A day or so ago, I was exploring around the rocks at this spot and looked up just in time to see a hummer diving straight for me out of the blue sky. Before I instinctively started to duck my head, another came at breakneck speed from behind me. A split second before the collision they both veered up and away, to circle about and do the whole maneuver over again.

Having that tiny thing diving right at me at about eye level, all I see is a round fuselage and the whirling propeller wings that look like a miniature WWI fighter plane diving right on target—shades of the Red Baron!

September 1, 1979

Killdeer

❀ ❀ ❀

How I love the plaintive call of the killdeer. All night I heard them high in the darkness, calling and flying about. They have been flying over for the past week or so, but this morning they seem more numerous than usual. Actually they are migrating, but in a most indirect manner, by flying about in circles, calling and generally acting as though they intended to stay as soon as they can decide on a place to land. But it appears that they linger for a bit to allow the stragglers to catch up to the main group, for I can hear the faraway birds coming closer; then suddenly they all drift off to the south, and their sad calls become fainter and fainter until they disappear over my hill. Perhaps in an hour or so another group will sail over, calling and circling. This must have gone on all night, for I heard them every time I was awake.

This same thing happens in springtime. One day, or very often one moonlit night, suddenly killdeer will be calling and flying, forcing me out of my warm bed to stand in the field in flimsy slippers and thin robe, listening to that wild gypsy calling until the chill of the early dawn drives me in again.

These little birds with their striped collars and long legs always remind me of swampland and sea shore, and they have in their penetrating cry something of the sea birds and salt spray that makes me say with John Masefield, "I must go down to the sea again, the lonely sea and the sky..."

I've known killdeer all my life, and I never tire of their incessant cries. I only wish I lived close to water so I could hear them through the summer as they nest and call to their little ones—and the fledglings answer with that high-pitched "beep" that can be heard over the noisiest of rushing waters.

September 22, 1979

Last Visit

❀ ❀ ❀

The creek runs muddy and swift through its once-dry gullies and depressions. Now it has at least two courses, both wide and tumbling, with long narrow islands between them. At the edge of the water on one of these islands, I see the dead stalk of the mullein I sketched the day the monarch butterfly flew over on its long migration to somewhere on the California coast. The stalk is still attached to the plant, and the brown seed heads bob and sway in the rushing water, but the tenacious plant still has a few small green leaves growing from the crown, and unless the water gets higher and washes it out, it probably will remain alive until our freezing weather later in the winter.

All of the scarlet mimulus are covered with at least a foot of rushing water, and the bank where I lingered so many times to eat breakfast is almost level with the surface of the creek. The little pool where the tiny fish jumped, and where I saw the green heron, is just a wide place with alder thickets on either side. No sand bars, no rocks, no clumps of sedge.

But all is as it should be for December, and I see tiny green leaves sheltered among the rocks, and grass sprouting thick on sand above the water's edge. Not too many weeks hence, the willows will be covered with furry catkins—even now, the tallest alders have their green and red tassels swaying in the breeze, and soon their pollen will lie like yellow dust on quiet stretches of water.

I can never quite become accustomed to winter being so short and spring coming so soon after New Year's Day as it does here. For me, winter is over when I find the first spring queen (*Snythyris reniformis*) on my dark hillside and the first pussy willow down beside the creek.

As I go home, I sample a few of the rose hips from the bush I sketched beside the log on the seventh of November, but they are sour and mushy, and I doubt if even the birds would relish them now. When I pass the old fire-scarred pines, I see they have not a single visitor. And all summer I never saw them without their company of birds—woodpeckers, jays, flickers, even a hawk occasionally.

Come to think of it, even towhee was absent from its old haunts today. It's rather unusual to be out anywhere along a stream at any time without seeing or hearing some kind of bird. When towhee and the jays have deserted you, the countryside is indeed lifeless and quiet.

I detour along the edge of the field, going downstream to see if I can spot the old leaning tree held up by the grapevine cables, but I'm unable to find it, or even where it ought to be. When the leaves are gone and the creek is running bank to bank with muddy water, all the landmarks disappear and everything is unfamiliar and strange looking. But I'm sure if it were still there I'd see part of it, so it must have washed out.

A hazy sun is setting behind my hill, and shadows deepen beneath the little willows, and it's time to go home, for winter evenings have their comforts—a cozy fire, a good book, and the sound of rain on the roof.

December 31, 1979

May, and the Return of the Birds

This morning is overcast and cool, but the birds sing as happily as they would on a sunny day. At first, when I came in April, only towhee sang from the willow thickets, and once in a while a robin practiced a few bars, but until now it's been too quiet. This is a late spring, and I'm relieved at last to hear the old familiar songs; just two singers, but at least they want me to know they're back. I guess I'll always remember those terrible "silent springs" of a few years ago when on a May morning I could stand on my hill and not hear one bird song (had Rachael Carson's "silent spring" visited Grants Pass too?). The hill was so alive with birds when we first came, it was impossible to hold a conversation with anyone more than a few yards away, because of the symphony of ecstatic song coming from every tree and bush.

Today the air is cool and tangy with the smells of a new season: alder, willow, and poplar leaves; wet sand, new grasses, and young plants; and just the smell of water and wet soil.

The first blooming plant I've spotted is the Scotch broom, but a legion of little ox-eye daisies will be a close second. Hundreds of plants with big, fat buds wait only for a warm day. And I never knew they were here, either. They must have died down by July last year, for I never even saw their leaves when we first came, that hot summer day.

The scarlet mimulus has sprung up all over the sand bars and among the rocks. The same clumps that bloomed last year, and were covered with water this winter, are green again and soon will be blooming. Even where the water piled up sand and rocks, the plants go right on as though nothing had happened. They just grow a few inches taller and send out their light green leaves as before. And I wondered about them when the water was so deep and muddy over their chosen spot.

But the plant that surprises me most is the tiny *Epilobium*, "farewell to summer," which blooms so late in the fall. It was the last blossom I found in October, and now the tiny plants are blooming again so early. Are the late ones a second crop from the seeds of these May blossoms? It hardly seems they could survive the torrid July and August days here on this hot sand.

And the sandbar willows! When I came in March and April, they looked as though they'd all died in the winter. And I worried about them. What would it be like here beside the creek without the lovely sandbars? How could they have all died through such a mild winter? And now I see tiny buds appearing on the topmost branches—so they aren't dead at all. They're still as naked as they were in January, except for those tiny swelling buds where the sun hits them. But why are they so late? Willows are the most impatient of the bushes along any creek or river. In fact, the other kinds are fully leafed out—have been since the first of April. And here the sandbars are just awakening! I'll never forgive them for making me think they were all dead.

Most of the birds are here again: I even saw a little band of killdeer going through last week. And black-headed grosbeak is singing almost every morning—nonstop as usual. As I come through the field, a meadowlark sings, and sometimes he's still on the same light pole when I go home again.

A few days ago I forgot my binoculars, and of course I saw a strange bird, but without the glasses I couldn't tell what it was. It stood on a rock downstream and was about the size of a killdeer, but it had an odd cry, like a sea bird, and I know I've heard that call somewhere before. So now I'm hoping to see it again—no luck so far, but I'm prepared if it does show up. No more leaving the binoculars at home!

May 22, 1980

Wild Rose Blossoms

❀ ❀ ❀

The little rose bush that last fall had so many brilliant red hips is now in full bloom, and what a sight it is. But long before it can be seen, it makes its presence known by the heavenly fragrance of blossoms and leaves. It's the old sweetbrier, or eglantine, and while not a true native, it's found just about everywhere a wild rose can grow. The dried leaves make a sweet-smelling tea, for they have the same scented oils the flowers have, and nothing quite captures the essence of springtime as a cup of this fragrant tea, made either from leaves or flowers.

Last year I didn't pick the bright red hips, as I thought to leave them for the birds through the winter. But last March, I noticed not a hip had been eaten; all were mushy and rotten on the stem. So this fall, if there is a good crop I'll take some, for even the red juice has a faint fragrance of the early blossoms.

This little bush is a special favorite of mine, and whenever I pass it as I go to the creek, I look to see how it's faring. Actually, I have several bushes like it on my own place, but they aren't in such a picturesque spot. This one, growing beside the old log, with alders, willows, and wild grasses for company, seems much more wild and free than do mine beside the driveway or at the corner of the house.

June 17, 1980

Loveliest Month Beside the Creek

❀ ❀ ❀

June has to be the loveliest month of all to come to the creek. Now the birds are singing so loudly they drown out the sound of the rushing water. Black-headed grosbeak, towhee, wrens, song sparrows—everyone seems so happy and carefree. I've been coming quite often since April, but June seems to be the month of flowers and birds. May was cold with only a few sunny days, and so was the first part of this month, but now the weather is settled and we can have our spring— although a good five to six weeks late.

I was amazed to see the extent of the cornflowers and California poppy colonies across the road from my place. The whole field is one patchwork of color, with the blue of cornflowers and the golden poppies predominating. Here and there, a stand of sorrel gives an Indian-red tint to the field, and farther toward the highway, swatches of bright yellow buckwheat look like spots of sunlight. But the blue cornflowers have taken over the place. They grow by the millions, and looking closer I see some are white, pink, or magenta—but still the blue tints the field like the reflection of the summer sky on water.

All these years they must have been there, but I never came over to see. No more than a couple hundred feet from my fence, and I never came to see them. What a waste of all those lovely summer mornings when the cornflowers bloomed and the birds sang along the creek, and the willows were misty green in the clear morning light—and I was too busy to look.

June 26, 1980

Case of the Agitated Sandpiper

Some time ago, I found out who the killdeer-like bird is that makes the haunting call along the creek in early morning. It's a spotted sandpiper. When I got a good look at it, there was no mistaking that odd bobbing motion, like a spring-loaded toy. Even when it's standing still on a rock, it bobs gently up and down, and I wonder if it can ever be motionless.

This morning the little bird was really upset, for ever since I arrived at six-thirty it had flown about, hopping between the rocks and calling PEET-PEET, so reminiscent of the cry of a sea bird. Normally it would be very philosophical, going about its business of collecting breakfast, not even noticing my presence anymore; something must have been different in its small world this morning. So I quietly took my usual place beneath a low alder and waited.

Just as I settled down, I got a quick glimpse of a doe gliding through the brush on the bank across the creek, and I suspected she was too close to the sandpiper's nest. Then in a little while, the deer emerged with a spotted fawn and both walked leisurely up the creek toward me; splashing and enjoying the water and early sun they came, never seeing me at all. They were facing the bright morning sun and the wind was at an angle so they never had a clue I was there. Then about twenty feet away the mother spotted me. She gave a low warning sound and bounded off into the brush on one side, and the fawn took off in the opposite direction. A few minutes later, the fawn came looking for its mother, and I'm sure it didn't know just what the warning was all about, for it seemed not at all frightened. It came back to where they had parted, and walked directly toward me in the middle of the creek. About four feet from me, it stopped and looked quizzically at that strange shadow beside the alder. But it still wasn't frightened. And I spoke to it twice before it realized I was something strange and not its mother at all—then it did take off, clearing the bank and bushes in a couple leaps that did credit to its youthful leaping ability!

After that, everything seemed to be frightened off, but now, half an hour later, the hummers are back exploring the scarlet mimulus, and the little sandpiper is calling in a less-agitated voice at the far end of the creek, where I'm sure its mate is sitting on the nest.

June 27, 1980

The Royal Visitor

❀ ❀ ❀

This morning when I went down to the creek, I walked quietly behind a group of young alders before coming out into the open—and it's a good thing I did. For just at the near edge of the little green pool stood the biggest, whitest, most regal and most elegant bird I've ever seen. A perfect copy of the blue heron, but just a mite less tall, and pure dazzling white.

Lately, since there hasn't been anything of interest to see in the mornings, I've been rather careless on my approach, and even this time I wasn't as cautious as I might have been. But again that blinding morning sun just coming up over the mountain saved the day, for the big bird never had the least suspicion I was there. It's hard to measure time in a situation like that, but I'm sure I must have watched it for six or seven minutes or more. I had time to put the lunch down, focus the binoculars, and get comfortable on one knee to observe it. The little alder I was behind wasn't nearly tall enough to enable me to stand upright without being on the skyline, and remaining still while half-crouching, half-standing would be almost impossible.

The bird was just standing and enjoying the early sun when I first saw it; then after a few minutes it moved very majestically out into the water and downstream a little, and poised in a waiting position. Still as an alabaster statue gleaming in the sun, with that backdrop of alders and willows, it made a picture I'll never forget. Then quick as a flash it speared something and gulped it down. It stood for a while, preening its immaculate feathers, then very slowly walked down toward the other end of the pool. Once, it stumbled over a rock and spread those huge white wings to regain its balance. How I hoped it would lose just one of those gleaming white feathers!

In all this time, it never gave any sign that it knew I was watching—and all this time I was like a statue myself, not daring to breathe or move, or hardly blink an eye. Gradually the big bird, picking here and there among the shallows, walked toward the sandbar willows at the far end of the pool; then very leisurely it waded across, hopped into the bushes, and disappeared from sight.

August 21, 1980

First Day of Autumn

❀ ❀ ❀

The killdeer are flying and calling on this clear blue morning, the first day of autumn. They must be very high today, for I can't see them; only their plaintive calls drift down out of a cloudless sky.

Today the creek whispers with a louder voice over the rocks, and the water moves with a faster pace through the little rivulets where the day before yesterday there was only a tiny trickle, or none at all. Always the creek does this, the age-old ritual of the returning of the water. One day there are only stagnant green pools, the next the sound of running water over the rocks—water that mysteriously arrives in the night, and from now till one hot day in July of next year that little stream will swell and tumble and roar along its rocky bed, bringing life and moisture to the willows, alders, cottonwoods, and the legions of tiny plants that depend on the annual replenishment of this vital element.

Many of the alders and willows are turning color now, but only the grape leaves show the brilliant hue of the coming season. For some reason there is no vine maple along this part of the creek, so there never is much of a show of color—except in those rare years when the grape leaves decide to turn every color you could imagine in fall. From palest flesh-pink, through fire-red, yellow, orange, bronze, to mahogany, the wild grape can be the most spectacular kaleidoscope of color ever seen in these parts—but they do it only once in ten to fifteen years.

A few days ago, the great blue heron came wheeling in but veered off when it saw me, and it hasn't come back since. The little birds are restless in the willows, and for a brief moment I saw a grey and white warbler sunning itself on an alder branch. But soon all will be gone and only old faithful towhee will call to me in the morning, and the little pool will be in shadow all day long.

September 22, 1980

Drought, Logging, and Development

❀ ❀ ❀

Much has changed for the small creek since Charlotte and I had our early morning tea parties so long ago. A drought has lasted nearly ten years, and more houses have been built along its once wild banks. But most devastating of all, hundreds of acres have been clearcut on the steep hills. Large homes have been built on the hillsides above the creek, and much of the latent ground water is used for these dwellings. In the early days, the creek always had pools where a slow trickle from underground kept the water fresh, even in the hottest summer. Now, in July and August, if any shallow ponds exist, they are stagnant and too warm for the tiny fish to survive.

Seldom does the creek run bank-to-bank with water from heavy rains or snow melt from the higher elevations. Consequently, its banks and sandbars are choked with tangles of blackberry, poison oak, and stunted willows.

Without pools of water every hundred feet, many birds—the heron, spotted sandpiper, yellow-breasted chat, and groups of robins—have disappeared. The new awareness of the value of undisturbed riparian areas came too late for the small streams that used to support a varied amount of wildlife even through the hot, dry months of summer. Now they're reduced to mere run-off channels in winter, carrying mud and silt from the cut-over land at their headwaters.

2
The River and Hellgate

The Setting

The Rogue River is short, as rivers go in the West. Starting on the north side of Crater Lake, the Rogue runs through the towns of Shady Cove, Gold Hill, and Grants Pass, then through many scenic gorges and finally emptying into the Pacific Ocean at Gold Beach.

One of the most interesting areas along the Rogue is the deep cleft of volcanic rock at Hellgate Canyon, twenty miles from Grants Pass. Here, the river officially enters the Siskiyous. Here too, the traveler encounters the first large outcroppings of serpentine and peridotite rock formations.

The north-facing hillside is cool and has more trees than the south-facing torrid slope. Both exposures have their own insect life and plant communities. I believe one is considered Upper Transition zone, the other Lower Sonoran. Certainly the climate, temperature, and moisture are vastly different for the two sides of the river at this point.

The river itself, just below the canyon, has another plant and insect community. Here the digger wasps love to excavate their tunnels, and Sceliphron, the mud dauber, gathers mud for her clay edifice. Here too, the tiger beetles play in the hot sand, and Bembix entombs her paralyzed flies.

But it is on the torrid rock faces far above the water that the Odynerus wasp and the resin bee ply their trade. And it is here the observer must lie for hours in the broiling sun to record the lives and loves of these fascinating, little-known creatures.

First Day at Hellgate

Today the wild geese flew over and called me away from my work. I knew there would be no use trying to do anything here at home, so I did something I've been meaning to do for months: packed a lunch and drove to Hellgate Canyon. It's only ten miles from here, but it has been all of nine years since I've taken the time to go there and explore those rugged cliffs.

The canyon was more beautiful than I had remembered. That cool green water so far below, the massive rocks, the cliffs across the river in deep shadow—how serene and quiet they all are. Why, oh why have I waited all these years before coming here to enjoy the peace and contentment of this wild place? How I regret the loss of all those sunny hours that I could have been among these quiet hills, or down on the warm sand at the river's edge. As I sat in the shelter of a rock, another flock of geese flew over. I can think of no other place in southern Oregon where I would rather be when the wild geese send their haunting calls across the autumn skies.

ABOVE HELLGATE BRIDGE   GEESE BEFORE THE STORM OCTOBER 29 '76

After lunch, I climbed around the cliffs and rock outcrops, admiring the number of little plants that grow here. The species and varieties that can grow in this barren place are amazing. What a rock garden it must be in springtime! And I know that I am forever lost now—for no matter how busy or hurried I may be next spring and summer, I'll have to come here to take pictures and sketch every few days, or at least once a week.

This must be a torrid place in summer, for even now, this late in the season, the sun is hot and the wind blowing from off the rock faces is almost unpleasant in its warmth. Now everything is dry and shriveled. The bunchgrasses rasp in the dry wind, and the leaves of the stunted plants scrape against the rocks, as did those of the trees and grasses of the far-off mesa lands of Colorado so many years ago. Standing in the shelter of a sheer rock cliff, I hear again those long-forgotten sounds and see again those sagebrush lands of home. The only thing missing is the sigh of the wind through the branches of the piñon pines, and the smell of the hot sage in the desert sun.

October 17, 1966

Plants of Hellgate Canyon

❀ ❀ ❀

This is a world of dwarf plants. Many are old friends I've known before, elsewhere. But here they are smaller editions of themselves. The huge outcrops of basaltic rock create many nooks and hidden shelves of soil where tiny plants attempt a foothold. Many plants succumb to the impossible obstacles of this harsh environment, as can be seen in the bleached stalks and dead wood of bygone summers.

The tiny rock ferns (oak, lace, and parsley) are the most amazing, for they seem to thrive where there is no soil at all, in the cracks high up on the sides of the rocks. Where they can possibly find their moisture throughout the long, rainless summer is beyond imagination. Facing south, these dark-colored boulders must become torridly overheated in the months of June, July, August, and September. And many years we do not have even a drop of precipitation during those months. I visited the small ferns before we had our first splash of rain last month, and most of their little fronds were green and healthy looking. Some I found in the most exposed places, dried up completely. And I'm watching with interest to see if, after the fall rains set in, these ferns send up new fiddle-necks early in the spring, or possibly sooner.

The over-wintering female *Polistes** wasps were flying in the hot sun and resting on the warm rock faces this afternoon. I heard and saw a few lively locusts among the dry bunchgrasses. And one daring little spider gaily sailed out over the abyss above the river, on its long, silken parachute. It was between me and the lowering sun, and looked like a tiny golden drop at the end of a silvery cord.

Occasionally a night hawk plunged toward the river with a sound like a falling rock. By the time I focused the binoculars, it was winging away. It was quite a bit larger than a killdeer, and all grey except for a broad, white, transverse stripe on each wing.

How those sheer rock cliffs remind me of long forgotten places. I thought they were forgotten—but they are all brought back to memory

---

* *Polistes* wasps. Make paper nests under eaves, in attics, in rock crevices. Beneficial, as they feed larvae chewed-up insect pests—flies, canker worms, etc. Non-aggressive if not disturbed. Mated queens over-winter.

again as I sit in the hot sun and hear that dry whisper of the bunchgrasses. Those little grasses that sound the same in all the wild and secret places of the West.

October 31, 1966

Spring Has Come to Hellgate!

Three weeks since I've been here, and even at this nadir of the year there has been much change. Unbelievably, some of the little white oaks are putting out new leaves! And all the tiny rock ferns have new fronds. I wanted to see their minuscule fiddle-necks, but they beat me to it. I did find, after much looking, one little frond still rolled up in a tiny ball at the end of a tinier stem. It was $1/8$" wide and the stem $1/2$" long. Under the hand lens it had a perfect little fern leaf rolled and compressed in the typical fiddle-neck of all ferns. Perfect in every detail, and almost microscopic in size.

The chokecherry is still in bloom since the last time I saw it. I passed it on the way to the far end of the canyon about 10:30 a.m., and I saw nothing flying about it at that time. But on my way back around one o'clock there were two or three kinds of *Erestalis* flies, and I think one dark fuzzy bee. This in spite of the fact that it rained lightly off and on, and the wind had come up brisk and chill. Found a small white sweet clover in bloom in a cleft in the rock down by the water, and I have no doubt it also had visitors in the brief sunny moments. A few of the yellow mustards are blooming sparsely too. I doubt very much that winter lasts more than a few weeks in this sheltered canyon.

The sun is much lower over the hill across the river now. I want to come near the winter solstice to see when it sets and how far to the south it is. I used to hate these short dreary days of November and December, but I've learned to enjoy them increasingly each year. The tide of life in woods and fields is at its lowest now. This is the time of rest and retrospect. The time to observe quietly and at an unhurried pace. I'm beginning to prefer it to the hectic turmoil of spring and summer.

As I look across the river, the little silver drops of rain shine like tiny jewels in the weak sunlight. Against the dark walls on the other side I can see again the small flying things dancing and flitting about. There aren't so many this time; shorter days and cold temperatures have ruthlessly weeded them out. How many thousands there must be in the warm sun of spring and the torrid heat of summer. Saw the *Polistes* wasps again flying about their winter retreats. Perhaps every sunny day in winter they will be out for a brief time.

Hiked over to the far point to the east that I hadn't explored before. There were actually two more rock points and one cove to check on. The river is too high now to see whether the little cove had a sandy beach and gravel bar like the others had. The last rock outcrop has very little vegetation on it. It is more level than the others and, being less sheltered, gets most of the cold east wind from up river. The river makes a sharp bend to the south just above, and the banks are wider and more open. The wind has a clear sweep until it hits this first rock bulwark of the canyon. There were numerous mosses, lichens, and a few grasses, but in comparison to the other ledges this one was almost barren.

Lest one be inclined to forget civilization in this quiet place, the stench of the river and the sewage it carries comes as a shock as you face that cold east wind on this first rock ledge of Hellgate. The river narrows sharply here, and at the base of the cliff is a bay or backwater that collects all the debris and litter that comes down from upstream. The main current of the river flows swiftly past, but the water here is stagnant and foul-smelling. Somehow, after seeing the old trees, tin cans, cardboard boxes, and other detritus of affluent society, the rest of the lovely landscape is a little diminished in beauty.

Found a small cave or entrance to one where it looks as though some animal lives (and it was cleaner and less evil-smelling than the people who dump their garbage in the river), possibly a raccoon or skunk. Also came rather suddenly and unexpectedly on a paper nest of the bald-faced hornet under a ledge. I'm thankful it was in December and not in the heat of July! How fast could one flee over these jumbled rocks with loose shale underfoot and an angry mob of hornets in pursuit? I hope to heaven I never find out! I'm inclined to think that with numerous snakes, yellow-jackets, wasps, and whatnot, this might not be an ideal place for a quiet stroll on a hot summer's day.

The river is brown and muddy now, and doesn't look nearly as deep from above as when it is dark and green. I often wonder just what that other canyon wall looks like in the bright sunlight. I've never seen it except in shadow, for the sun is too low by the time the fog lifts to see the south wall in bright light.

When the sun is out and I sit against a sheltering rock, I can forget it is the month of December. But when the sun goes behind a cloud and the wind whips the dry leaves off the ledges, it's not hard to remember! And I keep wondering—who of these tiny plants will be the first to bloom? And when? If this warm spell keeps up, it could be before the new year.

Had a glimpse of the big blue heron flying over the hill, but it disappeared and I never saw it again. Very few birds here now. Did hear a few chirps of some kind of sparrow, but they dodge among the rocks and I never get to see them.

December 1, 1966

First Butterfly in the Canyon

Perched on a white forget-me-not in the middle of a patch of bright green grass, it poised motionless for a second. I had just looked that way and knew there had been only the white of the small flowers and lavender stars of filaree—and now a dazzling luminescent orange spot had bloomed where there had been none before. The instant I moved, it darted up and away, but I knew before it flew that it was the first Sara orange tip of the season. Only that brief glimpse, no more.

Beautiful day again at the canyon. Arrived there earliest of all—9:30 a.m., and everything was fresh and dewy in the early morning sun. Got some sketches of the grass widows above the first cove. That flat stretch of mostly rock is comfortable to work on and has a breathtaking view of the canyon up-river. Sheltered on one side by a large myrtle (*Umbellularia*) bush, and several balanced rocks along the edge, the canyon forms a sort of hollow with a north exposure. Here the moss is thicker, the lichens softer, and the plants greener than at other spots more exposed to the sun. Numerous clumps of grass widows favor the place, and their bright magenta bells against the furry silver-gray moss are unforgettable. This silver moss grows only in certain places and isn't nearly as common as the green and brown kinds; also it is more shaggy and curly than others. So far I've been unable to identify it and may have to send a sample in to OSU at Corvallis.

Brought the water colors and hoped to get some reasonable likeness of the color tones of the canyon and rocks. But to my disgust, first I broke the pen point in the holder and had to improvise a branch to hold the new point; then, as though that wasn't aggravation enough, when I tried using the water colors I discovered the damn ink wasn't water-proof! So working on color was out, but I did get good sketches of canyon and river and dwarf trees in the rocks. Don't know if I'll ever have time enough again to try water color, but if I do I'll check on the ink beforehand.

Reluctantly left the beautiful spot and brought my lunch to a little grassy meadow where the filaree blooms thick among the short grasses. They seem to be the most numerous species in bloom now. Tiny yellow mimulus are increasing among the rocks and down the slopes between boulders. One dwarf manzanita about two feet tall is just coming into bloom, wedged in a cleft of a rock facing to the south. How it manages to survive in the heat, growing as it does against that rock wall with no relief from the scorching sun all summer, is something I just can't figure out. Found more wild gooseberries in bloom and they are alive with bees. A medium-sized black bee with hairy gray legs works both the willows down by the river and the berry bushes here. It may be a miner, and I hope I'll have time to hunt for her burrow and watch her work this summer. Speaking of the willows down lower, I saw a small, dull-colored tan butterfly working the catkins last Monday, and I think I've seen it here on the hillside today. It looks so much like a moth and flies so quickly and is so inconspicuous when it lands, I can't get a good look at it. But I think it may be a ringlet.

First butterflies in the canyon
Sara Orange Tip
Ringlet

    Heard a strange hawk-like call from across the river, but never saw the bird. It could be a fish hawk's nesting call. They should be nesting now, for the redtail hawks are calling and flying up on my hill at home. Will watch for it next time. If osprey use the same nest year after year, and I think they do, then they will be easy to watch. A large, dead fir across the river, high up against the skyline, has a hawk nest near its top, and that could be their home. Now I wish I had a good pair of binoculars—what is worse than a bird-watcher without them?

March 8, 1967

The Merganser and Her Babies

❀ ❀ ❀

Cool and windy at the east end today. As I climbed down the slope I thought of the coast and that sharp fresh wind off the headlands, and the warmth of the pale sun, and the murmur of tiny pebbles as they washed in and out with each wave. The river is louder than usual, and with a little imagination I could smell the salt spray and hear the sea birds of Agate Beach. That was a million years ago, and days were long and happy and brighter than they've ever been since.

New flowers have been appearing since the last visit ten days ago— numerous wild onions, and a tall, yellow daisy with sage-green leaves. I should know that daisy, but can't be sure of it. The little onions favor the slope below the spring, at the base of a huge rock. I've often wondered whether that spring would stay moist and dripping through the hot days of late summer.

Those plants I've seen all winter with woody, hollow stems and greenish-grey leaves are blooming now. There seem to be three varieties. One tall with very few flowers; another as tall, but with compact little white heads in a very loose umbel; and one, the showiest of all, shorter with very dense umbels of soft, foamy, creamy white blossoms. I believe all three are species of *Eriogonum*, or wild buckwheat. The big, showy ones (*Eriogonum compositum*) are the most numerous now and grow in large clumps among the bright yellow daisies with the grey leaves (*Eriophylum*). They make a beautiful picture against the grey rocks, with the backdrop of strange greenish water so far below.

That cold wind is blowing again, and very few insects are out. But it's only 9:45 a.m., and I've been here only an hour.

Last spring I found a tiny colony of strange little plants that grew in a rosette, with leaves very like the small saxifrage I saw so much of on the rocks along the river. I thought they were saxifrage, but they never bloomed when the other species bloomed. Now they have their odd blossoms, and the mystery deepens. The little stalk is eight to ten inches high, topped with a few bright lavender, four-petaled blossoms. They have a long corolla tube much like a radish flower, but are very much smaller: tube $3/8"$ long, flower $1/2"$ wide. They started blooming last time I was here, and today they are going to seed—and I think that gives away their secret! They have produced a long, thin, upright pod like the mustards.

Ate dinner high on a rock ledge above the river, surrounded by the foamy blossoms of the *Eriogonum compositum* and bright yellow daisies. Hoped to see butterflies coming in for lunch. But I'll never know whether there were any, for a merganser came swimming by on the other side of the river followed by a whole fleet of fluffy, bobbing, bouncing little ones! They all headed for a little sandy cove directly opposite, and all climbed out and took a sun bath. I never moved, and they sat in the sun for about a half hour preening and running about. Then the mother decided to go swimming and

1-29-68   MERGANSERS FLYING THRU HELL GATE CANYON

diving, and everyone plopped into the water and off they went. She took them back upriver against the swift current, but always close in to the rocks. Once when she swam through the rapids, the little ones climbed over a low rock outcrop and met her on the other side. When she dived, the whole bunch followed her on the surface, swimming along, head down, until she surfaced in the midst of them. Several times, three or four would climb up on her back and get a free ride. Then she would spurt ahead and off they'd slide, and then half swimming, half running on the water, they would take off after her.

I've never seen anything so buoyant and so fast. They bobbed on the water like corks, and they could swim as fast as their mother, for they kept up with her through rapids and cross currents and always up river. Before they disappeared around a rock ledge, I saw the drake waiting for the family to join him.

Later I heard some kind of bird calling in a high-pitched voice down below the last rock pile at the east end. Carefully crawling over the top, I saw one of the babies who seemed lost from the group, and just as I got the binoculars on him his mother came sailing around the cliff to rescue him. She didn't see me for some time, and I got a good look at all of them. Her head is reddish brown with a crest toward the back like a kingfisher. The little ones are still fuzzy in their baby down—there were eleven of them—with grey oblong spots on each side and of the neck.

Now I'm not so sure they are the same birds I saw in April. These seem duller and their feet aren't that bright orange I saw when they were sunning on the sandy ledge. It's possible, though, that they lose their bright color during nesting season and their plumage becomes less conspicuous. I had quite a hectic half-hour leaping from one rock to another, first one side of a ledge, then the other as they swam away. But I think I got a picture of them fairly close up. Now they've kept me from my work and I'll have to try to catch up. They are sunning themselves in the little cove again, so I'd better get the sketching and the notes finished and head for the west end.

The strange plants with the white cottony leaves will be blooming in a few days, and I'm betting they will have yellow daisy-like flowers. When they do bloom, they'll be the most numerous at the east end. Now I can see several things blooming across the river on the south wall. One bush looks like azalea or white rhododendron. And I think some of the *Eriogonum* is over there on the rock shelves where they get most of the sun. Also some of the yellow daisies. No chance of getting over there this year, but the best time would be in May, as this is the first time I've seen blossoms on that side.

Well, there goes the merganser family off the sand bar. She took them along the other side, and at the swiftest part of the rapids she crossed over on this side. All but three made it with her, but they just couldn't swim through that swift water. After trying, and being tumbled and tossed back several times, the three decided to climb over a rock ledge and detour the rapids. The last I saw, they were half flying, half running up over the rocks and disappearing over the other side. I never did spot them crossing the water farther up, but they must have, as soon as they got into quieter water. That little sand bar looks deserted now, and I guess I'll leave too.

May 24, 1967

Those Clowns the Tiger Beetles

❀ ❀ ❀

Jumping, running, flying—they play these last days of summer away. Seemingly without a care in the world, these metallic green beetles with cream-colored spots run gaily over the warm sand. Aimlessly here and there, back and forth, up a sand hill, down the other side, endlessly scrambling, looking, inquiring. They never seem to eat anything and they're not interested in digging out the burrows. Nothing to do but skim lightly over the bright sand on their long legs and tiny feet—that make not the slightest track in the driest sand.

Curious and alert to everything that moves, they never miss a thing. I discovered they love grape seeds, and will pounce on one the second it hits the sand. Often two will grab the same seed and a fight begins. It's not much of a fight though—a lot of scuffling and sand flying in all directions, then it stops as suddenly as it started and off they go, one with the seed in its jaws, the other in hot pursuit. Sometimes the one with the seed tumbles down an incline and lands in a heap on the bottom, but it never lets go the seed. By this time, the other beetle has lost interest and leaves for more profitable business.

Sometimes two will meet unexpectedly at the top of a tiny hill, and a quick cuff to the head is the usual greeting. A fast tussle and each goes merrily on its way without a backward glance. It often happens that one is resting, perhaps dozing, in the warm sun, and another beetle comes careening down a slope or around a curve and runs right over the first beetle, like a dog trotting over the door mat!

Ants they evidently don't like, for after running up to one and grabbing hold of it they quickly drop it and hastily go on their way. They act like they've made a nearsighted mistake and the sooner they can leave the better.

If they want to see something of interest, they raise themselves on their front legs to look around. But if they are wary or frightened and just ready to fly, they hug the ground and appear to have no legs at all.

Just now one tried to climb my boot, but slipped off when it reached the smooth leather. Each time it fell on its back, then quickly righted itself and came back and gave the edge of the sole a good hard bite—just to show it wasn't licked yet. Finally it gave up and nonchalantly went its way after a final nip at the sole, plainly showing its contempt for that blankety-blank object it didn't want to climb anyhow!

Sometimes two will get to fighting over something that couldn't possibly be important to them. A while ago several were pulling on opposite ends of a pine needle. Neither gained ground until one suddenly let go and the other fell over backwards.

The little clowns are fascinating to watch, and I wish I'd seen them earlier in the year when they were digging their tunnels for egg-laying. It must be a circus if they stay in groups as they are now. But of course they may pair off and each female dig in seclusion when she is ready to lay. At any rate, it will be interesting to see how they behave through the summer. I will be especially interested in knowing when they appear in spring.

October 12, 1967

Day to Climb a Mountain

❀ ❀ ❀

Ten-fifteen and the long climb begins. The sky is overcast and it may rain, but the mountain calls today. That little meadow high up on the hillside must be explored, for who knows what strange plants, birds, and insects live in that world eight hundred feet above the river?

It has been many long years since I climbed to a high mountain meadow, and though I know this won't be the same as those meadows at the edge of timberline among the hills of home, yet I'm excited and intrigued.

Thirty minutes later I'm at the lower edge of the "big meadow"—it's no longer a small clearing spanning an acre or two. Now I see it is a large, sloping, grass-covered incline. A place where one could lie in the sun and listen to the whisper of the wind in the grass—and almost believe the eternal glaciers were waiting up there above the tree line; that when the sun dimmed and the wind turned cold, the snows of winter would return to claim the lonely meadows as their own. I could almost dream I was in the high country again. Almost, I could believe the boulder-strewn slope was an alpine meadow I had known long ago and far away.

Almost, but not quite. Lest I ever forget these are the hills of Oregon, I lift my eyes to the line of trees at the edge of my meadow—and the lovely sun-tanned bark and green, green leaves of the madrone remind me of where I am, where I've been for all these twenty and more years.

But I love the meadow. In spite of the illusion, I fall in love with it at once. It is clean and open, and I can see for miles. Below, the river and Hellgate bridge and road seem misty and unreal. The south wall of the canyon is an etching in smoky blue haze that gradually clears as the pale November sun gains strength.

I've come for two things: to see what kind of plants call this meadow home, and to see whether the wasps of the canyon so far below also build their nests here. As I move up toward the middle of the grassy space, I see old friends beginning another cycle of growth: buttercups, filaree, saxifrage, forget-me-nots, and many others.

So I know the meadow isn't all grass, as I'd feared it might be here on this slope facing the torrid heat and brilliant sun of the south exposure.

All the way up I look at every rock outcrop, every chunk half-buried in the grass, but no wasp nests. Not surprising though. I figure they will be nearer the trees at the top of the meadow. The canker worms the wasps prey on probably would be on those white oaks, and there are more basalt rock clumps for building sites. Never have I seen a nest built on serpentine, so I won't search these grey-green chunks strewn over most of the open space.

Then, by pure chance, I put my lunch and Thermos down by a grey serpentine slab standing on edge in the middle of the grassy slope—and what do I see, on the NORTH side of the rock, and on the UPHILL side? Wasp nests! Three of them!

It has just occurred to me—I don't know a thing about the little wasps I thought I was so familiar with. They never build on slick smooth rocks, such as serpentine. They never build their nests on the north side, nor do they face them uphill. And they never build almost on the ground (these I just found are within two inches of the soil). So much for the so-called "experts."

All these nests are old, and all but one cell of the small one are open and being used by spiders. At least the opening is crossed by a thin, white, silky web. One is a six-cell masarid, one a two-cell, and the little one a single-cell cobble-stoned nest. The one sealed cell of the two-cell nest looked old and the occupant probably never emerged.

Later, a little farther up I found a very old two-cell nest full of holes and about to fall to pieces. Then, clear up almost into the trees at the top of the meadow, I saw a very low basalt rock with a five-cell nest, again on the north side. This was old, but still intact.

The sun has come out and as I sit in the middle of this open space and watch the clouds building up in the southwest I think I'd almost forgotten how wonderful it is to be in an unspoiled, "undeveloped" wild place away from noise and clutter.

Here there are no paper plates, no beer cans, no plastic bags to mar the landscape and diminish its wild beauty. No subdivision stakes, no fences, no roads. Nothing but the wild mountain and the untamed clouds.

Every so often a fitful cold wind blows across the meadow and the dry grass stalks shiver with a slight rustling noise. I had almost forgotten, too, how the wind sounds when you are in the middle of an open space where there aren't any trees or other obstructions to produce the familiar noises we all hear but seldom notice.

To complete the day, not fifty feet from where I ate lunch I found a completed nest of the resin bee* in a three-cornered angle of rock. And this I believe I can chip out and bring home. It was made of resin studded with tiny rocks and gravel, but wasn't quite as artistic as the one down by the river. Mostly because the gravel was practically all the same color. The first one I saw had various kinds of rock chips; several colors of serpentine, quartz, and lava. But I'm not complaining. This one is perfect and looks new and undisturbed. The sun was even warm enough to soften the resin a little, but I resisted the temptation to take it apart. I'd rather try to bring it home intact if I can. Didn't get it today though—there's plenty of time for that.

The clouds came back and the wind skipped through the short grass as I started down the long slope for home. It had been a perfect day to climb the mountain—and I found much more than I came looking for!

November 25, 1967

---

*Resin bee. Small bee that uses plant resins for nest building. One species plasters cracks and crevices in rocks with resin studded with tiny pebbles. Eggs and larval food are placed in a deep orifice of the rock, then sealed over with this unusual material. Not common.

The Merganser Babies and How They Grew!

❀ ❀ ❀

Pale December sunlight lies weakly over all the canyon today. Far above, in the stratosphere, filmy white veils of ice crystals warn of an approaching storm from the north.

But here, among the rocks, the sun is warm, and a faint roaring from the river below also warns of coming storm and high water racing through the narrow gorge. The river is still low, only a foot or two higher than last summer, but now it has lost that strange blackish-green color and is grey-brown with sediment.

Back in the dark recesses of one of the little inlets at the base of the opposite canyon wall I see something black and white washing to and fro with the tide. Through my binoculars it is just a formless, shapeless something bobbing about on the water. Is it a piece of worthless flotsam tossed up by the river during our high water of last week? Occasionally it turns end for end in a sudden whirlpool. Drifting a few feet nearer to the rocks, then pushed out again by the surging water. But I have a suspicion— and I climb down for a closer look. No piece of trash I ever saw was so shining black and gleaming white as this.

Yes, I'm sure of it—it's one of my mergansers of last spring! But my heart sinks. What is it doing so still there in that deep shadow? Is it hurt? Has someone shot it and left it to die there in this inaccessible place? Quickly I scramble over to the Grass Widow Point directly opposite for a better look.

It's a merganser all right; I can see its red bill. Nevertheless, still it bobs aimlessly in the still water of the little cove. I move closer, and suddenly that sleek black head turns in my direction and the long neck arches gracefully. It is watching me. Unhurriedly it swims out of the cove, dives into the swift white water and comes to the surface several hundred feet up river. I had caught it napping! How lucky it was that it was me, and not some fool with a gun.

As far as I could see it, I watched that graceful black and white form as it dove and surfaced ever farther up stream. Diving, swimming, then diving again always against that swift current racing among the rocks. What marvelous swimmers they are, perfectly adapted to their environment of swift white water.

I watched, hoping I'd see its mate up river, but it went its solitary way and disappeared around the bend.

After the interruption, I returned to the business of the day, checking to see what plants are growing, now that the rains have dampened this hard, dry soil. All my little friends of last spring are here: saxifrage, forget-me-nots, woodland stars. The tiny *Crocidium* has sprouted and is growing its second pair of leaves, and even the grass widows are almost an inch tall beside their sheltering rock.

Even this dry side of the canyon is a world of moisture now, moss cushions squish water like wet sponges when stepped on, the boulders glisten with oozing moisture, and the hard, red clay soil is slick with seeping water. The tiny rock ferns have some new fronds, and the evergreen *Garrya* have their long pendant spikes of blossoms ready for the first warm days of February.

Ate lunch at my lookout point above the second little cove, and as I came blundering down the trail, a duck (it looked like my pet duck, Dopey) jumped off the little sandy beach opposite and skipped away over the water before I got a look at it. If I'd learn to fall down this steep canyon quietly I might see more wildlife, instead of scaring the daylights out of them with all the noise and clatter.

After dinner I checked the plants at the east end. And as usual they are much smaller and less advanced than the others at the west end. There will be hundreds of *Nemophila* next spring, and very tiny forget-me-nots. Even found a goat weed plant (*Hypericum perforatum*) blooming in the shelter of the pile of rocks at the east end, where all the debris is piled by high water.

As I climbed down beside the level rock outcrop and the rocks where the Indian paintbrush grew, I heard a flutter of wings on the water below. Just as I turned, two large, grey-and-white birds with black heads and long necks flew downstream. At first I couldn't think what they might be—then I knew—the merganser babies of last May. As I stood watching them, two more came paddling around the rock wall and saw me. But they decided to go back, turned half in, half out of the water and flew back behind the flat rock outcrop at the east end.

Quickly I climbed to a vantage point just below the level top and lay down to wait for them to join the other two. For over an hour I waited, getting colder and colder by the minute. Those wet rocks and soggy moss cushions are less than comfortable to lie on. Finally, when not a thing stirred on the water or in the coves opposite, I gave up, too cold to care whether I missed anything. On getting up I discovered I'd been lying with my feet in a pool of water. In the excitement of watching for the birds I never noticed where I flopped down.

Then the thought struck me—had the two birds dived underwater, swum downstream with the swift current, and surfaced beyond where I could see them? As I walked back to the truck, I looked up in time to see four rather large birds with long necks flying companionably together up river after a day's sport in the swift water of the canyon. Somehow I think I've been had by a pair of adolescent mergansers!

December 9, 1967

Hellgate and High Water

❀ ❀ ❀

I've seen some of our Southwestern arroyos no deeper than Hellgate is today. The river is 16.2 feet, almost flood stage, and as I watch from above my favorite cove it seems to be frantically climbing the walls even higher. A great amount of turbulence is generated as the huge volume of moving water boils, surges, and careens through this narrow gorge; sometimes the center of the river is elevated in a mad, rushing mountain of water, then again it levels out and the sides rise and foam high up on the mossy rocks above.

Sitting here, not too far above the water line, I see nothing but a vast expanse of moving water with now and then a dead tree or log shooting down the middle with the speed of a runaway truck on a steep grade. No birds again today—even the mergansers would find rough going here in the canyon.

Behind me, in the rain pools left by the storm, I hear the frogs—our version of the spring peeper—singing their ancient vernal melody. Every so often one trills like a bird, then a big deep voice booms out "Shut up - shut up." Then they all join in and the chorus swells and fades away to silence. I watch intently, but never catch sight of them, though they're not ten feet from where I'm sitting.

I eat lunch at the little pool, then reluctantly depart for the west end to see how the river looks in that narrowest part of the canyon.

Lying here on the narrow ledge where the yellow daisies bloom, I watch the river below. It is even more violent here in this narrow spillway, and it leaps even higher up the sheer walls and through the clefts in the rocks. It is more than half-way up the citadel where the swallows built their nests. The little bays, coves, and grottoes are all under water, and now I can see why those lower rocks are so smooth, white, and rounded, and how those strange hollowed-out caves and indentations are made. Through eons of time, the scouring action of the relentless water has shaped and polished them into pleasing rounded contours that contrast strangely with the angular, jagged rocks farther up the walls.

The wild, leaping water is lapping at the moss line on the higher rocks, but I can see it has been much higher in years past. There is an unmistakable high water line the length of the canyon, and the river today is only halfway to that line. What a sight this canyon must be when the water reaches that highest mark. But if it were there, I wouldn't be here to see it, for parts of the road would be flooded before the water came near that elevated flood line of past years.

Some of the bees were out on the gold stars, but there are only a few flowers, and the sun is not bright. I thought I saw a Collotid,* but they are wild and won't come close enough for me to know for sure.

---

*Collotid bee. Small, solitary bees who make nests in hollow stems or empty beetle tunnels in wood. Brood cells are lined with silky secretions and stocked with pollen and nectar for larvae; perhaps a mason bee (Osmia).

The tiny saxifrages (Howell's?) are blooming on the rocks in the middle of the canyon, but none at this end. Found a wild gooseberry just starting to bloom below the Grass Widow Point. There were several Ceretinas there, and a medium-sized black fly with grey fur and long legs was sipping nectar with a long tongue. Thought it was my fuzzy grey bee-fly of last fall, but this one didn't have the proboscis.

Saw one of the large saxifrages in bloom and the grass widows have buds now.

Came down to the bridge and parked opposite the rock to the east of the tiger beetles' sand bar. It is entirely under water except for the top three feet. And it looks like it's almost in the middle of the river. No rocks, willows, or clumps of sedge can be seen where the may flies' little green pool stood. The water is up to the foot of the clump of pines below the old wrecked cabin across the river, and even on this side, the water seems close below the parking place.

I hope the receding river leaves a nice sandy beach and long, low bar for the tiger beetles to play on, and the black wasps to dig in, and the grasshoppers and katydids to sun themselves on. And for me to spend many idle, happy, peaceful hours sketching, writing, and picture-taking on!

February 23, 1968

Last Day of Spring

❀ ❀ ❀

Again I sit here opposite the swallows' ledge (the "citadel"), high above the river, as I've done so many times before in the past year-and-a-half. The water is low, exposing the little sandy beach in the cove below the swallow's nests. Not a sound comes from the river except the chirping of young swallows skimming the surface of the water.

My little wasps seem to have finished building for the year, and the canyon is dry and barren; only the last blooms of *Eriogonum compositum* (false buckwheat), and pennyroyal are left of the flowers of spring.

The wind coming up from below is almost cold, and even the sun is weak here among the rocks. But it's early, only a little before 9 a.m., and it will be hot later; right now all is pleasant and quiet, and I love to sit here among the dry golden grasses of the canyon and watch the slow-moving green water in the gorge. I always hope I'll see the little duck quietly eddying in and out of the bays and grottos on the opposite side of the canyon. But so far he hasn't appeared, and neither have the mergansers. I could sit here the rest of the day and watch the parade of things below, but there are other places to be checked, and other things to be accomplished.

Came over to the tiger beetles' sand bar and ate lunch. While I was eating and listening to the radio, I heard a crashing and thumping on the hill behind me, and here came a half-grown buck deer down to the river to drink. He never saw me sitting there beneath the willow, and happily splashing and running, he played in the water. He lay and sat in the water just like a big, friendly dog without a care in the world. His summer coat was a foxy-russet color and sleek as brushed nylon. The tiny horns were just sprouting and covered with bronzy velvet.

Then the wind changed! What a bounding, frantic retreat! And I felt guilty for having spoiled his refreshing bath.

This was a day to surprise wild things. After dinner I went over to the sand beach in front of the old wrecked cabin, then came back by the trail. Suddenly a mourning dove fluttered out of a low oak and flopped and staggered down the trail ahead of me. Stepping up on an old stump, I looked into a tangle of sticks and weeds in the oak; and sure enough, in the flimsy, haphazard nest sat two little, sleepy-eyed, dark grey doves. Their feathers were just coming out on their backs and wings and they were a dark gunmetal color. They never moved or uttered a sound. In fact, they didn't appear to be able to focus their eyes yet, and acted as though they never saw me. I left quietly, and I suppose the mother came back presently and resumed her maternal duties.

Then, as I sat on the sand bar again, finishing up the tea and crackers, the merganser family hove into view, gaily sailing right up to the tip of the little isle to the east of where I sat. I don't think they saw me, as they played and dived and seemed quite unhurried. She had eight or nine; I can't be sure, the fidget widgets weren't still long enough for me to count. They were almost as big as mother and cloaked in summer plumage.

About the time they paddled off around the bend, the big heron flew by, but it never said a word, so I don't think even it saw me this time. When it spies me watching something, it usually lets out a squawk that everything in the canyon, and up and down the river, can hear.

So all in all, I met most of my old friends of last summer, including the tiger beetles, who are very busy and not playing on the sand at all, but are down by the water's edge in the wet sand probably sizing up places for egg laying. Not a one appeared on the warm dry sand where they were so thick last September.

June 20, 1968

The "Bee Wolf"

❀ ❀ ❀

Came down to the river where the patch of milkweed grows at the edge of the willows and ran into a monarch freeway. They were coming from all directions, straight to the blooming milkweeds. The plants are taller than usual this year and green and vigorous looking, and the monarchs are taking advantage of them. All the monarchs looked new and bright as though they had just hatched.

The water has left more sand than last season and the flat is covered with great fragrant bushes of white sweet clover higher than my head.

Much cloud today, but when the sun is out the sand feels warm and the buzzing of the bees in the clover and the almost overpowering odor brings back memories of other clover fields and other times. But no matter where, or how long ago, that lazy buzzing of the happy bees in the blossoms is always the same, and always reminds me of warm summer days and carefree years that have gone.

Suddenly a very small, black-and-white wasp lights on the sand in front of me and begins digging rapidly. She digs just like my black and yellow *Philanthus** at home, but she is about a third the size. Then, a short distance away, another comes in and drops something yellow on the sand. Quickly going over to look, I see it is a small *Halictus* bee, yellow with pollen. So these digger wasps are some sort of *Philanthus,* or bee-killers. Known in Europe as "bee wolves," they prey mostly on *Halictus* bee colonies.

The one I'm watching takes an hour and a half to dig her tunnel, then comes home and deposits a bee, closes the door and leaves. Does she put in more than one? I'll wait and see. It's so pleasant here on the warm sand, this won't be any trouble at all. But the weather isn't favorable. After a time, the clouds roll in and it begins to sprinkle and the wind blows. But I wait, and soon the sun comes back, but it's now cool and windy. Presently my little wasp comes back without a bee, hurriedly goes in, shuts the door, and stays there. So now I don't know whether she intends to put in more bees or is just resting there until she builds another nest.

A little way off *Ammophila*** is also digging, but finally departs for the day, and I'm left alone with the monarchs, who are still fluttering lovingly around the milkweed.

**Philanthus,* the bee wolf. A small, black-and-white, or black-and-yellow ground nesting wasp who waylays and kills bees to put into its nest for food for the larvae. She looks very much like her victims, the Halictid bees.
***Ammophila*. Large, black-and-red digger wasp who paralyzes caterpillars (one specializes in cut-worms) and buries them in a tunnel in the ground, lays an egg on the victim for larval food, then closes the tunnel. This is a tool-using insect, but not all species of *Ammophila* do this.

The little song sparrow is singing in the willow, and I remember the first time I heard him in this very clump, that first October when I started coming to explore this new place. He never fails to sing, even in winter when I come to enjoy the sun. He must stay all winter among the willows and close to the water. But of course I haven't been down during the floods or in the snow, so I suppose he at least leaves off singing then, if he's still around.

The little resin structure that I had found on the big rock is gone, washed away by the water, and I haven't seen any other wasp nests yet. I wonder if they will build later, as it's now nearly as hot as on those rocks in the canyon.

It would be interesting to find out when things start blooming, and when the insects appear down here too. But I can't seem to get away from the canyon walls long enough to come down regularly to the river. I last visited during the high water of February. Some spring I'll have to come to the riverbank as often as I do to the canyon walls, and make a list of plants as they bloom, and of the butterflies and bees I find on them. I know I've missed lots of plants species I've never yet discovered, by not watching more closely. Just today I found a beautiful pure white milkweed I've never seen before. It probably has been here, but I've never been down when it was in bloom.

Each little world must be explored exclusively by itself to be understood and appreciated. Every day of each season brings something new and unexpected, and only the one who comes faithfully to watch and learn will be initiated into the secrets of these shy and unknown inhabitants of the wild places of canyon, river, and hillside.

June 28, 1968

Silent Canyon

❀ ❀ ❀

Stopped at the canyon this morning on my way down to the river to watch the digger wasps. The water is even lower than it was twelve days ago. The silence is disturbing and unnatural. As I gaze down from this height it seems as though I'm looking into a lake, or rather, a stagnant pool of green, sluggish, turgid water. The little grottos and bays all have their own tiny sandy beaches, and rocks that haven't seen the sun for years lie exposed and bleached above the water line. The water seems not to move at all, but if I watch one spot long enough I can see slowly turning eddies and whirlpools moving almost in slow motion. Occasionally a dead fish or floating eel drifts by, but that is all—no birds, no mergansers; even the heron has gone to more productive fishing grounds.

Here at the river as I sit in the shade of the willows writing up these notes, I see I have a little visitor. A tiny, short-tailed brown mouse comes scampering across the sand and stops right in front of where I'm sitting. I get up and walk up to it. It's so tame I can reach down and touch it. It acts like a pack rat when it's caught out in the daylight. Pack rats seem to be almost blind and very slow to react to danger.

The little thing looks very like a small hamster except he has a tail. Perhaps it's a pocket gopher. The fur on the back is very soft and chocolate brown, the face, legs, and paws (and presumably the underparts) are a soft golden tan. The eyes are very small and so are the ears. Head-on, it looks like a miniature beaver with its long cutting teeth, numerous whiskers, and wiggly nose.

After our little tête-à-tête, it begins to dig a burrow in the shade of the willows. At first, it digs with its front feet, then turns around and backs into the hole and bulldozes the mound of sand out with its nose and head. I offer it a piece of graham cracker and an orange peel, but it disdainfully heaps a mound of dirt over the whole thing! Now it's disappeared and I guess the interview is over.

July 13, 1968

Wild Geese Calling—Calling

❀ ❀ ❀

This is a day to set a gypsy's heart to singing! Scarlet leaves of sumac aglow among tawny drifts of pine needles—bright October sun, warm with the touch of departing summer—yellow maple leaves glittering among deep shadows on the hill.

The sun glows warm over my new-green fields, tall trees stand dark against the sky on my quiet hill, and a golden-crowned sparrow sings from the thicket—and I should be content. But that gypsy spirit that lies dormant

in the time that passes between winter's snows and the first red leaf of
Autumn is astir again.

I try not to remember other places where "all the suns and skies, and the
flowers of June together, cannot rival for one hour October's bright blue
weather."*

Then the faintest of sounds comes out of the north. A sound my ears
have long been tuned to hear. A melody I've held my breath to catch, in the
silent hours of the night.

Wild geese!

Coming closer, ever closer—their haunting music fills the sky and echoes
over fields and woods. That long wedge of dark bodies and flashing wings—
now streaking across the luminescent blue—again melding into the
overcast—wavers and curves as does the tide that breaks upon the shore.

As quickly as they come, they are gone. Their cries drifting back ever
fainter as they sweep over the hill, calling—calling.

Only a moment out of all the days of the year, but I'm a gypsy again—
seeing those faraway places where,

*On the ground red apples lie, in piles like
jewels shining.
And redder still on old stone walls, are leaves
of woodbine twining.* *

Again I stride against the cutting wind that blows across the sea meadows
before a storm—I lie in a golden drift of aspen leaves at the edge of a
mountain meadow—smell the sensuous perfume of piñon pine and
sagebrush on the high mesa lands of Colorado—hear the sandpiper's lonely
call on a forgotten beach. The faint bugling fades away—and the gypsy dies.

This evening the cricket sings loud in the grapevine, knowing it may not
sing another night. The pale clouds have turned to fire in the west and the
first evening stars are aglow.

I wait, listening, listening, but no wild music comes out the darkening
skies, no beating wings catch the last of sunset's glare.

---

*Helen Hunt Jackson's *October's Bright Blue Weather.*

It may be another year before that wild clamor sets the embers of memory aflame once more. But when it does, drudgery, worry, loneliness will disappear, and briefly, so briefly, my gypsy heart will soar with the wild geese to those almost forgotten faraway places.

October 16, 1968

The *Odynerus* Nests at Hellgate Canyon

❀ ❀ ❀

The *Odynerus** wasps of the canyon are beginning to emerge. Found several nests, both the blob and vertical tube types with holes in the closing plugs.

On one tube-type nest on the rock across from the swallow nests, at the west end of the canyon, the cast skin of some species of bee-fly parasite protrudes from the plug. But all the other holes seem made by the wasps themselves.

On the blob nest at the extreme west end, across from the swallow nests, I found four newly emerged wasps resting in their open doorways. Two are fairly active, putting their heads and antennae outside when the sun comes out from behind a cloud. But the other two are very quiet, only stirring when I reflect light down into their cells.

This is the warmest of the nests, and as I watch, a yellow wasp flies in occasionally; but it is shy and won't alight where I can get a good look at it.

About two inches from the nest I see last year's filaree seed stuck, like the shaft of an arrow, into the lichen on the rock. And the tiny "spring" is slowly rotating counter-clockwise as the temperature varies and the wind

---

* *Odynerus* wasps: Several species of black-and-yellow digger or mason wasps, about the size of a yellow jacket, though slimmer. Some dig tunnels in the soil, others use mud nests attached to rocks as brood chambers for the larvae.

shifts it about. But always the point remains in the lichen, gradually working deeper under the tension of that tiny spring.

I believe the wasps have just today opened their doors, but not yet ventured outside. Occasionally I see one of them biting at the sides of the plug as though gradually enlarging the opening. In fact, the holes seem much too ragged and small to allow the wasp to emerge comfortably. And under the magnifying glass I see all the wasps have soil particles on their faces. It's much too cramped inside for them to do any cleaning up, and I'm sure if they had been out they would have polished themselves long ago.

Stayed until 2:00 p.m., but they won't come out, as the wind is much too cold, and the sun flits in and out among the clouds, and never really warms up those rocks or the cold air.

May 1, 1969

Where the Boys Are

❀ ❀ ❀

Here I sit, high above the river at 10:00 a.m., and two little wasps are resting with their heads out of their doorways. A third wasp is a little way down, but the fourth is still way down in the nest and seems uninterested in what's going on outside its cell.

Temperature is only seventy degrees and the sun is quite often behind a cloud, and the cold wind is blowing from the river, so it may be awhile before they venture out—if they do at all today.

The swallows are flying and singing, but not yet nesting on the cliff across the river.

Have just checked the other open nests, and one also has an occupant. Two cells are open, but only the one wasp has returned.

11:20 a.m., temperature eighty-five to ninety degrees, sun's bright:

Out they come! The first popped out and began a fight with another one that was just sitting quietly in its doorway. After a tussle, number one flew a couple inches up the rock and began cleaning itself. Number two stayed in for a few minutes, then both two and three came out and began a fight, then both flew off without bothering to clean up.

These seem to be the same size and color as the little black-and-yellow wasps I saw around the poison-oak blossoms last year. Length about ten millimeters. As I look at them I think they are smaller than the wasp I saw provisioning the nest last June. So I'm reasonably sure they are males. The fourth cell appears to be empty, or else the wasp is way down inside. I didn't look closely when I came this morning, for fear of frightening the others. But now I can't see anything in the nest, so the occupant may have departed after all, before I came.

Several wasps are still flying around and one rested briefly at the base of the rock where the nests are, but didn't seem interested in the old dwelling.

May 2, 1969

"I Wandered Lonely as a Cloud"

❀ ❀ ❀

I wandered lonely as a cloud until suddenly on a hill I saw a host—not of daffodils, but of woodland stars and golden mimulus. They were dancing in a tiny mountain meadow where the wind blows cold and the yellow flowers lie like a carpet of gold across the sunny slope. And swaying above them was a white mist of woodland stars (*Lithophragma*)—more woodland stars than I've ever seen in one place before.

High on the south slope above Hellgate bridge I found the little meadow, about an acre in size and slanting southwest away from the river; so it can be seen only as I top the rise heading for the trail above. I had other plans for today, but such an inviting golden meadow was too much, and I sat down to enjoy my unexpected wealth—and there I stayed until time to go home!

When you are down on your hands and knees among the blossoms, you soon discover a numerous population of small, blue, tube-like flowers growing beneath the taller yellow-and-white ones. At first I thought they were purple penstemon, but now I'm not sure. They have no leaves, but seem to come up on a naked, two-inch-tall stem from a bulb-like root. They have four stamens and a five-lobed corolla. Are they *Orobanche*? It's been so long since I've seen one I can't be sure. But nowhere else in the canyon have I seen them. And there is another strange flower growing in this little meadow. On the barest, hardest, most exposed serpentine outcrops I found a two-leaved plant, with leaves like a miniature iris, but which sends up a flat stem with a top-heavy enclosed "bud" at the summit. At first I thought it was a bud, but found plants later that were almost bloomed out. And the "bud" becomes dry and papery, like the covering over the flowers of an onion. Inside, a cluster of white, star-like flowers look much like those of an onion or wild garlic—though it is neither, for it has no taste or smell. And, last year, just above and to the east I found those lovely white blossoms of *Lewisia oppositifolia*, which remind me of evening primroses. This hillside is indeed a strange place, where each little area is a tiny, self-contained biological world of its own.

Have seen no bees in all this sea of blossoms, even though the sun is warm when the wind is still. Several *Bombylus* hovered for a moment, and two Sara orange tips sailed over, but strangely there are no bees.

Across the river in the "big meadow" I can see patches of gold that must be yellow mimulus. And all down one side there is a hint of white that I think must be white popcorn flower (borage). But I doubt that I will be able to get over there again this year. And I doubt too that I will return to this golden hillside this season. Maybe another time, another year—always it's next year, next spring. Then one day there *is* no next year and all the sunlit hours that could have been spent among the golden flowers of spring are gone beyond recall.

March 31, 1970

Mud Daubers Beside the River

❀ ❀ ❀

They came by twos and threes and half dozens, the black-and-yellow *Sceliphron caementarium** mud daubers, at the edge of the pool, south of the sand bar. The mud daubers found the wet silt just right for their work.

They seem to have a small territory where each female comes back to get her ball of mud. She has to do a certain amount of biting out and excavating before deciding to begin the mud ball. But as soon as she has the right spot, she begins a low hum much like she "sings" when making the nest. It takes only a few seconds to get the ball rounded out, and of the right size, then off she goes. They all, every one, head out for the big rock at the river's edge.

Two days later, I climbed the big rock to see if I could find their colony, but no luck there. Since it is important that these wasps' nests be kept dry

---

* *Sceliphron*, the mud dauber. Large yellow-and-black wasp with a very conspicuous "wasp" waist. She constructs a series of mud tubes, stuffs them with paralyzed spiders, lays an egg, seals the door with mud, then plasters the whole edifice with a thick layer of mud. None of her buildings are waterproof, so she shelters them inside barns, sheds— even houses, under bridges and eaves. Very docile, she doesn't mind being observed and photographed.

until next summer, they must be building deep in the rock crevices, or perhaps even in hidden grottos. So unless I actually see them coming and going in some crack or under an overhang, I probably won't ever know just where they are building. It would have to be high up, as the water could get fifteen to twenty feet deep in flood time.

Came back to the edge of the pool and found one wasp flying about, but she doesn't seem inclined to begin work, as she's just lazily sitting on the sand preening herself.

I was mistaken! The first mud dauber was a male—no wonder he wasn't interested in going to work. I thought it was rather smaller than the ones I saw last time. A large female came in and began looking for a good place to get mud. The male pestered her for a minute, but soon flew off to sit in the sun on the rocks.

Now there are more females beginning work. It takes them five to fifteen seconds to roll up the ball of mud and fly off. When they first land, they bounce around here and there, trying one place, then another. They bite out the mud to get a little below the surface, then usually leave the spot and try an inch or so elsewhere. They may do this four or five times before they are satisfied. And bounce is the word! They walk as though they had springs in their legs. I don't remember seeing mud daubers walking in just this manner at any other time.

As soon as *Sceliphron* starts to dig out the mud, she begins her little song. She stands high up on her middle and hind legs—and at first on her front legs—but as she begins rolling the ball, she uses her front legs in the process. She digs down a little below the wet surface, probably because the surface of the sand is covered with a green slime of wet algae. I haven't yet been able to get within lens distance of a wasp as she makes the mud ball. She seems to dig out the stuff with her mandibles, backing up as she draws the pellet toward her. The farther she backs, the larger the ball becomes.

She's biting and scraping at the wet earth all this time—until she is clear out of the depression, and on the level surface. A little juggling and side-stepping takes place, then she's off with her load.

But the second she stops forming the ball, her low humming ceases. And by the time she has the ball almost ready to cart off, she is standing almost vertically, with her long abdomen up in the air at a most ludicrous angle!

They take only about one and a half minutes to go and return, so they can't be going far. The big rock where I thought they might be building is a good three to four hundred feet from here. And today I noticed some flying in the opposite direction toward the bridge and across the river.

The temperature finally got up to ninety-two degrees, but I don't know when, as I was too busy trying to get near the wasps.

Have stopped to eat lunch and will have to go soon. But if the weather stays warm, the wasps will work. I've often heard them singing their building song from my kitchen all through September, even after frost, as long as the days stay warm.

September 9 & 11, 1970

Cicindela's Larva

❀ ❀ ❀

Came over to the milkweed patch at the river to see whether the monarchs are about yet, and found a tiger beetle (*Cicindela*) larva in its hole at the edge of the water. Just for fun I tried pulling it out with a grass stem, and to my surprise it worked. After it got out on the wet sand, it ran about quite actively and wouldn't go back into the hole. After a bit, I became concerned that something might find it, so I tried to get it in, and once it did go in head first, with a little help from me, but turned around inside and came right out again. Then it flipped about on its tail like a springtail when disturbed. They can jump several inches this way. Finally, after resting a little, it began digging another hole. It used its shovel-like head and mandibles for the job. The three pairs of feet are used only to keep balance and to straddle the hole as it works. This strange little creature can double its head beneath itself exactly like a back-hoe at work. It bites out the sand, then pushes it about in a circular mound all around the entrance. It seems in no great hurry to get the work done, and frequently rests in the sun.

After about eight minutes or so, it has buried itself and all that shows on the surface is a mound of drying sand. This sand is very wet, having recently been under water, and there are several larvae holes at the edge of the wet area. This seems to show that the larvae of *Cicindela* remain dormant under water during the winter.

Ten or fifteen minutes later, I see the head has reappeared, the door is opened, and the larva is established at its new home. The burrow is evidently smoothed and rounded from the inside while the sand is blocking the doorway. Then when the tenant reappears, everything is in order and it sits at its leisure watching for a tidbit to pass by. Probably because I disturbed it in its old burrow, the instinct was to leave that spot and establish a new tunnel in a safer place.

June 18, 1971

Day of the Butterflies

❀ ❀ ❀

I visited the milkweed patch by the river, and the monarchs are back. The milkweeds are just beginning to bloom and are shorter than normal. Probably the late season this year had something to do with that. But the butterflies don't care, just so the blossoms are open and the nectar flows as usual. Others have succumbed to the lure of the flowers too. Monarchs chase swallowtails; tortoise shells and little checkerspots wave their wings at each other over a blossom head while bees and dragonflies sail about in all directions. The still air is heavy with the sweet scent of the milkweed flowers, and the hot sun beats down on the dry sand; the summer sky is deep blue and the clouds, white and fluffy as cotton balls, pile up against the mountain ranges.

June 19, 1971

Big *Philanthus* Is *Bembix**

❀ ❀ ❀

Came back to watch a big wasp and maybe see the prey she brings in, but she never opened her door until 11:00 a.m. I had been waiting, but it was hot, so I walked around a bit, collecting Melilotus seed. I saw her come out so I got down, focused the camera—and waited. Finally the sun got so hot I stood up—and in flew the wasp, dug out her door, and disappeared—all so fast I didn't have time to move! I caught a glimpse of something brown—could have been a bee, or a bug, or a hopper, or anything. Now I don't know any more than I knew before.

Had to come home, as it's really hot down there in that low spot beside the river with the rocky cliff facing south and reflecting all that heat back onto the sand. Will try again in a few days, not so much for a picture— standing on your head on that sand is almost too much—but to see what it

---

Bembix, a large, black- and grey-striped digger wasp that looks like a giant *Philanthus*. Often called a sand wasp, she is the only wasp who feeds the larvae progressively. She specializes in flies of various species. First she digs a tunnel in the sand, lays an egg at the bottom, kicks sand into the opening to close the door, then returns after the egg hatches and begins almost daily feeding.

WATER KNOT WEED

is she brings in. Then I'll know what she is: a *Philanthus*, or a *Bembix*. Could be either; only the victim will give the proof.

August 19, 1971

Found the big wasp using the same burrow as before. At last she brought in a black- and yellow- striped fly that could have been some kind of *Erestalis*. I got a good look at her as she dug out the door, and I'm reasonably sure it was a fly—I'd bet it wasn't a bee—so that makes "my big wasp" a *Bembix*!

Waited for over an hour to see her come in again, as I hoped to make her drop her prey, but she never showed up. If she's a *Bembix*, she wouldn't be coming in too frequently to feed the larva, which is only four or five days old—and two of those days were cloudy and cool. She'll probably be working oftener in a few days, if the weather stays warm. So I'll come when she's working and maybe will be able to settle the question of the prey, and get a picture or two.

August 24, 1971

Have come back and the *Bembix* never showed up. I waited from 9:30 till about 1:30 p.m., and no one came into or out of the nest. I'm sure something must have happened to her. It was plenty hot enough on the sand, over one hundred degrees, and the other wasps were very active. The little *Philanthus* are really working; I could have caught half a dozen of either males or females if I'd wanted them. One little female started her tunnel near the *Bembix* nest, so I took her picture, as I haven't any of *Philanthus* yet. Had a chance to steal her bee as she dropped it a second.

And in doing so I disturbed her doorway, and an hour later she was still looking for it! After that I left her strictly alone; I'd done enough to disrupt her work for one day.

Did see one of the large *Bembix* land on the sand six or eight feet from the place I was watching, but I'm sure it wasn't the female wanting to get to her nest, as it rested briefly then flew off.

I could be mistaken—they may be *Philanthus* after all, and don't come back day after day to provision. (Later, I found my large wasp was indeed *Bembix*, the fly catcher, who feeds the larva progressively).

August 26, 1971

Autumn Comes to the Milkweed

❀ ❀ ❀

On this golden September day—eve of Michaelmas—I visit the milkweed patch down by the river. The little forest of weeds that so enamored the monarchs of summer is now ragged and yellow-leaved, their ripened seed pods white and airy as burst pillows of goose down. On each vagrant breeze the wayfaring seeds depart beneath their silken parachutes. There is a feeling of desertion, as though something had gone that should be there on this quiet, sunny day with its pale sky and penciled clouds.

Gone are the lively, frolicking monarchs of June; gone are the females urgently going about the business of egg laying; gone are the newly-emerged adults of summer sailing and dipping and soaring on July's hot breezes. For one hot day in August, when the first red leaf of coming autumn blazed among the ripening grapes in the thicket, the monarchs heard the voiceless call that has stirred their ancestors for countless aeons; one by one they turned southward toward that great flyway that was old before man followed his first game trail in the forest.

But, occasionally, throughout September's shortened days and October's bright blue weather, a lone monarch or two sails forlornly over the milkweeds, wings ragged, color faded, flight slow and hesitant. These are the old ones, the remnant of the lively hosts who came sailing in on the soft winds of spring, who eagerly placed their new eggs on the tender leaves of the growing milkweed. Now the cold nights and short days of autumn have come upon both. The once gay monarchs and the once lush plants grow old together. Then one cold October day after a night of silver frost, the wilted leaves of the plants will lie in golden mounds beneath their bare stalks, and somewhere not too far away, the tattered wings of the monarchs will rest close to the frozen earth, as lifeless as the faded yellow leaves.

September 28, 1972

Farewell September

Farewell to blue skies and golden days, to endless hours beside the pool where mayflies dance and tiger beetles play—to the last purple aster and the first crimson leaf on the vine. Days and hours that never were—time that might have been, but was lost in the flood of everyday trivia. The suns and skies and flowers were in their appointed places, but I was not.

Now on this last day of September—a September that will not come my way again for forty-eight long weeks—I sit here on the hot sand by the river and watch the insects cavorting about the goldenrod. Again they soar and glide in the sun, their wings scintillating and flashing as they settle among the yellow blossoms. Their lives will be measured now not in weeks, nor days, but in hours. Short, sunny, ecstatic hours. A time of work for some, like the tiny bees still gathering pollen and nectar, but carefree hours for the brilliant *Erestalis* flies and late season wasps.

Sitting here with them, I, too, revel in the heat and light and gentle breezes of these precious dwindling days. But my enjoyment is touched with sadness. Never again for these happy creatures will there be another season. They've lived their intense lives, finished their exacting work, and these days of autumn are their sunset years.

All their short lives through they've lived beneath the suns and skies of summer, abandoned themselves to the gay blossoms of August, skimmed the gentle breezes of September. Then one cold day they will be stilled, covered at last by October's drifting leaves. But for now, the insects dance among the golden blossoms, the little brown lizard sits on its warm rock, and the blue heron glides majestically above the river, and I listen drowsily to the soft lapping of little waves as they wash in and out among the pebbles. For the moment, I, with the other creatures, am content to be a part of the autumn scene, with no more thought of the morrow than they.

September 30, 1972

Leaf-cutting Bee of the Serpentine

❀ ❀ ❀

Here, where the *Odynerus* colony used to nest, I sit patiently waiting in vain for the little black-and-yellow wasps to appear. But instead a small, stubby, brown-and-tan bee busily digs her nest and loudly buzzes her annoyance at my intrusion. At first I thought she was a wasp, as she dug a little then flew up and circled about before going down into the hole again. As near as I can see, she isn't transporting soil, as she kicks that out an inch or two in front of the doorway. She seems quite excitable, and I guess she just makes her aerial survey out of habit. When I get too close, she loudly protests and flies close to my ears, around my head, and even between my nose and the magnifying glass. However, so far she's all noise and bluff, and I doubt that she has the least intention of stinging.

When I first got here at 1:00 p.m., she had very little debris before her door, but now at 2:15 there is quite a pile of brownish soil and rock chips spread out on the grey serpentine, and it's quite easy to see that something is digging there. Occasionally she leaves for five to ten minutes, and always the doorway is left open. But she returns and begins the excavating again. She must be getting down some distance, for now she's bringing up small, reddish-brown rock chips, while at first they were the grey-green serpentine. The red rocks underlie the grey serpentine that covers these steep, exposed slopes.

In appearance this bee is rather short and stout, dark brown with narrow tan stripes on the abdomen, and reddish-tan fuzz on the legs, thorax, and face. I don't recall seeing a bee just like her on the flowers, and since she's the only one digging in the area, I imagine she's of a species not numerous around here.

This bee, whatever she is, is quite energetic and drags out large rock chips almost as heavy as she is. She isn't fussy about their disposal, but merely drops them far enough down hill to be out of the way. This is the first bee I've observed digging, and as near as I can tell she uses all her legs and scrapes the soil backward rather than kicking it out as the wasps do. She gathers a load beneath her and backs out with it under her abdomen, then scatters it about after she's a few inches from the entrance.

She's a LEAF-CUTTER!* She just now brought in a pale pinkish-lavender piece of flower petal folded neatly beneath her and carried with the middle and front legs. It takes her only twenty to thirty seconds to cut and transport her petal, so she must be getting them close by. In ten minutes she has brought in ten pieces. She stays inside ten to fifteen seconds arranging them. So why didn't I recognize her? She has been covered with the fine, brownish dust from underground, and when she stops to clean up a bit she is two-toned grey—just like my leaf-cutters at home!

The bee was gone for twenty-five minutes and I thought she would bring in a load of pollen, but here she came with another flower petal, and is bringing them in at ten- to fifteen-second intervals. Guess she must have knocked off for a nectar break. I could stand a little refreshment myself; the sun is hot, though the sky is somewhat hazy with small clouds.

I notice she backs out of her tunnel, so she must have just enough room to go in but not to turn around. Her petals are from the *Godeta*, I'm sure—the only flower close by of that color. She folds them in half lengthwise, so that from behind it looks like she's carrying a flattened tube or cone.

She dug for one and a half hours, and has now been carrying petals for almost an hour. Here it is 4:00 p.m., and she's still bringing in flower petals—fifty-eight so far! She took a ten-minute break, then started again.

She's getting the petals from a small group of *Godeta* about a hundred feet from the nest. What a lot of mutilated blossoms! Some with one petal

---

*Leaf cutter bee. Cuts leaf and flower petals to line underground cells in which she stores pollen and nectar for the larvae. One egg to a cell.

gone, more with two missing, and some even with three cut off. All within a small area of probably fifty by fifty feet. Nowhere are the flowers plentiful, but they're more numerous in this particular spot.

It is now 5:15 p.m. and she has been gone for over twenty minutes, so it looks as though the bee won't be back again tonight. I thought she might sleep in the burrow, and there is still an hour of sun before this hillside is in shadow, so she may be having dinner and will return later. But I can't stay, so only the little leaf-cutter knows whether she sleeps in her flower-bedecked apartment with the lavender-tinted wall paper.

May 16, 1973

The Leaf-cutter's Work Is Done

❀ ❀ ❀

The little leaf-cutter bee is gone, and so is the *Godeta*. The ceaseless wind blows the dry grass heads about, flowers are fast going to seed, and all is quiet here on the serpentine barrens. I don't know how many more nests the busy little worker made, but she seems to have her activities timed nicely to the blooming of the *Godeta*. Very likely she had been hard at work many days before I first saw her. When I came to the hillside, the flowers had been blooming for some time; in fact, I'd say they were past the peak of their bloom by a week or more.

If there is a summer generation of leaf-cutters, I wonder what they use for making their cells. It would be interesting to know whether there are two generations of both wasps and bees here. The season is certainly long enough and hot enough to produce another before the cool weather of fall. The limiting factor would be the lack of rainfall through the summer, and the scarcity of blooming plants through the hot months.

I've never been on this torrid hillside in July or August, or after the first week of June, so I could be very wrong in saying nothing blooms then. I remember how surprised I was to find thousands of a tiny species of buckwheat (*Eriogonum vimineum*) blooming here, and in the big meadow higher up the hillside in September and October, with hundreds of bees of all kinds working them over in the last hot days of autumn.

Usually I quit coming here, and to the canyon, after the last wasps have disappeared, but I've often wondered if in a month or six weeks there isn't renewed activity among those lovers of intense heat. In other parts of the country with a long, hot summer, many species of bees and wasps produce a summer generation that emerges late but still has time to produce offspring before winter.

Unfortunately, from my point of view, when it gets hot in summer here in southern Oregon, it never lets up until the fall rains in late September or October. And without the relief of an occasional cooling shower, wasp-watching on this hillside, or in the canyon below, might be more than anything could take—except another wasp!

So it's goodbye to the little leaf-cutter until one happy, sun-filled day next May or June. I'll be here when the first *Godeta* opens, watching for her descendants to begin their own little petal-lined apartments, close to where their mother worked this year, and where I enjoyed her tiny company.

June 2, 1973

Twilight and the River

❀ ❀ ❀

This evening the sunset sky is a colorless pale blue, washed with the faintest tint of gold, but its reflection on the river has turned to molten silver with golden ripples and eddies. Standing on the wet sand, their dark shadows betraying them, two almost invisible killdeer wait for the little wavelets to bring their supper. In the shallows of a little bay just up-river from the motionless forms, two domestic ducks dabble in the ebb and flow of the current. A large mallard drake, and a white Pekin hen, very happy to return to the element of their ancestors, seem not to have a care in the world. Then from out of the white-capped riffles comes a flotilla of mergansers—all dressed in the grey and brown, with a touch of white, of last year's brood. At first, it looked as though there might be a confrontation with the other ducks, but the mergansers preferred the swifter current, so they moved on upstream to play and dive in the fast-moving water. Then the dark silhouette of a blue heron silently flapped downstream to land in a clump of flooded willows.

Coming home from Briggs Valley; this is the first time I've stopped to watch the river so late, and it must be the best time of day to see the birds. Not since the days I sat motionless for hours watching the *Odynerus* wasps of the canyon have I observed so many water birds in one area.

April 5, 1983

Hellgate—Twenty-seven Years Later

❀ ❀ ❀

The canyon at Hellgate, and the serpentine slope above the north side of the bridge where the wasps and the leaf-cutter worked, are essentially unchanged since that summer of '66 when I first began exploring those fascinating slopes. But the habitat along the river has been greatly altered over the years.

In the early '70s, Lost Creek Dam was built on the upper Rogue River, and seasonal fluctuations in water level have been stabilized. Floods, which in former years scoured out the sand bars and cleaned the banks of brush and heavy growth, no longer occur. Now there is an almost impenetrable

tangle down to the water's edge where the milkweed used to bloom, and there is no longer a clean sandbar for the tiger beetles to dig their burrows, nor for the digger wasps to work. There are some mud flats for *Sceliphron* to roll her mud pellets, but they too have been overgrown and greatly diminished.

In the summer of 1991, part of the slope on the south side of the river above the bridge burned, and the thick clumps of grass, thatch, and brush that had accumulated for over forty years were completely consumed. The following spring, what had been for decades a hillside of mostly grass with a scattering of flowering species, exploded into a slope carpeted with grass widows, gold stars, woodland stars, penstemon, woolly sunflower, and mimulus. Most noticeable were the grass widows (*Sisyrinchium douglasii*), which covered the slope from top to bottom with thousands and thousands of their purple blossoms. In the late sun, that hillside was literally a haze of purple color. Now, two years later, the grasses have again dominated the scene, and the blooming plants have declined, to wait perhaps another forty years for their day in the sun.

The wasps of the canyon are very scarce now, as the hot spring weather of those early years has given way to uncertain, cool, drizzly days with a few warm spells, which in turn affects the blooming of the plants and the emergence of their prey.

In many ways, the fragile plants are more adaptable, though some—such as the red bells—are gradually disappearing from the rocky outcrops. But the tiny gold stars still carpet the slopes on the north side of the river, and the leaf-cutter's *Godeta*, while fewer, still bloom among the serpentine chips. And perhaps one day, conditions will again be favorable and the small inhabitants of this canyon will return and continue their life's work, where their ancestors of ages past surmounted all the obstacles of the rugged environment.

—1993

3
Chrome Ridge and Freeland Mountain

❀ ❀ ❀

The Setting

Chrome Ridge, an ancient sea floor remnant, is now a 4,000-foot plateau of weathered serpentine approximately six miles long; this ridge supports an astonishing variety of plant life, considering its barren, inhospitable appearance. Most of the ridge is open Jeffrey pine steppe with a heavy understory of manzanita (three to four species), huckleberry oak, rhododendron, and Garrya. Port-Orford-cedar colonies are abundant in sheltered canyons and on north and east slopes. Knobcone pine is scattered through the area, with a large forest of varying ages at the north edge of the ridge.

Freeland mountain is the most prominent peak, situated about a mile from the north end of the ridge, and it, too, has its own community of species not found elsewhere in the area; among them a rare anemone and Bolander's lily.

Both the north and south ends are slightly elevated rocky outcrops, supporting few trees with islands of shrub understory interspersed and grassy slopes on more mesic sites. On the very dry xeric slopes facing south and west, the small flowering plants have reached their greatest development. Geologically, Chrome Ridge resembles the rough and ready botanical wayside near O'Brian, Oregon. Although the 2000-foot rough and ready area puts on a better show of color, Chrome Ridge nurtures species not seen in the lowlands.

Both ends of Chrome Ridge are connected by an old road that surely must be the remnant of the original road through the area, for many of the drainage culverts are made of cedar staves, bound together with iron hoops—and still very efficient.

While both extremities of the ridge produce much the same plant life, the north end is the most interesting and varied. However, some species are found on the south end that do not grow on the north, and vice-versa. In appearance, these out-crops are open and barren, swept by hurricane winds in winter and sucked dry of moisture by a torrid sun in summer. The few trees that survive to old age are grotesque and twisted, reminding one of the tortured trees at timberline. Rare is the tree with an intact, growing crown. Most have been broken by heavy snow or wind, some almost at ground level. Continuing the struggle, but unable to send out a strong leader, the lateral branches take over and the injured trees grow almost horizontally, producing a contorted, gnarled growth like a giant Bonsai.

The ridge has much chrome in its makeup, and mining has occurred in times past, especially on the south end. Since then the ridge has existed undisturbed and unnoticed, except for occasional timber sales.

Here is a wild and fascinating area, old in time and rich in interest for those who study how plants respond to edaphic conditions. Here serpentine endemic species have established colonies under even more extreme conditions than those on serpentine in the lower, more sheltered sites.

Home Again—Almost!

❀ ❀ ❀

Here at Chrome Ridge, the melting snow runs in little rivulets down the road, the wind sighs in the pines, and spring walks lightly across the rocky ridges. At this altitude—4,000 feet—snow patches lie everywhere: along the edge of the road, on the slopes of the hills, in great white pools beneath the trees. Scattered groups of pine climb the hills, and the open spaces are rocky and sun-dappled. And I'm home again on a Colorado mesa, among the yellow pines, listening to the wind, and looking at the edge of the melting snow for the first wild flowers.

This is so different—and yet the same. Always the high country has its similarities, no matter where it may be. The clean, cold wind, the pines audibly responding to every breeze. The bright, clear light, the departing snow slowly yielding to the warmth of the returning sun, and always the sense of aloneness in a world untouched by greed and progress.

Today the sky is blue with the tint of April, soft at the edges, pale and misty overhead. Off to the south, the high Siskiyous are snow-capped and indistinct on the horizon. Here the breath of spring has touched the sunny spots, for the miniature *Claytonia lanceolata* var. *sessilifolia* is blooming among the rocks and at the very edge of the snow banks. Such a tiny pinkish flower, no more than an inch or two tall with thick, granular-surfaced leaves spread flat on the ground, it is so small I'm sure I walked over quite a number before noticing them. The blossoms are only ten to twelve millimeters wide.

Have climbed to the ridge—about one hundred-fifty to two hundred feet higher than the road—and on the south side, where the sun must have been warm for some time, the little plants are growing in a populous colony, scattered all down the rocky slope and even descending the red clay bank beside the road.

A hive bee and a wild black bee came in briefly to visit the blossoms, but found nothing and left. Under the magnifying glass, the flowers appear to be fading, and have no pollen I could detect. Probably they open in early morning, as so many of that family does, and now in afternoon, they are about to close up.

April 28, 1974

Trees of Chrome Ridge

❀ ❀ ❀

Silvered skeletons they stand, with their twisted limbs and broken tops. Weathered to the grey patina of driftwood, their bark long since gone, these old monarchs of Chrome Ridge, even after life has departed, stand defiant against wind and storm.

Nothing on these rugged serpentine headlands brings home so clearly the fierce struggle for survival as these gnarled giants of the past. Perhaps they're not "giants" in comparison to the huge old hemlocks of Lake Mountain, or the old-growth Douglas-firs down in Briggs Valley, but for their place and conditions, they attained a remarkable growth in their lifetime.

The largest I measured was thirteen feet two inches in circumference. Most were between nine and eleven feet, and perhaps one hundred feet tall. The most unusual feature of the dead trees is the twisting growth of the trunks; which is most noticeable where bark is absent. Fully ninety percent—both standing trees and downed logs—have this oddity to some degree. It reminds one of a large, twisted cable, and must have been caused by wind pressure on the growing tree. Trees of middle and lower elevations are seldom subjected to such force, and if they are, the trunk snaps or the roots give way. But on the high places, the tough old Incense-cedars and Jeffrey pines won't give an inch. Often their tops are broken off, and occasionally one splinters and falls, but mostly they continue to grow, turning away from that wild wind. With their roots anchored among those huge boulders, they hang on until old age and waning vitality finally takes its toll.

Long after the life-giving sap has ceased to rise, they stand against their enemies, the snows and winds and freezing rains of winter. Then perhaps one calm, warm day in summer, the old giant will crash to the ground in a light breeze—brought to earth at last not by the mighty gales of the storm gods, but by the unrelenting work of a colony of termites or carpenter ants. *"Sic gloria transit mundi."*

July 10, 1980

Bolander's Lily

❀ ❀ ❀

The beautiful, wine-red Bolander's lilies had a long blooming season this year because of the cold weather into July, so I enjoyed them for several weeks past their ordinarily short blooming period. In fact, I spent so many happy hours looking for them and sketching that I missed them terribly when at last they faded and began to set seed.

BOLANDER'S LILY

This has been an exceptional year for them, and I've found more in bloom at one time than I ever knew grew here on the ridge. One in particular was my favorite. It had three beautiful reddish buds that seemed to take forever to open. Finally, feeling sure it must be blooming, I arrived before sunrise and hunted it up, only to find it at about the same stage as it had been the week before. This was a perfect plant, not a blemish on it. So many I'd tagged, only to come back and find something had eaten a hole in the side of the bud and ruined the flower, or the stalk had been chewed off completely. So I took no chances with this one, but sketched it then and there just as the first rays of the sun touched it. The next week I went back and every bud had opened, and I think it was one of the most perfect plants I saw all that season. Also it has set two beautiful, fat seed pods in this last week of August.

I saw many dozens of these lovely flowers all across the ridge and Freeland Mountain this year, but the one that remains the most vivid to me is that lovely stalk growing out of the brush thicket with its three perfect buds on the wild, peaceful hillside on a clear July morning at sunrise.

August 25, 1980

Freeland Mountain and the Abandoned Lookout

❀ ❀ ❀

The view is superb; as I sit on the top of Freeland Mountain and the wind moans through a small Jeffrey pine, I wonder how many years it's been since anyone else has been here.

For more years than I can remember, I've wanted to climb this ridge of weathered serpentine on Chrome Ridge. Why I haven't done it sooner I'll never be able to explain. But this morning I set out with the exact purpose of climbing to the top, and now at 10:00 a.m. I'm here.

Last week, while sketching the Bolander lilies, I followed a hawk through the binoculars and happened to focus on the bare, flat summit of Freeland—and saw what looked like a small house or shack of some kind. And now I've found what it is—an abandoned Forest Service lookout from way back, probably before WW II. It leans at an angle atop its solid rock foundation, and I marvel how it has stood the gale winds all those years. And how was the material brought here to build it? Long ago, the ubiquitous brush eradicated any sign of trail or road. Very likely this and the little tower on Lake Mountain were built about the same time. There are the same cabinets and tables made out of rough boards and wooden dynamite cases, the same wire and old-time insulators for the phone lines. In those early days, the Forest Service had mule stations where the animals were kept to go into the back country, and no doubt the material for these small lookouts was brought up to these high peaks on pack animals.

The interior furnishings were crude: wooden cases for cupboards, homemade tables and file cabinets—even the range-finder table was made on the spot, of native materials. A large stump is embedded in the wooden floor, and a wooden platform built on top. Two slats, fastened to a two-by-four pivoted at either end by nails driven into the stump, served as a moveable support for the range finder—or it might even have been the instrument itself! Oh the age of simplicity! Now it would take ten thousand dollars worth of equipment to do the same job—and fifty thousand dollars of work projects, cost estimates, and appropriations to get it done!

INSIDE THE OLD LOOKOUT

A post outside the north end of the building must have had a battery-operated phone attached, as I found a number of the old cylinder-type batteries with a carbon core surrounded by a zinc covering. A rather large wooden box had been attached to the post, and a pair of heavy wires ran downhill toward the road at the four corners (Freeland Saddle). Probably there was another station with a phone in Briggs Valley.

The little building certainly was constructed with an economy of materials, for it is just high enough to stand up in, but to see out of the long windows you would have to be seated on a low stool at the range finder, or at a built-in desk in the corner that looks like it held the maps. There was a tin stove pipe hole in the roof, so it could have been quite cozy, though cramped—and the lookout people in the modern towers think they're roughing it!

The rafters and rooftree were cut from small trees here on the mountain, but the rest of the building was of planed lumber; the floor boards especially are quite smooth and well finished. But the snow and winds of winter have broken the roof in and only the west side, and the north end, are standing. The front, with its shed door and porch of sorts, has caved in, but I could distinguish a pile of kindling and small wood left beside the door for the little stove inside.

That restless wind moans around the ruined building, and I wonder what it must have been like to stay here on this isolated peak. When the mules came up from the valley below with supplies—that must have been an exciting day! And the storms—and wind—and nights of the full moon. Those people had all the luck and excitement, but I bet they didn't really think so.

The wind is growing cold and it's time to start back to the bus. This is the time of day I miss my old dog Sal the most, for it's a lonely trip back home with no one to share the pleasures of the day with. (Sal died in 1978.)

September 15, 1980

World of the Snow

❀ ❀ ❀

Sitting on a stump on Chrome Ridge with the snowflakes drifting down, I look at the pale afternoon sun and think "then came the snow, announced by all the trumpets of the sky."*

It's been forty years since I've seen a sky like this. Off to the north, the tall old trees of the ridge are steel etchings against a deep Payne's grey backdrop. In the west over Freeland Mountain, the sun is sinking into a sea of swirling grey, mauve, and white storm clouds, and the delicate flakes drift down like silver spangles against the dark trees.

It started out to be a day for picking alder catkins for their pollen, up Taylor Creek. Cold, drizzly and wet, it was more of a time to sit indoors, but I knew the alders were blooming, so I came, though reluctantly. Working until two o'clock, I gathered all that were ready, then thought about going to Briggs Valley to check the alders there. At the top of Lone Tree Pass I saw the snow on the ridge—and the call of a winter day among the trees of the high country was too much.

Drove about two and a half miles, then the road became pretty well covered with snow, and there were no tracks to follow, so I parked and started up on foot, without snow shoes! It was a good three miles to the top—and I knew what a hike it was in the snow, for old Sal and I had trudged up that long grade in January of 1976.

The snow was only about four inches deep where I left the bus, and as white and dry and fluffy as thistledown. The sun was out just enough to make faint shadows across that long, unmarked expanse of road ahead. There was nothing in the world but me and the snow and the trees. The temperature must have been below freezing, for nothing was thawing, and the tree branches were bent low with their load of snow, with tiny icicles at their tips. Occasionally, little animal tracks crossed the road, mostly going downhill. Rabbits, birds, and one pair side by side, that may have been a couple of foxes, and one larger dog track that undoubtedly was a coyote—probably seeking the companionship of the rabbits!

About half way up, the sun became a pale circle of light among the grey clouds, and a fine sifting of silver flakes began drifting down on the still air. At long last—one hour after leaving the bus—I rounded the final bend, and there was the big Jeffrey pine at the crossroads. What a sight! The line of trees that grow toward the north of the ridge was engraved in silver and white against that dark, stormy sky. It was then 4 p.m., and I knew I didn't dare stay later than 4:30, for it would take a good forty-five minutes to the bus and an hour from there to home. But I sketched an outline of the trees and skyline, and will try to reproduce that unforgettable scene tomorrow. But it will be a poor substitute for the exquisite beauty I've experienced on the ridge today.

---

* *The Snowstorm*—Emerson

❀ 65 ❀

Before I left—in fact before I finished sketching—the snow began and the sun disappeared in those threatening clouds. Suddenly I felt chilly and a little apprehensive. Suppose it snowed so much that I couldn't get out? The shadows between the trees were much darker, and I realized I was a long, long way from nowhere—and on my own. It's amazing how a tiny bit of sunlight, no matter how pale and weak, makes the world a friendly place, and when it's gone, almost at once the air is cold and you feel like a stranger in an alien land. I didn't hurry, though, even with night coming on, for I knew I might never experience another hour out of time such as this again, for many a year. After all it would be much easier going back, for it was downhill—and I could follow my tracks. But how I missed my old Sal! What I wouldn't have given to again hear that bell and see that cheery red harness on the trail ahead of me. And a day such as this needs to be shared with another wild spirit. So the beautiful day ended on a note of sadness, and longing for a dear departed companion.

January 29, 1981

Snow on Freeland Mountain

❀ ❀ ❀

The little lookout on top of Freeland is sitting in the midst of a snowy field today. Bushes, small trees, and rocks have disappeared beneath the blanket of white. A few of the more exposed rock outcrops are bare, but mostly the whole mountain top is covered—in some places I sink up to my knees where the drifts have covered the thick brush. There was no brush to fight coming up —but you never knew where your feet were, either atop the downed bushes or off a rocky ledge.

It took thirty minutes to climb the slope instead of the usual twenty; not bad, for the snow had drifted deep in spots.

When I arrived at 11:50 a.m., the warm morning sun was brilliant on the glittering snow, and a small breeze was moaning through the little Jeffrey pine at the corner. Ate lunch atop a bare rock, with my back to the sun, and with a grand, panoramic view of all the snow-capped peaks in the Cascades. While I tried to ignore it, I could also see the top of that damn fog that is choking the valleys again. Looking so white and innocent, it could almost be an extension of the lovely snow fields on these hill tops. How I wish that fog could be as attractive from below as it is looking down on it!

Now at 2:00 p.m., the breeze is picking up and the sun has gone behind dark, stormy-looking clouds coming up fast from the west. It's incredible how a perfectly clear blue sky can become overcast in such a short time. As soon as that cheerful sun disappears, the air feels cold, and unless you get up and walk around, it can be most uncomfortable.

So the sketching is finished for the day, and I'll go back to the bus, and drive to the other end of the ridge near Taylor Mountain, where I can see the tiny dark silhouette of this little building and finish the tea and the rest of the lunch—and long for my old Sal to be there to help me eat it.

February 4, 1981

The Arabis of Freeland Mountain

❀ ❀ ❀

Today I again sit beside the little ruined building on Freeland Mountain and wonder why I didn't come sooner. It's been two months since that day I sat in the snow and made a painting of the light and shadow, of the clear blue sky and the weather-beaten structure in a winter setting.

This is more like a day in fall—hazy and smoky with a cold wind from the north. When I first arrived here at 10:20, there was faint sunshine, but gradually a pall of smoke has spread over all the area. And I see a great plume of wood smoke over toward Grayback, and I think the burn is somewhere close to Pepper Caves partial cut, a grove of huge old hemlocks they were going to log last year. So now I suppose they're burning the slash from it. And it's just as well I'm this far off seeing it, for I'd never want to walk through that lovely, dark, primeval company of trees again and see the destruction they have suffered. Now, at 2:30, none of that range of mountains can be seen at all, and the pale sun is more like the sun of December.

Few flowers are blooming here on the ridge yet, but a lovely little *Arabis* has opened its purple blossoms among the rocks at the very top of Freeland. Only within a radius of 150 feet around the old lookout can I find them. Mostly they grow atop the large rock outcrops, seeming to prefer those deep crevices to the loamy soil of the open places. Scattered in small colonies, they seem to be the same arabis (*Arabis koehleri*) I've seen on both ends of the ridge. Very scarce, always growing in the harshest of conditions, these little plants are one of our rare Siskiyou endemics, found only on dry serpentine outcrops.

NOV 18- 81   AFTER THE STORM

Also a few phlox are just beginning to bloom—*Phlox diffusa*, another inhabitant of the serpentine ridges. And scattered about like miniature squirrel tails a tiny dwarf sedge (*Carex concinnoides*) sends up its yellow, furry pollen spikes with its yellow anthers and chocolate-brown heads. What a strange place for a sedge on this xeric, barren ridge top with its cold winds and blistering summer sun.

The wind is moaning louder through the little Jeffrey pine and it will soon be time to go.

May 1, 1981

Lost Canyon

❁ ❁ ❁

The morning sun was bright and the water splashed from pool to pool as I made my way down "Cobra Canyon." On the map, a small pond or marsh shows at the lower end of this canyon, and today I hoped to find it. I started from the end of the road, and had to go downhill farther than I'd thought before finding the canyon. But from there on for some distance, the water runs steadily, and the cobra lilies are lush and green, nestled between the roots of the old Port-Orford-cedars. I walked for an hour, then decided to eat lunch. "Walked" is not really the word—crawled, climbed over, under, and around, would say it better! I never saw such an obstacle course in my life. Beyond the end of the road the logging stopped, and this is virgin forest, untouched, unexplored. The brush is almost solid azalea, and their perfume was overpowering. The canyon becomes steeper in places, and detours have to be made around large rock outcrops. But the detours aren't any easier; they go through brush so thick you can walk on top of it until you lose your footing and sink into it waist deep. If you walk along the water, the rocks are so slick you can't stay upright; if you go along the edge, the brush covers the outcrops and drop-offs and you fall into the tangle. So in many places it's simply easier to get down and crawl. After an hour of this, I was ready for lunch!

Some time before I stopped, I'd been seeing leaves I was sure were California lady slipper—and sure enough, beside a little pool ringed with ferns and cobra lilies, I found a lovely stalk in full bloom. So here I had lunch. Maidenhair fern and a tiny saxifrage grew among the wet rocks, and just up the hillside I saw a large plant of *Ribes sanguineum* beneath a tree. Bolander lilies grew within a few yards of the stream, and numerous small trillium leaves were scattered about. Possibly they may be the rare little *Trillium rivale*.

I debated about turning back after lunch, as I'd come a long, hard way and I was already tired. Knowing it was all uphill and with just as many logs, stumps, brush piles, and huge logs to get back over made me uneasy about getting any farther from the road. However—against my better judgment— I made the decision to go on for another half hour, and if the pond wasn't in sight by then, turn back. It was only noon and the days are long this time of year—and such is the mentality of the plant explorer, that better judgment is sometimes ignored!

Unfortunately—having been born stupid, and never having gotten over it—I had decided to leave the knapsack and the rest of the lunch and go down without it. Crawling through that mess with a load is no picnic—in fact, it's no picnic without *anything* to encumber you. Somehow, caution did win for a moment—and I tied a red ribbon on the tree above the knapsack. Actually, I'd tied several of those ribbons on trees as I came down.

As soon as I started downhill again, I hit a stretch of canyon where the water went underground and came out some distance farther along. In fact, there were several stretches like this, until finally the canyon widened, a cool breeze blew up from below, and I found a lovely small pool with ferns and lady slippers—but absolutely no sign of the pond. A wide old log the color of driftwood stretched across a little sandy beach beside the pool, so I lay down for a quick nap; I was exhausted.

When I awoke it was one o'clock—not late, but the sun had changed and shadows were lengthening in this deep canyon. And this time, I heeded that better judgment and turned back to pick up the lunch and knapsack. It must have taken a half hour to go the distance back—and somehow I went up a side canyon in a place where there wasn't any running water to follow. An hour later I realized what I'd done—and that I was lost!

At no time in my life have I come so near to panic. Those shadows were long, and the canyon would soon be dark, and I was getting really tired. I had to go back and find where I'd made my mistake—and how much strength and daylight did I have to do all this? Now I can see why people who are lost do the foolish things they do. That veneer of civilization and logic we live with all our lives is extremely thin. And something like this strips everything away that we've ever learned, strips it down to bare instincts.

I felt like getting up and running as fast as I could toward the direction of the road. So I sat down on a log and told myself I wasn't alone; I wasn't in danger; I had enough strength to get out if I acted rationally—and I said a very earnest prayer. After resting a bit, I started back down to find the knapsack. After about twenty minutes—there was the red ribbon on the tree! So now I at least had my vital equipment; food, matches, and a survival blanket.

But now I had to pick up my leaden feet and do the whole thing over—and take special care not to lose the main canyon again. I consoled myself with the thought that I'd tied a long red ribbon on a big cedar where I met the canyon coming down from the road, so I couldn't miss my turnoff spot.

But I did miss it! After hours of walking, I was almost sure I'd passed the spot without seeing the marker. Theoretically then, all I had to do was start up the hill and hit the road. But I still wasn't absolutely sure I'd come far enough to be past the end of the road. If I started up the hill too soon, I could just keep on going and never find the road at all. So I walked a little farther, just to be sure, and still no red ribbon on a tree. Things were beginning to look unfamiliar, so I was reasonably sure I hadn't come down this way in the morning. At this point everything was solved, and there shouldn't have been any more problems. I could go on up the canyon and come out at its beginning just below the road, or I could strike uphill through the brush and hit it within a few hundred feet or so.

Never before in my life have I come so near to being at the end of my strength. But this time I knew there was a limit—and that I'd almost reached it. I didn't know how much farther up the canyon I'd have to go, and couldn't take much more of climbing around, over and under those rocks, stumps, and logs. So I decided to make off uphill, and hope to heaven the road was there somewhere.

The hillside was covered with manzanita and Sadler oak, and on these steep, south-facing slopes the brush all grows downhill! But by working around through little open spaces and crawling under, I got quite a way up the slope—but the brush was so tall and so dense it was impossible to see whether the road was up there. And for a little bit I was almost sure I'd come out past the dead end, and missed it altogether. Right then I wouldn't have given a cent for my chances of getting home before night. A few more prayers and a lot more crawling through the brush, and I came out onto a small clearing—and there, a couple hundred feet uphill, was the bare, sloping, red bank of the road cut! I threw the knapsack off my back, lay down and fell sound asleep.

About twenty minutes later a couple of quarreling flickers woke me, and refreshed, I made it to the road shoulder. I had come several hundred feet beyond the dead end where the bus was parked, and when I rounded the curve and saw the little bus sitting there I couldn't think of anything in this world I'd rather be looking at!

It was then a quarter to six. I'd been down in the canyon climbing around for four and a half hours! I think if that road had been another two hundred feet up the hillside, I wouldn't have made it.

I can look back now and see the stupid mistakes I'd made. Not checking my direction before I left the bus—not taking the compass—not marking enough trees in unfamiliar territory—and leaving the knapsack. I know— and should have remembered—that going one way in bright morning sun, and coming from the opposite direction in afternoon shadows can make even a familiar area look strange and unnatural.

I'm still puzzled about the markers—how could I have missed those bright red surveyors' ribbons? I tied them higher up on the trees and branches, but I think they should have been on logs and roots nearer the ground, for in that kind of terrain you can't look up unless you stop to rest and look around. And you could be within ten feet of a marker and not see it in the heavy brush. But the lessons have been learned—and I'll never live long enough to forget that feeling of utter helplessness and panic when I first realized I was lost in such an inaccessible place.

As I left, I looked back down that darkening canyon and I knew, as far as I'm concerned, it will always be "Lost Canyon" to me.

July 9, 1981

The Cobra Lilies of Lost Canyon

❀ ❀ ❀

Of all the strange and unusual plants in the Siskiyous, the cobra lilies (*Darlingtonia californica*) have to be the oddest and strangest of all. These plants were found in a deep, narrow canyon below Freeland Mountain that I call "Lost Canyon" (because I was once lost there!), where a small stream runs over the serpentine rock outcrops and forms little crystal pools beneath the roots of virgin old-growth Port-Orford-cedars.

Only filtered sunlight dapples the watercourse, and in July, the air is heavy with the perfume of blooming azalea. Even at noon, shadows are long and the old trees and downed logs make the canyon a remote and vaguely unfriendly world. Certainly the large colonies of green-hooded darlingtonias enhance the feeling of eeriness as they peer from behind trees, crowd against old stumps, and thrust through the downed brush and debris along the stream.

Beautiful, though, in their own right, the cobra plants are interesting in their response to the changing seasons. When I first saw them in May, the old stalks were weathered and mottled with brown, and quite ragged from winter rains and frosts. But when I went back in July, the new growth was a lovely apple green, very soft, and easily bruised. Then by September they had hardened into a darker leaf green with scarlet "tongues" and red veins crisscrossing the upper part of the hood. At this time, a good amount of

yellow suffused the green of the hooded part and upper tube. Actually, it's not surprising to note these color changes when you remember that the stalk, tongue, and entrance to the hollow tube are in reality the leaves of these insectivorous plants.

The flower too, as befits such an odd creation, is on the bizarre side. Growing on a scape two to four feet tall, the purple-red corolla is enclosed in five narrow, strap-like sepals that are pale green at first, then upon expansion turn a yellowish straw color that surrounds the nodding flowers like a ragged halo. The petals of the blossom never open wide, but have small orifices near the closed tips where tiny insects may enter. As the sepals wither, they straggle down around the little skull-shaped corolla like pale witches' hair. Eventually the flower parts drop away, revealing a large, green seed pod that, as it ripens, turns upward, and opens in several sections much like the seed capsule of an iris or lily.

After seeing these unusual plants in such a setting, one can't help but wonder what tales and superstitions the American Indians had concerning the strange plants and the gloomy canyons and secret places where they grow.

July 1981

Fern Canyon

❀ ❀ ❀

The little marshy place started in a most unlikely spot, in the midst of a hot, dry, manzanita flat surrounded by logging slash and huge stumps—all that is left of a cool, green forest.

Ringed with willows and covered with sedge and swamp grasses, the water could be heard gurgling underground until it finally came to the surface in a small pool choked with moss and algae. Clumps of fern grew in little, isolated islands, and two tiger lilies in one rather large clump made a brilliant orange spot in all that lush greenery.

So today I decided to follow the canyon down and see what grew in the cool depths of the untouched part. This time I didn't get lost, as it's a small canyon, and I didn't intend to go very far. And I had the compass. Fifteen or twenty minutes later, I found a lovely little flat open space carpeted with a species of small saxifrage, all in bloom.

Sitting on a log and listening to the water splash over the roots of the old Port-Orford-cedar, I felt like I could stay there all day. The dappled sun and shadow, the silence and the tiny flowers created an enchanted little fairy glen so out of character for this dry, rocky serpentine country; I could hardly believe I was up on old Chrome Ridge.

But the soul of an explorer is never at rest, and I had to know what strange and rare things might be growing in the depths of the canyon farther on. Knowing that Taylor Mountain was behind and to my right, and an old logging road was up the hill to my left, I felt perfectly at ease climbing into the dark, steep canyon that got steeper and darker the farther down I went. Here again was virgin Port-Orford-cedar, with huge logs across the canyon, tangled brush, and rocky outcrops. Not as dense and impenetrable as Lost Canyon, yet no easy hike either. And again the water went underground for a short distance to come out in little waterfalls and pools among the ferns. And the ferns! I've seen nothing like them anywhere in this southwest part of the state. I don't yet know what species they are, but they're different from any other fern I've ever found. There were huge patches growing in a dense jungle along the stream bed and over the rocks on either side. A waist-high, feathery tangled growth caught my feet and tripped me up, as I slipped and staggered over the rocks I couldn't see. But so airy and intriguing—like the sirens of ancient mythology—they beckoned me on and on. I knew there had to be ladyslippers somewhere in this cool, moist, dark place, and sure enough there were. But they weren't in bloom— so what are they? *Californicum* perhaps, like the ones in Lost Canyon, but again maybe some other rare *Cypripedium* not found in any other canyon on Chrome.

I went as far down as the ferns grew. Then the water went underground, and I turned back. Just as I started back, a patch of sunlight shone on a tiny plant I'd never expected to see here—*Listeria*, or twayblade. Only two to three inches high, with tiny greenish-white blossoms, it would have been almost invisible except for that one little ray of bright morning sun picking it out from the debris on the canyon floor.

Looking back up the way I'd come, those tangled ferns on that steep hillside seemed even more impossible to go through, so I decided to strike uphill to the left and hit the old logging road, then walk down the road to the bus.

Well, it's no easy thing to fight the brush going uphill anywhere in this area—and I knew that—but the old road couldn't be more than four to five hundred feet up the hillside, so off I went. I climbed, and climbed, and climbed—but no road. Since I had the compass, I knew I was going in the right direction, so rather than go back down in the canyon I kept on, and sure enough I topped the hill and found old skid roads where the logs had been taken out. So of course that had to lead eventually to an old road that connected to one of the main roads I knew. It did—an hour later—on top of Taylor Mountain!

When I started out in the morning, Taylor was on my right, and I climbed out of the fern canyon on my left—and never crossed another canyon of any kind. So how could I be on Taylor Mountain?

In the future, I have a suspicion that I'll come back the way I went and not be tempted to take any "shortcuts!"

July 30, 1981

Spring Comes to Freeland Mountain

A cold wind moans through the little Jeffrey pine, and the old building creaks in the sudden gusts—but the small lookout still stands. However, the snows of March did almost as much damage as the winds of November, for the south and east ends are completely down. Only that high peak and the northwest side still defy the elements.

It's unbelievable that the old building could have withstood the violent weather of last winter. It may have been made of rough lumber, and crudely put together—but it's done better than many a modern structure in the valley!

There were a few snow banks on the mountain coming up and several here on the shaded side, but it must have gone off in the last week, for there was a lot more just ten days ago when Charlotte and I followed the snow plow up to the four corners, at Freeland Saddle. But a ninety-five degree day, and several in the eighties, melted it in a hurry. Still, there is some snow across the road above "Wolf Alley," which will be the last snow bank here on the ridge.

On the way up I saw the tiny pink *Anemone lyallii* blooming among the numerous-stalked *Trillium ovatum* scattered in the manzanita brush. Here on top, the lovely purple arabis are in full bloom among the rocky outcrops, and the tiny *Claytonia sessilifolia*, and a few wedge-leaved violets. Wonder which opens its blossoms first?

I can see Lake Mountain and Elijah and know the snow banks must be well over ten feet deep this year. And for sure there will be a deep, cool, last snow bank on the north of Lake Mountain in September, but we won't go and see it, old Sal and I. So the flowers will bloom in the meadow and on Elijah, and beside the hidden pond without us again this year—as they did those many years before we came.

May 26, 1982

The Sleeping Bear

Fern Canyon needs to be explored today; it's been two weeks since I saw the tiny buds I think are queen cup, or *Clintonia*. But when I arrived here at the little waterfall and the pool where they grow, I found to my disappointment the little plants haven't bloomed yet. But those single stalks with the one bud are much bigger and must be within a few days of opening. At this point, I'm not at all sure I'll come back to see them again, for on the way down I had a rather startling encounter. I was carefully picking my way along the watercourse and really not making much noise, when I suddenly heard a loud thrashing in the dense brush, looked up, and was practically eye to eye with a black bear! About forty feet away stood a big, sleepy-looking bear trying to decide what was invading its territory. I'm sure it must have been asleep in the brush and never heard me coming until I was right beside it. Evidently the wind was from the wrong direction, and it stepped forward to get a better look at whatever the disturbance was. Then it got the scent! For something so big, it sure moved fast. It whirled about and started up the hillside at a lope I envied. How I wish I could climb out of a deep canyon with so little effort. A couple hundred feet up the slope it stopped and looked back. I think it was just curious—and it occurred to me it might come back after its first fright. Now I know why it is I don't like canyons—there's no place to run to, and you can get lost in them! I'd been having trouble enough just walking through that thick brush and around slippery rocks without trying to run anywhere. So before old bruin got its courage back, I clapped my hands and yelled as loudly as possible, "GO HOME—GET," and it went.

But all the while I was eating lunch, I wondered if it might get a whiff of the pungent Polish sausage and sharp cheddar cheese I always carry for snacks. This time I didn't linger long over my lunch break, but I did get the plants I wanted and made the notes I'd come for. Not even a bear was going to keep me from that part of the work.

Since there was no other way out of the canyon but the way I came in— and I wasn't about to try any shortcuts again—I had to go back through the same area to get to the bus. And I just hoped it wasn't near the bear's den, or something it considered its territorial right. However, coming out was without incident, and I learned one thing—next time I go down into a deep, dark, wild canyon, I'll tie a bell on my knapsack, or carry a police whistle and let the wild creatures know when I'm around, for I'm sure they don't appreciate being startled by an intruder any more than I like stumbling over them unexpectedly.

June 23, 1982

The Old Fritillary

❀ ❀ ❀

I saw her on a sunny day, but with a cold wind out of the northeast. She came into the rabbit brush, the last blooming plant on all of that rocky hillside.

How she ever managed to become airborne is a mystery, for half of her hind wings had been torn away, probably by some bird. The once bright color had faded to a dull tan; even the black markings on the upper surface were more grey than black. But she sailed and soared, dipped and danced about the flowers with as much energy as on the day she had emerged from the chrysalis.

She would alight on a blossom for a little, then glide off in the wind, making a wide circle across the road, up the hill, across the road again,

down the hillside, then back to rest a
moment on the yellow flowers. She
sipped a little nectar, but mostly
seemed interested in flying for the
pure joy of skimming the endless
air.

Only the week before, I'd
seen four fritillaries
cavorting about that same
bush, but today she was
the only one left. Had she
outlived all her younger
relatives? Or was she the
last of the four I'd seen?
As I remembered, all the
others were bright and new-
looking. Nevertheless,
sometime in early September I
recalled seeing a faded fritillary
among the others, but then its wings
were undamaged. This species does fly
about a good part of the summer, and it's
not unusual to find some with dull, tattered
wings, but mostly the ones who last till cold weather
have hatched later, and are young enough to take the frosty nights and
windy days of these higher elevations.

However old she was, she completely and thoroughly enjoyed the sunny
hour, and when I left at three o'clock she was still sailing happily in the sun,
though the shadows were long across the road and the chill of coming
evening was in the air.

September 30, 1982

Day of the Fritillaries

I didn't know there were so many fritillary butterflies in the world! Here, in
a half-acre patch of rabbit brush near the top of the south end of Chrome,
dozens fly about and feed off the bright yellow blossoms. This is the most
extensive colony of *Chrysothamus* I've found outside of Rough and Ready
Flats in the Illinois Valley. And since these are the last plants to blossom in
this barren serpentine hillside, they call forth butterflies from all around—
maybe miles around. There are a few crescent spots and skippers, but mostly
the bushes are covered with fritillaries—I lost count at thirty on one bush.
Possibly several varieties are represented: *Speyeria callippi, S. hydaspe, S.
zerene,* and maybe others. They are in all stages, from brilliant newly

emerged, to tattered, faded individuals with color so pale they hardly look like fritillaries at all. *Speyeria zerene* especially likes to congregate by the hundreds on thistle and rabbit brush, so that may be who we have. But no matter which they are, all need violets to lay their eggs on and provide food for the caterpillar. Are there that many violets on this hot, rocky hillside? *Viola macloskey* grows among the manzanita brush and in more sheltered spots all across both ends of the ridge and down into Briggs Valley; so presumably there are enough plants to supply food for these myriad butterflies I see today. But how far do they travel looking for the blossoms? How would the fritillaries fifteen hundred feet lower in the valley know about the rabbit brush up here?

Across the road, a little gully comes down off the steep slope and a small pool of water has collected among the rocks, and here I eat my lunch. There is a little trickle from up above, so the water is fresh and clear. A number of water striders play about, and as I'd hoped, there are other visitors to the little pool. A California sister butterfly, a little wood nymph, skippers, a *Trypoxylon* wasp gathering mud for her partitions, and last of all, a gorgeous, newly minted red admiral—the first I've ever seen!

The most surprising find of the day was part of a dead scorpion that had been run over on the road. That hot, rocky, southeast facing slope is evidently attractive to more than the heat-loving rabbit brush!

September 21, 1983

Ragged Wings and Faded Glory

❀ ❀ ❀

This morning was thick with fog, and not a wing fluttered as I watched the flowers of the rabbit brush on the road to Chrome. But presently, about 10:00 a.m., the fog lifted and blue sky appeared. Soon the sun came out, and almost before you could think about them, the butterflies were on the wing—sailing, gliding, and soaring for the sheer joy of seeing that bright light again.

Now the fritillaries on the flowers are much fewer in number, and many are old, tattered, and faded. "Feeble, and full of days," as Fabre said. Still they fly and cavort in the warm sun. Surely they sense their remaining hours in the warm air and bright sunlight are short indeed. But to look at them playing across this slope among the blooming bushes, you'd never think they had a care in the world. And maybe they don't. Perhaps they have been given the better part; to play the happy summer days away, then to sit in the late sun one autumn day with no regrets and no dread of the cold winter nights creeping ever closer over the hill.

I watch with admiration—and a touch of sadness for you, old fritillaries, with your ragged wings. And I watch you with a bit of envy also. To me is given memory of the past, and foresight of what the future may bring. But you are happy in this moment, in your hour of warm sun and blue skies. You know not the past, you have no fear of the future. For you the warmth, the sun, the soft breezes, and the fragrant blossoms are enough—how I wish I could say the same!

October 5, 1983

Lunch with the Cobra Lilies

❀ ❀ ❀

Sitting here at Mud Springs with banks of snow all around, I can see a patch of darlingtonia seemingly lifting their heads to see whether spring has come. And it has at last. Though there is about three or more feet of snow across parts of the road and under the trees, the wet spots where the cobras grow are mostly snow free. The plants look surprisingly good after being covered with tons of the white stuff since December. They are amazingly hardy things, and many of the stalks look green and alive, while others are bent over and turning reddish-brown. I wonder if the older ones are the ones that look so ragged, while the younger leaves are still green. I'm going to mark some to see how long they stay green and alive. I know some of them are a year old, maybe older. They certainly don't die down as most other leaves do when the cold weather in late fall gets them.

The mountain chickadees are here and so is a little warbler of some sort. It sounds like one I have at home. And a pileated woodpecker is off in the woods somewhere close, drumming on an old tree.

Walked in to the hidden bog to see the cobras, and almost missed them in the snow. They're almost buried back there on the north slope. After I found the lower end of their log, I could see that some were upright and as green as they were in summer. But that was only in the patches where the sun has melted most of the snow. The others are still buried a foot deep, or more.

On the way back, I stopped at the cliff where so many of the tiny saxifrage grow, and all the bees were out. All kinds—big

STREAMSIDE TRILLIUM   BUNCHBERRY

carpenter bees, medium ones, little ones, *Ceretina*, *Andrena*, and hive bees. Was hoping to see some butterflies, but only saw one odd moth that at first I mistook for a butterfly. But the antennae didn't seem right, though it was built much like a skipper. Later I found out it was a spotted forester moth; deep brown with big, white polka dots is the best description I can give it. I don't think they're too common, as I've never seen one before. But it sure catches your eye if you are watching for moths or butterflies!

April 15, 1985

November Pool—And a Brand New Butterfly

❀ ❀ ❀

Again I sit beside the tiny pool at Butterfly Bend and realize that in almost nine weeks I've only been here twice—during the summer I was coming as often as twice a week.

But no matter. At this moment, the sun is brilliant, the sky of November as blue as that of October, and the water striders are cavorting on their little lake as though it were still summer. The rabbit brush has only one or two bushes with a few yellow blossoms; all the others are tawny, fuzzy, seed heads sending little puffs of fuzz off on the slight breeze from the canyon. A couple of hive bees were out and one beautiful golden-metallic drone fly, but all the old fritillaries are gone—victims of frosty nights and windy days.

But while I was eating lunch beside the pool, who should come sailing in but a beautiful, newly minted California sister! All velvety black-and-white with big orange spots bright as signal lights on each wing tip. She made several passes, then alighted on a rock, waved her wings, and took off again, until I despaired of ever getting a good look at her. But suddenly she came over and landed on my lunch box and basked in the sun for a good fifteen minutes. Turning and folding and unfolding her pristine wings, she gave me a perfect chance to see all the flashing, iridescent colors of lavender, pink, and violet in the stripes under her wings. I could even see her tawny-reddish eyes with feet and proboscis to match, and her face and head of soft pussy-willow grey. What an elegant ensemble!

But finally that warm sun and soft breeze called her away, and I never saw her again.

As I was on my way to Mud Springs I didn't linger long after she left, for the sun sets early these days and early afternoon has shadows long as summer's evening twilight.

The cobra lilies look wonderful, and I went around and saw everybody. The last time I visited them was in August, and it was like greeting old friends again. The bog on the northeast slope is mostly in shadow now, and the little field where the Mariposa copper butterflies played among the western tofieldia is cold and drab and wintry looking. Only small spots of sunlight touch the field and bog for brief moments, and one would never guess how much life and color and action existed only a few months ago.

Walked around among the lupines (*Lupinus macronulatus*—Waldo lupine) on the road where the pileated woodpecker tree is, but soon the sun was getting low and the shadows longer, so I headed for Ducky's Pond to eat supper.

The alder leaves are piling up on the gravel bars of the creek, and it's almost too shady and cool to eat under the old alder any more this year.

Tried to shake down some apples for the little animals, and did get a few, but I need a pole to get the upper ones, as they really hang on tightly, although I know they've been frosted a number of times this fall.

All too soon, the sun headed for the south hill and I had to leave. Stopped at Flicker Pond, and didn't see or hear any kind of bird, but this morning as I came in I paused and saw several big, blue dragonflies sailing about over the new pools of water. Each little rain sends a bit more water into the pond, and a number of puddles in the low spots weren't there two weeks ago.

November 2, 1985

Discovery of the Mariposa Copper Butterfly

❀ ❀ ❀

Sometime in the middle of June, 1984, I first saw the little Mariposa copper butterflies at Mud Springs, a few miles west of Chrome Ridge. I'd discovered the darlingtonia bog above the road, and was watching butterflies in the area. Tortoise shells, checker spots, wood nymphs, and a dark skipper flew about, along with a medium-sized brown-orange butterfly with light, ashy underwings. While I was seeing only a few of the other butterflies, the orange ones with whitish underwings were quite numerous, flitting about in twos and threes every few minutes.

Since I'd never seen a butterfly quite like this, I became interested and watched them closely. They were some kind of copper, for sure, but none of the pictures in the guides looked like them. After I arrived home, I checked all my insect and butterfly books, but no copper had those ashy grey hind underwings. Not in this area. Dornfeld (The Butterflies of Oregon. *1980. Ernest J. Dornfeld. Timber Press, Forest Grove, OR) mentions the coppers of the Cascade crest, and so does Neill & Hepburn* (Butterflies Afield in the Pacific Northwest. *1976. William A. Neill and Douglas J. Hepburn. Search Publishing, Seattle, WA). But both books show greyer underwings with more dark markings than ours. It looked like I'd need help on this. It was August 13, 1984 before I again spent a day at Mud Springs. This time, I collected two of the strange little coppers and sent them to Paul Hammond (Oregon State University lepidopterist) of Philomath, Oregon, for identification.*

On September 17, 1984, I was notified that the copper butterflies at Mud Springs are Mariposa coppers, Lycaena (Epidemia) mariposa, *a species of* Lycaena *not known before from the Siskiyou Mountains.*

About this time, I'd noticed the blue ribbons of a timber sale in the area of the Mariposa's habitat. In fact, the equipment was already in place to begin harvesting! I immediately contacted Robert M. Pyle, whom I'd heard of through the Xerces Society. The word was out! And things began happening. The result was modification of the timber sale, and the Mariposas of Mud Springs live in peace on their fifty-two acre sanctuary. But without the help of those experts, it's doubtful I could have protected this rare species by myself.

The search for the food plants was long and arduous. Mariposa coppers in other areas used some member of the Polygonaceae for larval plant. There was no member of that species at Mud Springs, but there was a lot of Vaccinium—*three species*—V. scoparium, V. membranaceum, *and* V. myrtillus.

Finally, it was determined that a colony of Mariposas on Mt. Shasta was happy with a species of vaccinium. *Several people from U.C. Berkeley came to Mud Springs to investigate and shook out caterpillars from the leaves of* V. myrtillus, *and later we found the adults ovipositing on* myrtillus.

Until I left the Siskiyous in 1992, we monitored the Mariposas every season from the middle of June to August 15, and they have held their own, or are increasing at a moderate rate. The Silver Fire of 1987 came very close, but spared the interior of their preserve.

For several years during and after my discovery of the Mud Springs population of the Mariposa copper, I visited the area often, observing the adults and searching for the larval host plant. Several of my journal entries follow; they present a chronicle of this period.

1984-1986

The Mariposa Copper of Mud Springs

❀ ❀ ❀

Today is to be a butterfly hunting day, for as much as I hate doing it, I have to catch a butterfly up here at Mud Springs and send it away to be identified. I think they are Mariposa coppers, but unfortunately the only way to be absolutely sure is to have one examined by an expert in the field.

Never in all the places I've been watching butterflies in the past two years have I seen any quite like these here among the cobra lilies. So I'm spending the day just sitting and observing the activity in this little open spot among the old trees and the cobras. The morning sun shines bright and warm, and the helenium and senecio are blooming among the darlingtonia. A few Volmer lilies are left, but most of them have faded some time ago. I've been hearing a frantic buzzing somewhere close, and finally located where the sound is coming from. A big bumble bee is imprisoned in the tube of one of the cobra lilies. A neat slit in the side of the stem soon lets her out—and I'm sure she appreciates what a lucky bee she is!

Have seen quite a few butterflies—and are they fast. For a while I wondered if I'd ever get one as I haven't a real net, but had to improvise a snare with an old, filmy, nylon head-scarf. But I notice the little things love to sit and sun themselves, and if you stand still long enough in the middle of their territory, sooner or later they'll drop down to rest on some convenient weed or flower stem. But you'd better be quick! Got two, which I think are a pair. I purposely caught the faded, worn ones, as I think they have already mated and laid their eggs for the season, so haven't much time left anyhow.

August 13, 1984

Day of Discovery

❀ ❀ ❀

Have found the little butterfly at Mud Springs is indeed a Mariposa copper—and unknown in this locality. Exciting news. Always did wish we had our very own rare butterfly—and it looks like we have it.

Today I'm looking for its food plants, which are supposed to be knotweed. But there is no knotweed at Mud Springs that I've seen. Nor any other member of that family. Not even our common false buckwheat (*Eriogonum*), or curly dock, or sheep sorrel. So where are the plants; or does it substitute something else if it has to? Haven't found the answers to that yet—but I do know something else. More cobra lily bogs are located at Mud Springs, in the forest, than along the nearby road and its adjacent stream.

An old logging road leads northeast from the main road, and there is a sort of watershed seven or eight hundred feet up that road. It's a gentle slope, and at the top it starts almost imperceptibly downhill again, and the runoff goes in opposite directions at the "hump" on the northeast side. And off the road about two hundred feet, two beautiful darlingtonia bogs are hemmed in with thick azalea brush and Sadler oak. You first come onto a smaller bog, then fifty feet or so farther in is a larger one, with a big old silvery log lying across the middle.

These are the healthiest-looking cobra lilies I've ever seen. Fully as tall— at least three feet—as the ones at Woodcock, and of a bright Kelly green with no sign of the mineral deficiencies of other bogs. They are unusual, too, in being an almost pure stand of darlingtonia, with very little competition from the usual sedge and bog grasses.

The darlingtonias are on a northeast exposure, and the tree overstory is rather dense except for their little clearing, so they aren't subjected to the hot summer sun that the more open stands are. Actually, I'm betting these two bogs aren't more than eight to nine hundred feet from the one above the road where I found the Mariposa copper. Are the butterflies here too? Maybe their food plants are on this side of the hill? Since it's so late in the year and many of the earlier plants are gone, I'll just have to wait until next year to explore for the plants.

Did see quite a number of California tortoise shell butterflies flying around and sunning on old trees and logs.

5:00 p.m.—Now, as I sit under the old alder beside Horse Creek, the sun is unusually hot and a California sister is cruising up and down the stream. A little way above me, at a bend in the creek, one bush of red osier dogwood is flaunting a deep maroon-colored branch among all the green of summer.

At the little pool beside the old log in midstream, a thin line of dead alder leaves have piled up on the little gravel bar. Soon that thin line will be a great company of autumn leaves waiting to sail downstream after the first fall rains.

Off in the field toward the apple trees, I hear a cricket tuning up for evening. Too soon—too soon the happy summer days are vanishing.

September 17, 1984

The Striped Caterpillars

Really came today to hunt either for caterpillars or eggs of the Mariposas on some of the plants in the little clearing where so many of them congregated last week. Stood on my head, crawled around in the wet, got hung up in the brush looking with the magnifying glass for signs of the larvae of those butterflies—and found not a thing! Did gather two black- and orange-striped caterpillars feeding happily on senecio that I'll take home and raise to see what they are. From the looks of them, their color and the fact that crescentspots are flying about, I'd guess that's what they are.

August 4, 1985

New Discoveries at Mud Springs

❀ ❀ ❀

Ate lunch at Flicker Pond, though it wasn't very warm, and was pretty cloudy. But about 11:00 the sun came out and I thought maybe I'd better get up to Mud Springs and look for butterflies, at least see whether the larvae are hatching, though it's rather early.

Turned out to be nice and warm there, so it was a good idea to work up on Flat Top today. Saw a car parked at the turn-around, so I drove on and stopped farther up the road and went about my work. Wasn't able to find any eggs or larvae—and I soon found out why.

Later I talked to two gals walking down the road and discovered they're botanists too, just out looking as I usually am. They sometimes do work for the Forest Service people, and we both have seen each other's names on reports and such, but never met till now. And they told me that along with *V. scoparium* and *V. parvafolium* there is a third vaccinium species—*V. myrtillis*. Now I wonder, which species do the Mariposas use as food plants for the larvae?

Both *scoparium* and *parvafolium* are quite scarce, but *myrtillis* is all over the place, especially in the sheltered area under the trees on the outskirts of the bog. It also grows in the outlying open spaces where I saw the butterflies idling about last summer. So maybe I've been looking on the wrong vaccinium for the eggs and larvae.

But I looked all afternoon, and neither one did I see. But no wonder, there are little patches of snow all about under the trees, and the nights must still be freezing up here.

May 14, 1986

Mud Springs and Good Companions

❀ ❀ ❀

Today I'm looking again for Mariposas at Mud Springs—and did see one just as I got off the bus. It rested briefly on a western leucothoe blossom, then was gone.

Veva Stansell and Helen Planeto (my companions of May 14) came up after I'd been here an hour or so, and we had a wonderful time keying out plants and discussing some of the rarer ones.

They helped me look for butterflies, too, and Helen spotted one just before we left at 2:30. It was so fast, and disappeared so quickly, we couldn't be sure it was a Mariposa. But it was little and dark, and speedy, so very likely it was.

The logging has begun across the road, so we were treated to a lot of noise and dust. They're a good bunch though, and all seem interested in the butterflies. Clarence, the catskinner (bulldozer operator) was quite excited as he was sure he'd seen one crossing the road the other day. He couldn't wait to tell me about it. Then one of the truck drivers stopped and asked me about a bird he'd seen going down Taylor Creek. From his description, I'd say it was a western tanager, as they're pretty conspicuous with that red head and bright yellow and black. He was really pleased to have it identified—so there is a positive side to this too. When you can get the people in the woods looking at other things besides trees, they will be more inclined to save some of the rare ones when they find them.

June 2, 1986

Chrome Ridge and Freeland Mountain

❀ ❀ ❀

Portions of the serpentine ridges and flats around Freeland Mountain and Chrome Ridge were declared a Botanical Area as part of the 1989 Forest Plan for the Siskiyou National Forest. They must have listened to me! I hope this area will be protected from mining and logging. On those high serpentine ridges, there are numerous rare and sensitive plant species, many with a narrow range, and endemic to the Siskiyou Mountains of southern Oregon.

Though Freeland Mountain itself was spared, the Silver Fire of 1987 ravaged some of the old trees of Chrome, and many of the most picturesque trees are gone. That primitive little look-out cabin on Freeland is completely down now, but surprisingly, the old pole that held the hand-cranked phone still stands!

Wine-red Bolander lilies still bloom among the manzanita brush across the rocky ridge tops, and the small plants of the serpentine are still thriving, in spite of drought and fire, as they have for many aeons past.

—1993

4
Briggs Valley and Horse Creek

The Setting

To think of the Siskiyous as only wild rugged peaks and lonely ridges with breathtaking views, and to ignore their other features, would be to present only part of the character of these unique mountains. Many streams and small rivers run through sheltered meadows and hidden canyons. Warm, protected places tempt one to stop and rest in the sun or wander along the creek for the sheer joy of exploring. One such spot is the narrow, level, grassy field beside Horse Creek, whose headwaters rise on the west slope of Onion Mountain. This little valley with the steep, fir-covered hills surrounding it may be an ancient alluvial outwash, for the red soil, while gravely, is deep and loamy. It's been years since the last homesteader left, but a rich growth of wild and domestic grasses produces a hay crop that—in good years—is waist high. The upper end of the valley is very mesic, with a heavy cover of a large, clumpy sedge, and here water always runs in the old ditches, no matter how dry the year. This little valley, a mile or so long, opens out into Briggs Valley at the foot of Chrome Ridge, where Horse Creek flows into the larger Briggs and Myers creeks.

These little watercourses are a riot of color in autumn, much more so than the creeks of the lowlands of the Rogue Valley. At this elevation of 2,000 feet, many stream-side plants are also different. Several kinds of willow grow here, including a very large tree willow not often seen at lower elevations, plus Pacific dogwood, red osier dogwood, and vine maple. If the days are warm and sunny, and nights frosty in late September and early October, then the color display along these little creeks is the best this part of the state has to offer.

A number of old apple trees are scattered across both Briggs Valley and along the narrow field beside Horse Creek. It is generally thought that Briggs, for whom the valley was named, planted them, but the Forest Service says that James Farrin (or Ferren), who staked out the Barr Mine sometime in the 1860s, brought them in. It's not known just when the trees were set out, but they are very old, and some are more dead than alive but still producing hard, juicy little apples with a tangy taste not found in the commercial crops of today.

At the upper end of the valley where Smith Creek enters Horse Creek, there used to be a small house, several outbuildings, a corral and possibly a barn, and most certainly animals. Now all that is left are a few charred timbers from the house, and a corner post and three or four broken rails from the old corral. The year 1914 is carved on one of the large alders near the creek, a little way from the house site. Perhaps these people came a number of years after Farrin, Briggs, and the others who settled the larger valley to the west.

After the Forest Service acquired the property decades ago, the old pasture reverted mostly to wild grasses and sedge, except where the Oregon Department of Fish and Wildlife helps maintain forage areas for elk and deer. The old fruit trees are slowly losing their battle against time. No small part of the charm of this area is in trying to visualize the peace and contentment of living and working in such a beautiful place. It is all part of another, vanished era, almost as remote as the beginnings of these mountains under that shallow sea of prehistoric times.

Briggs Valley and Horse Creek are only a few miles away and 2,000 feet lower than Chrome Ridge. Many of my journal entries in this chapter begin on the exposed Chrome Ridge and end up down in the comparative seclusion of Horse Creek.

The Happy Wanderers

❀ ❀ ❀

The hills and hollows are aflame with vine maple and dogwood this last week of October, and as Sal and I sit on the bank of the little round pond at the east end of Horse Creek, the sun is warm and a half-dozen dragonflies sail and soar on the still air. Off in the middle of the pond, a tiny water boatman sculls his little craft toward shore. I've always seen them before in the bottom of shallow streams and ponds, but here it is on the surface plying its long oars with the speed of a miniature power boat, and making a small wake across the still water. The little body of water is only seventy-five to one hundred feet wide at most, and appears to have been scooped out at this end of the field for wildlife to drink in summer.

Sal and I came here only once last spring looking for maples, then when the snow melted in the high country we couldn't stay in the lowlands. But now snow has isolated those high peaks in solitude, and we're happy enough to be exploring these little creeks and meadows.

This is a long, narrow field that at one time was part of the homestead. Now, all that remains are a few rods of broken-down fence and a half-dozen old apple trees. It must have been a beautiful setting for a home, and there seems to have been plenty of water, as remains of old irrigation ditches still carry a good head of water.

Now, at 2:30, the cricket sings as loud as on a summer's eve, and the sun throws shadows as long as those of 5:00 p.m. on a July afternoon. Sally and I found a shallow pool in the creek, and I'm sitting on the bank looking down into its clear water. There was much more life in the little pond where we ate lunch than here. No water striders, no dragonflies, not even a tiny fish. Probably the pond's water is warmer, being out in the full sun, while here it barely penetrates through alders and willows. But gradually that sun will dip behind the hill until one day in November there will be no sun at all.

Today we have been the "Happy Wanderers," Sal and I, for we have explored the length of the field, found where the old house stood, visited the mint patch, and stirred up numerous sassy little winter wrens in their brush piles.

The shadows are deepening in the little pool now, the cricket sings louder, and it's time to go. How quickly the sunlit hours of October slip away.

October 27, 1976

The Little Golden-eye

❀ ❀ ❀

Thursday, November 3rd: A minute too early, a few seconds later, there would be no story to tell, and the little golden-eyed duck would have never entered my life.

On the road to Bigelow Lakes I found her. A hawk had just captured her, and was poised for the kill when I drove up and frightened it off. The little duck naturally tried her best to elude me, and after a zigzag chase down the middle of the road I finally caught up with her. She was bloody and almost paralyzed with shock, and I feared she was injured beyond help.

The road is narrow at that point, with trees on either side and no spot to pull over, so I drove with her in my arms a half mile up the road to the gravel pit and stopped to examine her. After the blood was washed off, I saw she had only one puncture wound in the breast at the base of the wing, and otherwise seemed unhurt. What to do with her? Fortunately, I always have a box of some kind in the bus, so I made her a bed of a soft sweater and covered her over so she'd feel secure.

I was at least halfway to Bigelow lakes and didn't feel I should turn back and go home. I know these little wild things are delicate in many ways, and handling them when they're injured very often kills them, so I didn't really expect her to live more than a few hours anyhow.

When Sal and I arrived at the lakes, I set the box in the sun near the back window and left her, for I knew she needed rest and quiet more than anything else at that time.

Four hours later, when I got back off Lake Mountain, the fog had descended thick and cold, and I dreaded looking at my little passenger for I was sure she was dead. But the moment I opened the door, I heard her stirring and knew she had at least survived so far. There had been a few hours of sun before the fog came in, it was quiet and peaceful, and I know she felt secure in her hideaway in the box.

Now the long trip home worried me. It was more than forty miles, and the little duck had already traveled twenty miles over rough roads with the unfamiliar noise of the engine to frighten her. But she was a good passenger and never once did she fly up or appear disturbed by the strange rumbling and jolting. From the beginning, I noticed she seemed calmer than most wild birds, and allowed me to touch her and even pick her up without much of a struggle. This was all to her advantage, and if she would cooperate by eating and remaining calm and resting, I might just be able to help her.

When I got home, my mother and I examined her thoroughly and could find no other injury. She was a beautiful little creature, about the size of a call duck ("show" duck), with green-grey bill and feet and a ring of lighter grey on the bill. The breast was mottled grey-brown; the head and back a deep, rich brown. On each wing was a broad band of soft grey-blue, bordered by a narrow, dark stripe. In the sun the eyes shone with a beautiful luminous golden yellow—and to me she will always be a little golden-eye. But as near as we could discover, she was a ring-necked duck, probably immature, as she lacked the white patch on the breast and eye ring. Since the bird was of a rather calm disposition, I believe it was a female. However, she was injured and probably not inclined to make a fuss, still being in shock from her unhappy experience.

Friday, November 4th: The little golden-eye is still alive, and last night after I left her in a box with a water pan, she cleaned herself up and splashed water in every direction! Since ducks love to dabble, I put grain, some grass, and a few bean sprouts in the water and she sampled all of them.

Later in the day, I was able to find a number of earthworms, and my little friend much preferred them, with a side dish of bean sprouts.

We have examined her again, and already the wound is healing over, the feathers are clean and smooth, and you'd never know she was hurt. Still she makes little protest when I pick her up, and will even stay in her bathing pool when I enter the room—earlier she would always hastily hide in the corner of her box when she saw or heard me.

Saturday, November 5th: Today is the day. The little duck is restless, eats everything in sight, and constantly plays in the water. I won't keep her any longer, though I hate to release her on a weekend, as it's hunting season. But I have in mind a perfect spot—the little beaver pond in Briggs Valley. Hidden among the willows along Horse Creek, a quiet spot that few except

Forest Service workers know about, I feel she would be safer there than anywhere else. Henceforth, to me and all who know the story, this place will be called "Ducky's Pond."

It is an overcast November day, and the slightest breeze sends showers of golden leaves whirling to the ground. So I take Jeth, who is alone and lost after the recent death of her husband, and we head up Taylor Creek with our passenger. The dogwoods are still flaming on the hillsides, the maples luminescent with golden light as though the sun were shining on them, and the rain and mist swirls through the narrow canyon.

As we walk across the broad field beside the creek, the sun comes out briefly and the red dogwood and yellow willows stand glowing in the pale November sunlight. The beaver pond is three times the size it was two weeks ago when Charlotte and I saw it. We release the little duck at the water's edge, and with a joyous leap she flaps her wings and paddles away, leaving a small wake that ripples across the quiet surface from shore to shore. About a hundred feet out, she turns and looks at us, stands up, beats her wings, dips her head a few times and sends a spray of water cascading around her, then silently the tiny dark form disappears among the willows around a bend. All that is left are the gently bobbing red and golden leaves on the surface of the silent pond, and we turn happily homeward, each cherishing this little moment out of time, each knowing that it will be something never to be forgotten in all the years to come.

November 5, 1977

The Little Golden-eye—Epilogue

❀ ❀ ❀

This is the kind of day in late Autumn you dream about—misty blue and gold, and wind in the willows.

I couldn't stay at home and work, so we headed up the canyon, old Sal and I, to visit the little duck at the beaver pond. Now when the fog lies thick, or the cold rain slants down, and I have to work outside because I couldn't resist the call of the pale November sun and the autumn wind blowing free, I'll have no one to blame but myself.

We arrived about noon, and slipped quietly up to the edge of the pond, and sure enough, there was the little duck. She quickly darted into the shadows among the willows, but I saw her and know she's all right. Then we sat on the bank and ate lunch. Later, Sal took a nap and I sketched, but the duck didn't appear. I spoke to her, and I'm sure she knows my voice, but I'm glad she's cautious. I wouldn't want to tame her for anything.

As I lingered there, the pale sun moved in and out among the clouds, first casting a grey pall over the water then lighting it with dancing reflections. Only one vine maple and one red dogwood, standing together, had any leaves left, but their reflections in the quiet water brightened the day, though the wind was cold and the sky mostly overcast.

Just before we left, Sal found a mouse nest and decided to dig it out, so I walked quietly along the creek bank above the pond—and startled the little duck dabbling among the weeds along the shore. She flew over the surface of the water for a little way, then paddled back toward the deeper part of the pond. The sun was out and the water a pathway of light, with the little dark form rippling the silvery surface as it swam out of sight.

November 7, 1977

Our Green and Gold Day

❀ ❀ ❀

It is now a dreary winter day of fog and white frost, but I haven't forgotten that soft blue and gold and green day last April when Sal and I went up Minnow Creek for maple pollen. There are so many small maples all along the creek bank and beside the road that we spend a good part of the pollen-collecting season in that area.

This was one of those soft spring days you dream of all winter—blue, blue sky; a few white, fluffy clouds; and the new-green leaves like a mist on the hillsides. The trees we had come to harvest were along the road fifty feet or so above the creek, opposite a high, steep hillside. Thick with maples and alders, the creek could only be heard, not seen, and that dark hillside looked cold and gloomy. But we were on the sunny side at a wide bend in the little-used logging road, so as I worked I let the old dog explore.

Usually when I'm collecting pollen, I get right down to it and try to have at least half the work done before we eat. For I know only too well that if by some mischance I see a bird or a strange bee or butterfly, or start looking for plants, we end up getting nothing done until late afternoon, very often arriving home after dark!

The trees in this spot grow below the bank and their tops overhang the road, so with the pole pruner I can reach the best panicles without too much trouble—the trick is to snap the cut branches onto the road instead of letting them roll down the incline. But after twenty-seven years of practice, this isn't much of a problem anymore. And Sal has been with me so long that she knows how long to explore, and the exact moment to come back for lunch.

Finally, that highlight of the day arrived. Sal had come back some time before and lay in the shade with that expectant look, so I gave in and quit work. I sat on the edge of the road with my feet hanging over the bank and that canopy of new maple leaves overhead. Looking up, I saw swatches of blue sky and fluffs of white clouds sailing by. A soft breeze shimmered the green leaves, turning them this way and that in the bright golden light. As we rested, we were lost in a little world of green and gold and blue, the only sounds the murmuring creek below and the rustling leaves above.

Then to make a perfect day more perfect, a winter wren began to serenade us from the dark forested hillside across the creek. He sang the whole time we were eating, a soft little treble warbling that somehow was the very essence and voice of the deep forest with its mossy aisles and ancient trees.

I have many lovely memories of April and the beautiful big-leaf maples that have been my livelihood these many years, but the sweetest, happiest, and most vivid is of that day beside little Minnow Creek when our world was all gold and green blended with the melody of a tiny wren singing to his mate in the deep darkness of that peaceful hillside.

April 1978

Horse Creek and the Spirit of the Siskiyous

I've come again to the little meadow beside "Ducky's Pond," and while it breaks my heart to be here with all the memories of Sal, after a little, the peace and beauty of the spot assert themselves and I'm content and almost happy to be exploring here again.

Lately, in my writing, I've been concentrating almost entirely on the high peaks and rocky serpentine outcrops of the Siskiyous, to the exclusion of this lovely little valley that the "happy wanderers" were so much a part of for so long. While my rough monograph "The Spirit of the Siskiyous,"* is intended primarily to describe the high, wild places with their rare plant colonies and the ancient storm-battered trees, why ignore this peaceful little spot where we spent so many happy sunlit hours? Until today I've always considered the lowlands as being so commonplace, so unexciting, that I'd never thought of them as being part of the spirit of these mountains too.

---

*Editors' note: The monograph "Spirit of the Siskiyous" is an unpublished manuscript of Mary's; parts of the manuscript were used in this book—Brief Natural History, and Settings for each chapter. To us, Mary *is* the Spirit of the Siskiyous.

But when the winds howled over the ridges and the snow piled yards deep across Elijah, then Charlotte, Sal, and I were glad enough to come here to the creek and explore among the willows, walk across the meadow, sit in the sun, and capture autumn's vivid colors on paper. When the fog lay thick in the valley below, there was no place this side of heaven we'd rather be, and when that pale sun set behind the little round hill, there was no place we'd rather not go back to than that fog-shrouded valley at home.

Quiet and beautiful, but in no way spectacular, these little, sheltered valleys played a greater part in the history of these mountains than did the rugged peaks and high ridges where the rare plants grow.

All down the length of this open space, and into the larger Briggs Valley, the old apple trees stand as mute reminders of those early days. Often I've sat here in the warm sun beside the old trees and tried to visualize what it must have been like in that faraway time when they were young whips just putting their roots down in this untamed land.

Now the field has gone back to wild grasses and sedge, but once there was a house and probably a barn, and most certainly farm animals. But that was in another time and another world, so different from the one we live in now.

In late afternoon, as I'm heading home, I like to imagine what it was like when people lived quietly in this peaceful valley: cattle slowly coming to the shelter of the barn, dogs barking, children at play, chickens clucking; and a little later, just before dark, the small light in the window of the modest farm house, wood smoke curling up from the chimney as the evening meal is prepared.

How easy it is to visualize these scenes of another era—for a lifetime ago I, too, was a part of just such a homey scene; I, too, came in weary from the field, smelled the pungent wood smoke from the old kitchen range, and gratefully ate supper by the pale light of a kerosene lamp. I'm afraid another world must evolve in another universe before such a time and such a people will be seen again.

January 7, 1980

The Ancient Jeffrey Pine

On the hill across the road above Horse Creek, about a half mile from where the house used to be, one grey, weather-beaten old dead tree towers above the young forest of green firs like an ancient patriarch from ages past.

This giant of a vanished race is so startling amid the lush greenery of the young trees that you notice it at once on rounding the curve in the road. This is no indeterminate dead stub with a broken top and splintered branches, but rather the presence of a tree whose life began in that dim and distant century when the climax growth of these hills was nearing its zenith.

Ever since I first spotted it, I've been curious about the old tree, so today I climbed to its base and measured its circumference: 14 feet 2 inches—almost 5 feet in diameter—without the bark. The slabs of bark lying about identify it as a Jeffrey pine. It's the largest Jeffrey I've ever seen, compared to the smaller, stunted pines of the Ridge and the Jeffreys on serpentine slopes like those of Eight Dollar Mountain. There seems to be no contemporary of the old patriarch in the immediate vicinity. The nearest large pine near the road is only 10 feet in circumference. In fact, the whole hillside has the appearance of a new, vigorous young forest springing up in an area that has had no disturbance of any kind. The young Douglas-firs around the old tree range in circumference from 3 feet 9 inches to 6 feet, while the largest madrone trunk is 2 feet 10 inches.

The hillside has never been logged, but there are faint signs of a fire decades in the past. None of the young trees are scarred by fire, but I did find two old downed logs uphill with fire scars at their base. One, a Jeffrey, was between 7 and 8 feet in circumference and 135 feet long. The other, a fir, was too rotten to check for thickness, but was about 75 feet long.

It appears that the hillside had contained scattered large Jeffrey pine and Douglas-fir, later destroyed by fire. This was probably a climax growth with little hardwood

understory. Now the madrones, California black oak, and some canyon live oak make up the understory, with Ceanothus as scattered brush cover.

Scouting around the old tree a little, I found enough bark, limbs, and small branches to keep us in kindling for years! One piece of bark 6 feet long and 3 feet wide, and surely weighing 50 pounds, was 24 feet away on the uphill side of the old tree. Quite a storm it took to tear that off and fling it so far. Smaller limbs and bark chunks can be found 50 feet away on all sides.

There's no way to determine when the tree died, but the base seems quite rotten, and all but a few slabs of bark around the bottom have fallen off and lie in great piles on the ground. Sixty feet up or so, huge limbs angle downward and look like they might fall at any moment—some are as large as the poles I used to build my studio!

Somehow I had no desire to linger any longer than it took to measure the trunk—I felt much easier admiring the old giant from a respectful distance. When that ancient one is finally brought to earth, great will be the fall thereof, and the sound will resonate all across the length and breadth of this quiet valley.

Estimating the height of the tree did pose a problem, but I worked out a measurement of sorts—very unscientific, and probably very inaccurate.

After I got back to the bus, I walked down into the field and thought at first I might measure the height of the bus, and then, by triangulation, the height of the tree on the hillside—but the tree was much too far uphill for that. So I estimated that the lower part of the trunk I could see above the smaller trees was about four feet in diameter. Holding a small ruler to sight by, the trunk was just $1/16$ of an inch wide. Allowing for the lower part I couldn't see through the trees, the trunk was 3 feet high.

There are 52 sixteenths in that many inches, and 52 feet times 4 feet equals 208 feet. As I say, probably that isn't very accurate—but anyone looking at that old, silvered, dead tree spot-lighted against that hillside of green firs can see that it very nearly measures two hundred feet in height. If I'm here when it falls, I'll try to count the rings, for it would be intriguing beyond measure to know in what century that giant was a seedling.

(This tree fell in 1992—and was so rotten the rings couldn't be counted.)

February 2, 1981

"Some Days are Diamonds"

❀ ❀ ❀

The sun is warm as summer, here by the old apple tree next to Ducky's Pond. In the willows beside the creek, a fox sparrow calls and a gentle breeze ruffles the colored leaves of the red osier dogwoods.

Charlotte (she's eighty-seven this year) and I have come to sketch and walk across the old familiar field, to explore the creek and talk of all the good times, and remember the happy days we've shared together. It's a rare treat for both of us these days to be off exploring like this. So many months have slipped away this year without our seeing each other. But we have to be home by 3:00 p.m., so we don't feel we have the whole day as we usually do. But half a day is better then none! We got up before dawn, and were here making a fire to boil coffee at 8:00 a.m. It's been many a long month since I've gotten out before sun up—not since the days when old Sal and I used to be on top of Lake Mountain or Elijah at sunrise.

When we arrived, the sun was barely touching the far end of the field, and frost covered the grass under the old apple trees. Charlotte was freezing, so we built a fire in the stove in the bus, and while she warmed up I put the coffee pot on the grate outside. When the coffee was ready, we decided to eat lunch—at nine in the morning!

The mist rose in clouds from spots where the warm sun touched the cold earth, and the one pear tree among the apples looked like a torch in the clear, bright, morning light. Now, as we walk back in the afternoon sun, we can see that bright scarlet beacon among the golden apple trees at the far end of the field. Like the song says, "Some days are diamonds, some days are stones." Tomorrow and many days after will be stones—but today is one of those rare diamond days of autumn that neither of us will forget through the dreary days of winter ahead.

October 18, 1981

CREEK BANKS ARE AFLAME WITH THE RED OF DOGWOOD AND GOLD OF WILLOW.
NOW THE CRICKET SINGS LOUD AT NOON, AND THE SUN THROWS SHADOWS AS
LONG AS ON A MIDSUMMER EVENING.

"The Good Grey Rain"*

❀ ❀ ❀

Today the mist obscures the little round hill to the west, and a quiet, drizzling rain slants across the field beside Horse Creek. The old apple trees have lost every leaf, and stand black and naked in a sea of dead grass and sedge. To some, this would be a dreary, miserable December day—and at home, in the lowlands, it would be so for me.

But here, as I walk across the long, rolling field and hear the rush of water among the alders and willows, and see tiny birds flitting about in the bushes, I count it a beautiful day. Not as cheerful as a sunny one, not as exhilarating as a snowy day, nor as inspiring as a golden afternoon in autumn. But there is something of special beauty in winter days; the "good grey rain," the gentle mist that softens far hills; clouds of December that blend the subdued colors of early winter into a calm, restful mosaic of peace.

When we first came to Oregon, even before I'd become accustomed to this "rain forest" type of weather, I loved it. Now after more than thirty years, I still love it. Perhaps more this year than ever, for now, after six years of drought and low rainfall, we are having a normal, wet winter. This country of the Siskiyous is meant to have rain in its season, and nothing is so heartbreaking as seeing the old trees dying on the hillsides, and colonies of rare plants slowly disappearing because they have too little moisture to survive. Heat and dryness, brush fires, long periods of high temperatures in summer they can take in stride, for they have been born and bred to those conditions through millions of years on these rugged serpentine ridges. But when the fierce suns of summer cool to the pale light of December, the

*Ben Hur Lampman's favorite expression for the soft, gentle rains of winter.

waiting reservoirs of life must have their annual renewal of both raging storms and gentle mists from the not-too-distant sea.

There have been droughts before, and there will be again, and we know not how many species have disappeared from their ancestral sites because of them, but for this year, they will flourish and increase, and soon lift the heart with their breathtaking flowers in the wild and secret places of the hills.

December 2, 1981

The Wasp Watcher

It's been many a long year since "the wasp watcher" sat for hours recording the visitors to the flowers in late summer. But today, east of Freeland Mountain, I'm sitting beside a clump of pearly everlasting and rediscovering the old enchantment in seeing the small, winged creatures who come to these late-blooming flowers. Tiny *Ceretina*, the bramble dweller; a black-and-yellow wasp of elegant shape who may be *Eumenes*, the jug maker; little *Passeloecus*, the resin wasp; and a small, dainty *Ammophila* that I've never seen before, with three-and-a-half bright red stripes on the abdomen.

All the years of wasp-watching from Rough and Ready Creek, Shasta Meadows, Mount Elijah, and the dusty trail to Lake Mountain, come back in a rush of memories I thought I'd forgotten. And again I have a desire to draw their portraits and the flowers they love to visit when their summer work is finished. So today is a time to sit quietly and observe, and remember.

Now, beside the creek below "Ducky's Pond," I gather my notes on the bees and wasps of Briggs Valley that I started August fifth, when the star-thistle began to bloom and the buckwheat was nearly finished. And I wish I'd started earlier in the summer, for now my little friends' season of work and nectar-sipping is about over. The little, heat-loving creatures of summer decline and soon disappear when the cool nights of autumn

arrive. And sometimes, even before the first frost whitens the tawny fields, they have gone from their favorite haunts.

But I'm looking forward with a good deal of anticipation to seeing them and recording their comings and goings next summer, when their favorite blossoms invite them back again.

August 17, 1982

All the Friends of Summer

The field lies bright and inviting under a sun as warm as early September, this blue October day. The bumble bees are working the last of the star-thistle, and butterflies flutter about on the still air. But in the thickets beside the creek, the red flames of dogwood and vine maple burn ever more brightly among the still-green willows and alders. Now the cricket sings at noon, when a few short weeks ago he was heard only at twilight. In the still backwaters of the slow-running creek, the first withered alder leaves pile up in long windrows, awaiting the swift currents of the first rain to send them on their way.

But as I sit on the edge of the road and observe busy visitors to the last star thistle flowers, I see a large bumble bee with a heavy load of pollen slowly lumbering from blossom to blossom, and collecting yet more of the yellow powder as she goes. Hasn't she felt the coolness of the nights? Doesn't she note the shorter days and the lowering sun? The cricket singing at noon? Doesn't that tell her there's not time left for another brood before winter? Maybe, like the old wasp Fabre observed digging tunnels when she had no more eggs to lay in them, the bumble bee—from force of a lifelong habit—must collect her pollen and nectar and fill her little honey pots though she has no more broods to tend.

How I love the small creatures of summer, and how my heart aches for them when their happy, busy days are finished. Some frosty night, the tiny spark of life will be extinguished and they will be seen no more. But some bright April day, the contents of the tiny eggs that were tucked away so carefully, the waxy pupa that hung so securely through the storms of winter, the tough chrysalis buried safely underground, will, like Lazarus, arise and come forth, to begin the ancient story of summer over again.

As I walk down the hot road, the locusts rise and sail about as they did in the heat of August. Huge dragonflies from the small pond dart about on flashing wings that make a dry, rustling sound as they pass.

But the sun sets earlier behind the hill every time I come, and now at five o'clock, the shadows are long and only a small part of the field still catches the sunlight. The bees have gone, the butterflies have found a safe perch for the night, and the breeze from that shaded part of the hill springs up cold, and I too must turn toward home and shelter.

October 11, 1982

Last of Summer's Butterflies

Across the sloping field above the road on the south-facing hill of Horse Creek, she flew about as though it were yet summer. A lone sulphur—the last of summer's gay crowd. Even the hardy bumble bees were absent. Only a few half-alive grasshoppers and locusts feebly jumped about, and in the Ceanothus thickets a half-dozen tree crickets still sang their cheerful serenade, no doubt dreaming of warmer days.

The red osier dogwoods have lost their leaves, and only the late willows display their chrome yellows in bright patches along the creek and up the hillsides. How quickly this year the bright leaves of autumn have come and gone, and with them the blue-and-gold days we wish could stay forever.

I'm eating supper under the old alder beside the creek, probably for the last time till next spring. The water is higher beneath the old log now, and some alder leaves are stranded in the eddies and backwaters along the shore, but most have gone on down the creek with the increased rush of water.

This morning at 10:00 a.m., when I arrived, it looked like I'd never sit beside the creek again this season. Every grass blade, seed stalk, and bush down the length of the field was sheathed in glittering crystal in the first rays of the sun. I walked down from the road into a fairyland of exquisite lace and silver etching that no artist could duplicate. So dry and cold was the air that the little crystals fell in showers of fine, glistening powder on my boots as I stepped among the tall grasses. Along the exposed bank above the road, delicate columns of water had been extruded and frozen by the cold until they were several inches high. As the morning sun touched them, they fell apart one by one with little tinkling sounds almost inaudible to any but the sharpest ears. Fascinated, I watched the tiny crystal palaces fall apart and roll down the slope to rest in silvery piles among the dried leaves and seed stalks in the ditch.

Sometimes, on enchanted mornings such as this, it's easy to believe in the fairies and leprechauns who peopled the quiet hills in the simple days of old.

November 2, 1982

Memories of the Little Golden-eyed Duck

❀ ❀ ❀

Once again I rest on the hillside above the road and eat my lunch in the pale sunlight. But today no yellow butterfly sails across the open spaces, no grasshopper jumps about in the dried grass, and only a few juncos fidget in the ceanothus thickets.

And I think back to a day five years ago, and the little golden-eyed duck we brought to the beaver pond and released. And of how happy she was to be free again. That was a day of mist and rain and scudding clouds. But for a brief moment, as the tiny duck swam away, the sun touched the red osier and golden willow leaves and painted a picture I'll never forget.

And I recall how Sal and I came back to see whether the little duck was still there, and we saw her twice, and the third time I couldn't find her and decided to cross the creek to look from the other shore—and fell backward into the icy water, and how Sal was so concerned she stood over me whining and would hardly let me get up!

That was in the dark ages before I acquired the little stove for the bus, so I sat around four hours in wet clothing before finally coming home and calling it a day. I never saw the duck again, and whether she was there that day or not I'll never know. After the commotion we created, I'm sure no wild creature would have come within a half mile of the place!

We had snow a few days later, and I came back the first chance I had, but no sign of the little duck—no pile of feathers along the creek or in the field—so I hope she flew out and had long since joined her friends in some faraway marshlands to the south.

November 5, 1982

Stars in a Fallen Galaxy

❀ ❀ ❀

On this first day of February, a million scintillating stars wink at me from the snow as I trudge up the unmarked white expanse of the road to Chrome.

Today the snow has a textured appearance, like the thick pile of an animal's fur, and under the magnifying glass the surface is made up of linear filaments of tiny, flat crystals, each strand about a quarter-inch long, and all lying in more or less the same direction—no doubt the work of the wind. With the bright morning sun at my back, the tiny crystals catch and reflect the light intermittently. And as I walk, they flash and twinkle like the countless stars of a thousand fallen galaxies. The sun is warm, the sky blue—the kind of day you dream about as you drown in fog and despair in the lowlands.

Could only drive about two miles up the road, then had to park and walk the rest of the way. But much to my disappointment, I couldn't make it to the top. Got within a quarter mile of the cross roads and had to turn back; the snow was two to three feet deep and beginning to soften, so walking over the surface without breaking through was no longer possible.

Ate lunch on a high bank facing that blessed sun—which we haven't seen for days in the lowlands—and enjoyed the silence, the pure unmarked snow, and the distant song of robins hunting madrone berries in the canyon below.

3:00 p.m.—Now I'm eating supper under my little golden willow above the road at Ducky's Pond—and could almost believe I dreamed that magical walk among the fallen stars on Chrome Ridge this morning! For when I got back to the bus several hours later, the crystals had melted in the warm sun and the snow was just ordinary white snow.

A black-and-yellow *Eristalis** fly just stopped for a moment to tell me spring will soon be here, and the pair of rain (tree) frogs answering each other—one in the culvert, the other in the brush on the hill—just announced the same thing.

Today made up for the rather unpleasant visit I had here two days ago. That was one time when I'm sure Ma had a better afternoon at home than I had found here. It had drizzled, fog rolled in, and finally the rain turned to half snow—so I left! I didn't wait to eat, but went on past the two snowy curves below the top of Lone Tree Pass, and pulled into a little road that overlooks the valley below. Started the fire in the stove, had my dinner, and wrote to Charlotte.

February 1, 1983

A Slight Bit of Excitement

❀ ❀ ❀

What a difference a week can make. Today I'm sitting at Freeland Saddle watching the dark thunder clouds over Lake Mountain as they slowly work their way across the valley. Never yet have I been fortunate enough to be on the ridge when a thunder storm came over—but today may be the exception. It's only noon, but the sky is overcast with everything from dark, rainy-looking stratus to big, white-and-lavender cumulus clouds on the horizon.

It's one of those days when I haven't felt like doing much of anything, but I came to finish the backgrounds on some of the butterfly sketches, so will go over to the south end and work on the picture of the painted lady I saw on the top of the ridge between Flat Top and Chrome.

Climbed the ridge, finished the sketch, and explored around a bit, then as nothing seemed to be happening on Chrome I came down to Horse Creek to do more sketching and eat supper under the old alder.

---

*Black-and-white, or yellow, *Eristalis* (Syrphidae) flies. Very beneficial, as their larva feed on aphids and scale insects. Adults feed on nectar only.

But about four o'clock I could hear thunder coming closer over Onion Mountain, and decided this little enclosed valley along the creek, with its head-high dry grass, would be no place to be caught if we have dry lightning. And too, I didn't want to miss the storm, which seemed to be on the other side of the hill. Took the little short-cut road out to the Onion Mountain road, but that was a little scary, as it is very narrow and closed in, and a very bad place to be if a tree came down or a fire started; there is no place to turn around to get back out. Didn't see any lightning, but heard several loud cracks of thunder that seemed too close for comfort—so was quite relieved when at last I came out to the main road at the other end.

Then as I rounded the first curve, I saw a huge old fir all afire like a giant torch! I missed seeing the strike by a minute or two. But what a spectacular sight! About a third of the old tree was dead from the top down. It must have been rotten all the way down the trunk, as it blazed like a chimney, with spurts of fire showing the length of the bole. Fortunately, it couldn't have been in a better place, as the tree was about two hundred feet below the road at the edge of an old logged-off area, with not too much else to burn unless it exploded and showered hot embers over the surrounding brushy hillside. It was in plain sight of the Onion Mountain lookout, so I knew the Forest Service crew would be showing up soon.

About forty-five minutes later, a tanker truck from Galice came along and the crew went to work on the tree, which was still blazing away like a giant blow torch.

I stayed until almost dark, and it was still burning as fiercely as at the beginning. Maybe a lot of crystallized pitch in the heartwood kept the fire so hot. The crew said they'd cut it down later, then douse the remaining embers. It was a large fir, and very green and alive below the dead top, and even up to the time I left, not a green branch ever flared up. Everything seemed to be on the inside, but quite large chunks of blazing bark were beginning to fall off, and I'm really glad I wasn't the one who had to cut that inferno down.

It seemed a strange place for a lightning strike, as there were higher trees on the hillside above the road and in the groves on either side. But it was the largest fir on the uphill side of the logged area, with its dead top standing above all the madrones and oaks around it. Still, it isn't a spot I'd especially think of being susceptible to being hit by lightning. Believe me, if I'm ever up on the ridge when a thunder storm comes in, I'll stay away from those big old Jeffreys with their dead tops standing there like lightning rods just waiting to be hit!

August 22, 1983

Of Snow and "Lowland Candle Flames"

❀ ❀ ❀

The sun shines warm on the north end of Chrome Ridge today, and I sit on the tip-top pinnacle and survey all the snow-capped peaks in every direction. Snow is all around and the old Jeffreys look like they're in a park, with all the brush covered over, and long vistas of white stretching to the far hills. Makes me think of the yellow pine forests on the mesas of the southwest, where you could see for miles through the tawny trunks, with no brush to clutter up the landscape.

Had to park about two miles below the top, but did get around the bad snowy curve that always stops me. At first the snow was about six inches deep, but just before the top it had drifted almost knee-high in spots. When I got to the four corners I just had to climb on to the summit and survey that view while eating lunch.

Years ago I made a full-color picture—a sunset scene—of an old gnarled tree growing out of one of those rocky outcrops, and ever since, that has been the "Sunset Tree." But now it has lost some of its limbs and isn't as picturesque as formerly, but it's still a good subject to sketch in the snow.

3:30 p.m.—At Horse Creek—again I'm amazed at the contrast between these two worlds—the valley and the ridge. In less than ten minutes, one can go from mid-winter to spring and opening flowers and butterflies! Was going to eat my second lunch under the old alder, but the skunk cabbage are blooming, so had to sit among them. True, it smelled to high heaven of old swamp water and skunk, but it was sweet perfume to me, for I love the "lowland candle flames" above all else this time of year.

As I got out of the bus along the road, a mourning cloak butterfly sailed by, just to let me know it was there. And from the willows among the alders a fox sparrow sang his sweet song—and allowed me to see who the singer was. Now I know who that melody belongs to that I hear so often in spring along the creeks and at the river at Hellgate. This was a day to remember indeed.

March 22, 1984

Cemetery Hill

❀ ❀ ❀

Came right to "Ducky's Pond" today, as I wanted to complete several butterfly sketches—and there was logging on the north end of Chrome, so the road may have been closed. Had sort of wanted to go up there to see how far the snow had melted since last week.

Not an especially warm day, with clouds and wind, but when the sun is out it's lovely and warm for a little while. After lunch I climbed the hill to the east of the little round pond; I've never explored that slope at all. As so many of these small, steep hills are, the top is a long hog-back that slopes down sharply on either side, but it's almost level along the ridge.

All across the top a strip of dead, bleached manzanita bushes just lie there. Only a narrow swath, maybe fifty feet wide with green, growing bushes around the edges. Was sort of an eerie sight, like a lot of weathered bones or antlers. None were fire-scarred that I could see, but there were chips and pieces of charred bark on the ground and some larger hunks of charcoal, so it must have been a fire. It must have been fast and hot, and run the length of the ridge, with little damage on either side. Anyhow, it's a strange sight, and I imagine by moonlight it's downright spooky! And I will call it "Cemetery Hill."

Now I'm sitting among the skunk cabbages and the sun is setting in a sea of grey clouds that reminds me of the stormy skies of December. But how bright the "lowland candle flames" burn among the alders and old tawny sedge leaves. There are dozens more than last week, and still more coming up in the dark mud and among old sedge tussocks.

Will have to eat supper soon if I want to do it in comfort, as that dark bank of clouds is rising fast—and so is the wind.

March 30, 1984

Green Mansions

Today is wild on the ridges, with wind and racing clouds from a storm coming in off the coast. Looks really dark and stormy on the south end of Chrome Ridge. It's windy enough down here in Briggs Valley, and this is a lot more sheltered than up there.

Climbed "Cemetery Hill" to see if anything might be in bloom, but only the *Tauschia* has a few pale-yellow umbels open. A gale was really blowing up here too. One old sugar pine, with its needles all gone except on one branch, was singing in the wind so loudly that as I walked across the top of the hogback to the far end, I could hear its music a good quarter mile away. If ever there was an Aeolian harp, that tree was it.

Lots of interesting things are coming up on that hillside, but it will be some time before they bloom.

After lunch, I decided to walk up the little creek that comes down opposite the tiger lilies, where Charlotte and I ate lunch last year. Always thought that little canyon might have something interesting like lady slippers, or maybe even darlingtonia. So while the wind tore through the old trees overhead, I went up the narrow canyon. Wasn't as bad as "Lost Canyon," but I sure had to either crawl under or climb over, and very seldom could walk upright. Saw a lot of interesting leaves, but no orchids or cobras. Some maidenhair fern, and lots of saxifrage, but again, nothing in bloom.

Almost at the top, a large log lies across from bank to bank, and underneath is a little secluded room carpeted with ankle-deep pale green moss. All around it's enclosed by the bright green, new leaves of vine maple. On a sunny day it must be a vision of pale sunlight and various shades of green. All I could think of was "green mansions." What a cool retreat on a hot summer day. I'll have to come back on a sunny day and eat my lunch in "the green room."

May 13, 1984

Butterfly Bend

The rabbit brush is in full bloom—and so are the fritillaries! They were all over the flowers again but not in such numbers as last year. But since there are many more blossoms to open, perhaps they'll become more numerous later. This year there seem to be more hive bees than I've ever seen before. I thought at first they were heading downhill, but some go in other directions, so I bet there is more than one bee tree around here.

Stayed with the bees and butterflies from nine a.m. to three p.m. and discovered two pairs of andrenid bees I don't remember seeing here before. Also an anglewing butterfly at the pool that may have been a zephyr.

It's been warm and humid today. Had a little rain just as I finished lunch, and everyone disappeared. Then the sun came out and they all came back again. Now, under the old alder beside Horse Creek, it's still hot, but the sun is about to set in a cloud bank, and tomorrow is supposed to be rainy.

Chickadee is calling, and so is foxy, the fox sparrow. While it's warm and summer-like, I can look up on the hill and see a clump or two of yellow among the willows that I'm sure wasn't there two days ago. Has it been so long since the fox sparrow sang his nesting song?

September 19, 1984

Mysterious Little *Anthidium placitum*

❀ ❀ ❀

Have come looking for the little yellow-and-black bee of south Chrome— and as usual I'm almost too late. I've lost track of the years that she's fooled me and had her work finished and her nest closed by the time I came looking for her. This year, though, I know who she is.

Last summer (late again, of course) I captured one and sent it in to the Bee Lab at Logan, Utah, and they tell me she is rather scarce, has been seen on the Cordylanthus flowers, and that's about all that is known of her life history.

I think surely her activities are tied in very closely with the Cordylanthus blossoms. Only two other plants bloom on the ridge at this time: the sulphur Eriogonum, and Indian or false caraway. The Eriogonum is almost gone, and the false caraway will linger awhile yet and is the last blossom on these rocky, dry serpentine ridges.

Although the caraway attracts bees, butterflies, and flower flies, I've never seen little *Anthidium* visiting these blossoms. Somehow I've never thought to watch for them on the Eriogonum. This year I did find one, or perhaps two, *Anthidium* collecting pollen from the Cordylanthus, so I'm greatly encouraged, as this is the first time I've ever seen them doing anything but loiter in the sun. Next year I'll start looking for them and the nests at about the time the Eriogonum begin to bloom, and maybe I'll have better luck than I've had these past years.

These two were busily collecting and flying off, but where? It was impossible to follow them over the stony ground—and to confuse the issue, several others were just loitering about—and I'm not sure who was collecting and who was just idling in the sun.

Then to add another distraction, I spotted two large dragonflies patrolling back and forth over the rocky, most barren part of the Ridge. Can you imagine dragonflies in such a setting, in August? Where did they come from: Mud Springs, Flicker Pond, or the little pool along Horse Creek?

They seemed so out of place, I watched them for awhile, and forgot about the bees entirely!

Today the locusts are really clickety-clacking all over the open spaces, the roadway, the rocky outcrops and even among the manzanita brush; can autumn be far behind?

Went down to the old alder for supper, and as the days are still long, I had time to stop at Flicker Pond and watch the birds.

Last week I stopped on my way home and saw two or three pairs of cedar waxwings enjoying themselves and catching insects over the mushy, swampy spot left in the middle of what last spring was the pond. They acted just like flycatchers, and I thought at first that's what they were, until I got a good look at their heads.

But today there's no one in sight; neither waxwings, nor anyone else. The water is almost dried up, except for a few pot holes of brownish, bubbly, stinking water in the low places.

After I'd sat on a log for a while, I did hear a fox sparrow, and a little MacGillivray's warbler sat in a willow and chirped to let me know that not everyone has gone yet. And now, just at sunset, a wood pewee is sitting high up on an old dead branch of an alder and whistling "fe-u fe-eu" in that clear voice that can belong only to a pewee.

Most of the birds are silent now, summer is almost gone, and the brackish water attracts nothing but groups of either gnats or tiny mosquitoes.

August 2, 1985

A Bouquet of Butterflies

❀ ❀ ❀

Here at Flicker Pond, at the edge of Briggs Valley, on this sunny April morning, the little blue butterflies are having a holiday, or a convention of some sort, on an old, half-submerged log at the edge of the water. Two old stubs have been leaning for years and looked like they might fall into the water any moment. Well, last winter one did, and broke into several pieces, revealing the soft, punky heartwood. Whatever is in that wet, spongy stuff, the butterflies are wild about it. They alight, drink awhile, get jostled off, fly up, circle around, land again, shove someone else aside, and drink some more.

There are about two dozen as near as I can count—ever try to count a fluttering, agitated bouquet of blue wings and waving feet? And I'm making a guess they are spring azures (*Celastrina*) (also called echo blues), as they seem to have no tails or orange spots on the underside.

Also saw one of my tiny veined whites, like I have at home and can never identify. Not many birds here yet, but the swallows are back and looking over the only dead stub with holes in it they have left, as the "twin" is gone. Presumably there are other dead trees on the hill with holes in them, as I see quite a few snags among the evergreens; but these two stubs in the water were special favorites of a number of birds, from swallows to woodpeckers, and either wrens or wood pewees.

April 7, 1986

Dance of the Blue Grouse

❀ ❀ ❀

Headed for Mud Springs today, and after I left the fog at the top of Lone Tree Pass, it was a beautiful blue-sky, bright-sun kind of day. It was so bright and clear I decided to go all the way to Flat Top. Although the new ring and valve job on my Volkswagen bus has less than five hundred miles on it, I figured if I was careful and didn't push it too hard it wouldn't hurt the engine. So I rested it often, but it never heated up or appeared to be in distress, and we went right on up. When we reached Mirror Pond, there was a little snow in the road, and farther up that long slope, more snow. But had no difficulty until where the road turns off to Mud Springs, and the main road goes around east of Lobbii Ridge. Right there I stopped, turned, and headed out. The snow was about four or five inches deep, but I didn't want to get stuck and race the new engine getting out.

Walked around the bend heading for Lobbii Ridge to eat my lunch, where I could have a nice view of the north slope of old Chrome.

Along the road near a large pile of old half-burned logs, I found more grouse tracks than I've seen in a lifetime! The snow was literally churned up in an area of about fifty by fifty feet, and leading to it and on all sides were more tracks in the new snow. The grouse must have been dancing—nothing else could account for the twirls, gyrations, pirouettes, rotations, circles and whorls recorded in that soft, white snow.

Some places one walked in a straight line, then hopped, both feet at once, then veered to one side and left an impression of a wing tip in the snow. Another jumped, skipped, and beat the snow, evidently with the "elbow" of the wing, as there were several straight lines very evenly spaced alongside the tracks. There must have been dozens of birds, judging by the disturbance. I estimated a good one hundred-fifty by fifty feet along the road and down the bank was used as the dancing area, or "lek." Do blue grouse have leks the same as prairie chickens? And this time of year, almost the shortest day of the season? In March or April I might understand it. Anyhow, I never saw anything like it before.

Came back to the Mud Springs road, walked in to see the cobra lilies and gather a few to keep for the winter, as I imagine this will be the last time I'll get up there for a while. I hope so—it's been much too dry and warm for so late in the season. Now there should be several feet of snow on Flat Top and Chrome Ridge too.

Went down to Horse Creek for supper, and found it was much colder there than on the higher ridges. I had eaten lunch on Chrome Ridge in comfort without my jacket; but for supper, although the sun was out at the little pond at the end of the field, it was almost too cold to sit out on the hillside. And as the sun headed for the little hill to the west I was glad enough to get in the bus.

December 16, 1986

Magic of Moonlight

❀ ❀ ❀

The moon is full, the hour is late, and snow crunches softly underfoot as I walk that long stretch of road above Horse Creek meadow.

What might be abroad tonight? Coyotes surely; a cougar perhaps? An elusive pine marten? In the deep shadows of the high, wooded hill across the creek a great horned owl calls—silence, then it calls again. Faint little bird twitterings from the thick Ceanothus bushes beside the road. Does the mournful hoot of the owl stir ancestral memories of the silent grey hunter?

The snowflakes have turned to ice crystals that glint like a thousand fallen galaxies. Faint tracks criss-cross the white field, but where are the makers of those tracks tonight?

Unfortunately, the cold, crisp snow has telegraphed my coming to all the listening ears in the vicinity. Vainly I sit quietly under a bush, hoping someone will venture out onto that bright, moonlit meadow. But I have the place to myself—even the owl is silent now.

Has the small adventure been a failure? Not really. As the stars twinkle overhead and the mist rises along the creek bottom, I feel the awe that John Muir spoke of when he was alone in the wilderness. Few of us can travel to faraway places, as Muir did, nor is there any need to. There are many quiet spots here in the Siskiyous where we can retreat from the traffic, noise, and confusion of daily life. Nor is it necessary to freeze your ears sitting under a bush in the moonlight!

Though I never saw anything unusual that night, I will long remember the white and glistening field, the lonely owl, and that big hunter's moon transforming a familiar place into a scene of mystery and beauty.

This experience coaxed other memories from the recesses of my mind. One January morning a few years ago, I arrived at the old apple trees opposite where the house stood, just as the sun broke through the morning mist. Every frost-covered tree and bush along the creek stood etched in purest silver against those dark trees in the background, while wisps of fog rose on the still morning air warmed by the sun.

One December more than twenty years ago, I visited this area on the shortest day of the year. Six inches of snow had fallen the day before, and when we arrived in midmorning, the bright sun sparkled and danced on that long, sloping expanse of white. I had Sally with me, and as we walked the length of the field, there literally was no square yard of snow unmarked by the prints of some animal. Sal was in seventh heaven following the strange scents, while I identified the prints of coyote, martin (or fox), rabbit, meadow mice, skunk, coon, quail, juncos, jays, deer, and elk. This is the domain of the elk, though they are seldom seen. Their immense prints left deep in the snow looked like those of a plow horse, beside the dainty tracks of the deer!

By early afternoon, the sky became overcast with the feel of more snow in the air. Still we couldn't leave that fascinating snowy pasture with its recorded travels of the unseen inhabitants. Sal and I crisscrossed that snowy field half a dozen times, until we finally had to give up and head for the bus, our feet chunks of ice—with noses to match. As we left, I saw the full moon coming up over Onion Mountain. What an adventure it would have been to stay and see who came out to play in the moonlight on that diamond-studded meadow!

February 9, 1989

The Wanderer Returns

❀ ❀ ❀

This mile-long field beside Horse Creek below Onion Mountain has long been a favorite of mine. From the first day Sal and I explored its intriguing grassy meadow until I left for the east side of the Cascade mountains, the hills, creek, and open spaces here have called me back time and again.

Flowers, especially rare ones, are not numerous here. Tiger lilies and lamb's tongue reside on the creek bank, but for the most part this area is uninteresting to a botanist looking for unusual plants.

Again I sit beneath the shade of the old alder at Horse Creek. It's been fifteen years since that November day we put the little ring-necked duck in the beaver pond, and she promptly took a bath, showering silver droplets all over the surface of the water.

Now the beavers and their pond have disappeared. Gone too are the clumps of scarlet mimulus that brightened late summer days with their color. The big old alder that Charlotte and I ate our lunch under for so

THE LITTLE POND IN WINTER

many autumn days is almost dead now, showing only a few leafy branches on one side. Years ago the beavers chewed almost all the bark off its large trunk, leaving only a strip down the side for the life-giving sap to reach the top. For awhile, it looked like the old tree was making a comeback, but seven years of drought and scorching sun have taken their toll. In a year or two I'm afraid the gallant old tree will be no more.

But the snails are back! They appeared as suddenly and as mysteriously as they left ten years ago. These small black fresh water "periwinkles" were in all the creeks when we came to Oregon in the 1940s. Then, so quietly that no one noticed, they were gone. Now as silently, they're back, and seeing them on the rocks in the dappled light beneath the alders, the small world of the creek seems more secure.

Several years ago, the Forest Service installed gates in this area to limit access to protect the elk and other wildlife. This effectively stopped the destruction of the field by four-wheel-drives and the spotlighting of game, and quail hunting out of season.

So for now, Horse Creek's animals, birds, and insects seem to be adequately protected. But that could change, and those of us who love this quiet, undeveloped place will have to be vigilant in keeping it that way.

—1993

5
Bigelow Lakes and Mount Elijah

The Setting

Bigelow Lakes nestle deep in the Siskiyous above Oregon Caves National Monument. At an elevation of 5,900 feet, they are considered "high country" in this area (and remind me of the "high country" of southwest Colorado, my childhood home). And indeed they do have severe winters with much snow, late springs, and a high elevation forest of Shasta red fir and mountain hemlock. Soils are derived from quartz diorite, gabbro, and scattered inclusions of other rock types

The two lakes, divided by a low hill, are actually shallow lily ponds nestled in a glacial cirque. The high rocky wall to the south is Mount Elijah, and from its top on a clear day, I'm told, the Pacific Ocean can be seen on the horizon. Meadow mountain trail starts at the road below the big lake and continues to the top of Elijah, crossing several sloping meadows covered with a wealth of flowers (some of them rare), then through a deep, dark, coniferous forest to the top. Here, in September, if you're lucky you can see golden eagles crossing the Siskiyou ranges on their way south.

A High Mountain Meadow and Memories

This October afternoon I'm sitting beside the little pool where the yellow water lilies bloomed last June. The late sun slants low across the water, and dragonflies soar on silver wings in the still air. Here in the high country where my heart has always been, I find contentment I haven't known for twenty-five years.

Here, high in the Siskiyous, are two bodies of water known as Bigelow Lakes, and a green open space slants down to the upper lake. Meandering through this meadow, a channel of water feeds both lakes—in reality they are large lily ponds—and in June and July, flowers bloom in a profusion unknown in the lowlands.

This is the fifth trip for Sal and me, and now I'm sitting in the golden October sun at the edge of the lower lake. Long shadows of the trees on the far side creep slowly across the quiet water, and the dragonflies glide and sail in October's bright blue weather as though they knew the frosts of winter are only a range of hills away. The grasses of summer have ripened and scattered their seeds to the restless wind, and little brown birds chirp with an urgent note among the willows along the shore.

This morning as we started up the trail, frost was heavy in the shadowy places, and on the high ridge a lonely wind stirred the stunted trees—and I remembered that in these high places the voice of winter is heard in the sighing of the wind and the rustling of the grasses, long before the first snowfall.

There isn't too much color here in this meadow, which is a disappointment, but in the morning sun on the rocky outcrops, a species of huckleberry burns with a crimson flame, almost like glowing embers. Dogwood and vine maple were alight in the canyons lower down, and occasionally a lone bigleaf maple threw a spotlight of brilliant yellow on a rocky crevice far up the hillside. But here at 5,600 feet, the predominant colors are tawny yellow of the grasses and grey-green of willow clumps, with the dark green of alpine firs ringing the water and climbing the hillsides.

Earlier, we climbed to the top of the ridge—6,281 feet—on Meadow Mountain Trail. From there, wave after wave of blue mountains march off to the hazy horizon, and to the southeast stands Mt. Shasta in all its glory! That was an unexpected bonus for the long climb. As we looked, a great golden eagle—the largest I've ever seen—cruised by. There was no doubt it was on its migratory flight. Its wings were rigid as those of a glider, the tips of the primaries turned upward in graceful curves, and straight and true he glided on a long slant across the hazy canyons until lost to view.

And now, here beside the little lake, the day's exploring over, memories of other high places come to mind. The mountain meadows of Colorado; high mesa lands in October; winds of autumn in the piñon pines; gold of aspens deep in a hidden ravine; summer lingering on a sunny ledge of rimrock. But somehow, this time the old familiar memories are less painful, the sense of regret and homesickness less sharp. While these meadows aren't the meadows of home, perhaps they will be sufficient until that distant time when the memories will have become reality.

Now the shadow is almost to the edge of the pool where I sit. Across the open space between the water and the willows, each tawny grass head is outlined in pale golden light, and the dragonfly wings are molten silver. Dark and mysterious as the forest primeval are the firs on the other bank. Off to the right, a fallen log has the weathered sheen of ancient driftwood.

Among the clumps of willow still in sun, the little birds chatter to each other. Overhead, the dry rustle of dragonfly wings mingles with the hum of late bees, and I see a tiny grey frog and a bright green one sitting companionably side by side in the last bit of sun at the water's edge.

It is time to go, and with dragging feet we turn homeward. If the snows of winter come soon, the better part of a year may be history before I return, and through the long winter months I must wait in patience. But come the melting snows of spring and the thousand, thousand blossoms that follow, I, like the bees and dragonflies, will follow my heart to the mountain meadow, and while these may not be the hills of home, I will be content.

October 4, 1973

Farewell to the Meadow

❀ ❀ ❀

There's a bright golden haze on the meadow, but the crimson leaves of October are brighter still beside the willows and on the hills as I bid farewell to the high country. October's sun lies warm upon the tawny grasses and rustling seed heads of departed summer, and yet I linger, unable to leave without a backward look. A cold wind plays through the firs beside the trail, and shadows lengthen, but yet I stay my lagging footsteps.

The brown leaves, all that is left of summer's gaiety, rustle in the passing breeze with a lonely sound while that warm sun caresses the long slope that was so full of life and color a few short weeks ago. I hear the voice of winter as the golden willow leaves scatter before the wind, and yet I linger.

"When all the lovely wayside things their white-
winged seeds are sowing.
And in the still green fields late aftermaths
*are growing."**

Now the last sun is sparkling on the dark waters of the pond far below. All I can see is a glitter between the trees as the wind ruffles the surface. In an instant it is gone. The shadow of that far hill has extinguished the dancing points of light as it creeps ever upward along the length of the meadow.

---

*October's Bright Blue Weather—Helen Hunt Jackson

I would stay until the last ray has vanished, but the homeward road is long and autumn's night descends and the hours of freedom have silently drifted away. Now it is still—even the firs are mute, and the willows stand motionless in the sun, a lone bee drones by and I close my eyes and think of summer.

A murmur starts among the trees on the hill, a cold blast ripples the dry grasses and runs on silent feet across the meadow, and I know I must be on my way.

Years ago I gave my heart to a high mesa with fragrant sage and piñon pines, with purple penstemon, and Mariposa lilies, with sunflowers and fall asters and golden aspens on a dark mountainside. But as I pause at the far edge of this mountain glade, for one last look, I am satisfied. The hills of home are far, far away, but the bright golden haze on this meadow is very close, very real; and I with the flowers, the birds, the butterflies, can wait for the melting of the snows and the coming of spring, and I walk the shadowy homeward trail with a light heart and no regrets.

October 17, 1973

Wind on the Ridge

On the highest ridge of Mountain Meadow Trail, the wind of winter scatters the last of Autumn's yellow leaves. No bird sings, no insect stirs, no flower blooms. When the fitful wind is stilled, there is a sense of expectant waiting. The urgent duties of life have come to an end. Summer's flowers have turned to autumn's seeds, and the winds of the high country have scattered them far across meadow and hill.

Two honking birds sail southward on shining wings, and a ruddy-backed hawk follows swiftly down the invisible flyway between the towering mountain ranges.

October's haze lies blue across the far hills, and the pale sun has no warmth even at mid-day. This may be the final trip to the high country, depending on when the snows come, and as I sit here among the tiny plants on this barren outcrop of granite with a dark green wall of hemlock at my back and the cutting wind on my face, I feel a great reluctance to depart.

Always the high country has been my fondest memory, and now that I have found it again, I could stay here forever; for once gone, who knows whether there will be another opportunity to return?

That cold sun is lower now, and for minutes at a time the wind forgets to blow. Shadows lengthen across the trail and it is time to turn homeward. Back across the brown and sleeping meadow, back through the darkening firs, and home. This has been a day to remember—a day to live again and again throughout the long, foggy winter. A day to savor until that bright golden hour in June when the flowers awaken, and the wind across the ridge is gentle with the breath of spring. A time when the sun will be warm, the air filled with the glinting wings of insects and the song of returning birds. The October haze will be a sweet memory, and all the suns and skies and flowers of June together will spread their magic across the meadows and over the ridges of the high country.

October 18, 1973

Snow on the Meadow

❀ ❀ ❀

The first red leaf of August predicted it, the biting winds of November announced it, and today, "heralded by all the trumpets of the sky,"* the snow drifted down across the meadow, ringing the dark waters of the pond in white, softening the rocky outlines of the ridge, and extinguishing the once flower-bordered trail.

The red-and-yellow leaves of autumn are buried in soft whiteness. Sculptured pods of summer's bounty scatter no more ripening seeds; the tawny grasses of the meadow are gone as though they'd never been. Only the snow-laden firs and hemlocks seem alive, their varying shades of green sparkling against that brilliant white of the new snow. The waters of the pond are deep and black, and below their cold surface in the soft ooze of mud, myriad tiny frogs sleep side by side with the legions of next summer's dragonflies.

Last night, the earliest snow in my twenty-five years of recordkeeping blanketed the valley floor and piled yards deep in the high country. Now, twenty-four hours later, the rain pours down and the snow falls in the mountains and no one knows what it may do. Will it all melt off in a sudden thaw in a few weeks, causing floods and hardships? Or will it continue to be stored on the reservoirs of the hillsides, to produce abundant water for next year's crops?

But no matter what it does here in the lowlands—snow early or late, snow piling up ten, twelve, fifteen feet deep—it's nothing new to the plants, animals, and insects of the high ridges and meadows. Animals hibernate, birds migrate, insects die, and only the eternal trees meet and conquer the

---

* *The Snow Storm*—Emerson

foe; and just how relentless that foe is can be seen in their contorted branches and bent trunks. Year after year, and decade after decade, the weight and pressure of the snow bends and shapes the boles of the hardy trees living at this high elevation. From the first year as tiny seedlings, the trees feel the weight of that merciless snow. As they grow in height, each increasingly bears the signs of its struggle, until in middle age and maturity the great thick, hoary trunks are bent into beautiful, graceful curves below their first whorl of branches. It seems as though—with one accord—in years past they all leaned in one direction either away from or toward something. But in reality, it is the soft, unyielding snow that—quietly falling, flake by flake, month after month, year after year—exerts that tremendous pressure on the uphill side of each and every tree that survives and grows in this high mountain country.

Next spring, Sally and I will go back and walk the familiar trail, and many a casualty of winter will be seen. Huge trunks split like kindling, young trees in the vigor of their youth uprooted and dead, branches stripped the length of one side, tops broken out—but always there will be the survivors, feeling the surge of renewed life with their blossoming "candles" bright and green against the darker branches of earlier years. And this endless shaping and pruning and searching out of the weaker ones will produce a more breathtakingly beautiful and hardy growth of forest than ever the milder, kinder climate of the lowlands can create.

November 5, 1973

"Oh Suns and Skies and Clouds of June"*

(Sequel to "Farewell to the Meadow")

June has come to the meadow, and we have come also. Gone are the memories of October's skies and November's wind and winter's snow and cold. The breeze is the breath of April, soft and sweet—as I knew it would be. The sun is the sun of early spring and the blossoms are the vagrant flowers of May—as I knew they would be.

When last I saw the willows, the chill wind of winter had scattered their golden leaves among the tawny grasses. But now the frogs in the pond far below are singing their vernal melody, the vibrant green leaves of summer cover the length of the meadow, and white marsh marigold and yellow buttercups spangle the living carpet of green like fallen stars.

A cold wind blows off the snow banks on the ridge, but it is the wind of summer to come. It bends no dying grasses, nor scatters the red leaves of autumn, but rather speaks of asphodel, of daisies, of gentians and asters and all the life and color that will belong to this high meadow in the months ahead.

---

*Helen Hunt Jackson

Short and poignant though the seasons are, here in these high places, before the winds of winter turn the leaves to scarlet and gold, a parade of birds and flowers and insects will file past, each in its appointed time, and each with its small part to play in the pageant.

Today the frogs sing and the buttercups unfold, and winter's snows still lie thick and glistening on all the slopes and even to the middle of the upper lake.

On the trail, snow lies six to eight feet deep in the shadow of the firs. The north slope of the ridge has drifts so deep that even the trees are buried yet. But here at the edge of the meadow, where last October I heard the voice of winter in the wind off the ridge, the sun is warm, the birds are singing and the little willows are sending out grey-green leaves and furry catkins. Acres of giant hellebore are coming up in patches in the open spaces. Hardly a foot tall now, in a few weeks they'll be five or more feet in height and one could easily become lost among their rustling leaves and giant stalks.

Water is rushing off the meadow from melting snow above, in numerous streams and rivulets—and the sound of their many voices almost drowns the song of the birds.

Butterflies by the dozens flit about and frolic in the misty air over the cold snow banks. Queen bumble bees are exploring every hole and crevice for nesting sites, and even a few honey bees are working the blossoms of wild plum at the upper edge of the long slope.

June has come to the meadow, and her breath is sweeter, perhaps, for the eight months of waiting and dreaming of this day.

Now, for the first time in many years I can say, "Oh suns and skies and clouds of June, and all the flowers of June together, you can and do, rival October's bright blue weather!"

June 17, 1974

July and a Melting Snow Bank

Although it's July, June lies gently across the meadow, and her breath is soft and scented and cool—as I knew it would be. No searing July heat yet penetrates to these high places, even as summer wilts the fields and dries the streams of the lowlands.

Snow still speckles the hills surrounding the ponds, and five feet or more lies across the trail in the upper reaches. Strange birds I've never heard before nest in the willows and among the alpine firs beside the trail. Buttercups and bluebells bloom in the meadow, and the sun is the sun of April. Spring is tardy here in these high meadows, but when she does come, she lingers long and lovingly.

Sally and I have come alone again and feel free to go where we will and stay as long as we wish.

It's a beautiful day of sun and warm breezes. The meadow is bright and gay with the first blossoms of the season. Birds sing from every direction and no thought of storm or dreary skies can mar this perfect day. We stopped beside a snow bank on the other side of the willow thicket, on the lower part of the trail, and the yellow fawn lilies (glacier lilies) bloom beneath the shelf of overhanging snow. That brilliant morning sun made the snow translucent; by lying down and looking into this miniature snow cave, I see an elfin world of living green leaves and vivid yellow flowers. As I watch, entranced, a drop of melted snow, radiant as a cut diamond in that morning light, falls from the glittering roof onto the thick, brown leaf mold and moss on the floor of this fairy cavern. One by one, the released drops of water run along the melting rim and drop without a sound into the rich earth below.

How much we overlook, by standing upright most of our lives. So much of earth's exquisite beauty can be discovered only by lying prone among her tiny plants and close to her living soil.

Spent most of the day at the upper edge of the meadow taking a census of bees visiting the bitter cherry bushes. There, in the full glare of the sun, it is hot, but always a cool breeze off the snow relieves the sun's heat.

Struggled to the top where the old tree stands guard and ate lunch, for this is my favorite spot to take a rest and have refreshment. The snow banks still are hard to climb over, but are melting slowly, even in the deep shade. Just below the tree, I found more glacier lilies blooming. Some thrust their buds right out of the snow, as though they are too impatient to wait for it to melt. Only inches away from the actual mass of snow, the lilies are in full bloom and a busy black bee gathers the pale yellow pollen into her pollen baskets. The sunlight filters through the Shasta red firs and picks out the yellow flowers, making the snow sparkle; the sound of bumble bees working in a blossoming wild gooseberry bush make this spring morning so perfect I could stay among the golden blossoms the whole day. But most of the bees are lower down among the bitter cherry blossoms, so the yellow lilies and melting snow were left to the hardy black bee collecting her pollen.

Earlier, at the cleared space just inside the gate on top, I saw literally hundreds of small black bees aimlessly flying about. Not a one seemed interested in digging, exploring the flowers, or even looking for nesting sites. These are the ones I saw the first time we were here on June 17. But only a few were flitting about then, and often resting on the ground. I'm sure they had just emerged and were males. They actually had just emerged from the very edge of the receding snow, as I saw their emergence holes only a few feet from the melting bank.

But today, these are a little larger, and are so numerous I'm sure they're the females getting ready to begin work. Probably, if the weather stays like this, they will be getting down to business next week when I come.

Stayed late at the edge of the meadow listening to the bees working the cherry blossoms. But finally, when the sun was low over the upper lake, we packed up and headed down the trail. Found a trail crew working on the lower part, and they've made a little camp just at the edge of the willows where the water comes rushing down from the meadow. How I envy them! How I'd love to stay here and listen to the sounds of the night and see the moonlight on the meadow—for there is a moon tonight. And no doubt they envy me—my freedom to come and go about my work as I please with no clock to watch and no boss to please.

But I have no complaints. It's been a perfect day, and as I start home I see the little elderberry trees in bloom, so I take a few blossoms to make elderberry pancakes tomorrow, which will start my day with pleasant memories of my well-loved meadow.

July 2, 1974

Journey into April

❀ ❀ ❀

The soft breath of April blows warm across the ridge as I sit here among the penstemons on the highest point of Meadow Mountain Trail. Last October, the stunted bushes shivered and dry seed pods rattled in that chill wind from across the blue ranges of mountains to the south. But today was a journey into April as we walked across the top of the trail and down into the meadow above the upper lake.

Anemones and larkspur were blooming in the shadow of fallen logs and across little open glades as we started up the west end of the trail. Higher up, manzanita and service berry were beginning, and surprisingly, at the very top, among the tumbled boulders on the wind-swept ridge of Mount Elijah, a legion of white Washington lilies (*Lilium washingtonianum*) were just opening their first buds.

Another surprise: the manzanita berries along the top of the ridge were at the same stage of ripeness as those I found at Chrome Ridge two days ago. So were the penstemon blooms. The two places must have very much the same growing conditions, as both face south and are well drained, although the soil is very different, and there is a 2,500-foot difference in altitude.

Snow lies across parts of the trail yet, and below the dead tree near the gate the drifts still are three to four feet thick. Drifts linger along the south rim of the upper lake, and all through the trees up that hillside I catch glimmers of white patches in the open spaces where the sun strikes them for a moment.

And still, the fascinating pageant of the advancing glacier lilies continues. Although the banks of snow have receded greatly since I was here two weeks ago, the lilies still come up through the edge of the melting drifts, opening wide a few inches from the vanishing snow, and setting seed less than six feet farther down the hill. And I wonder how much longer the bulbs still buried in the deepest part of the drift can wait for their day in the sun. At the edge they come up through three or four inches of snow, but those in the middle will have to wait two or three weeks yet. Is there no end to their patience?

The black bees that were so plentiful in the open space beyond the gate have disappeared, and I suspect they've dispersed to the hundreds of penstemon, owl clover, phlox, and other flowers blooming along the bluff above the lake. And several black bees are working the glacier lilies for nectar and pollen. The longest-blooming plants of all are the bitter cherries along the edge of the meadow. They opened their tiny white blossoms when I came to the upper edge of the meadow on June 17, and now they still bloom, although the upper bushes are setting myriad tiny berries or fruit. If they were wild plums, I'd come back and gather some for jam—how good that would taste through the long, dreary winter, and what memories it would evoke!

July 15, 1974

Blue Penstemons and Mount Elijah

❀ ❀ ❀

Here on Meadow Mountain Trail I've seen more blue and lavender penstemons than I've ever seen anywhere before.

They're blooming down by both lakes, in among the rocks and up the hillside. They bloom on the trail near the old dead tree. They bloom in Shasta Meadows, and clear across the top of the ridge. The highest point of the trail on the ridge is Mount Elijah—how it ever came by that name I haven't yet discovered.*

And always when I see penstemons I wonder if that rare masarid wasp lives and works among them. For she collects pollen off the penstemon and phacelia, and no other flower. Down at Rough and Ready Creek I found her busily working on the penstemon, and even found two mud cells she had built on rocks. Up on Chrome Ridge I found a whole series of her mud cells, and there, too, the penstemon bloom. Here the flowers grow in a profusion I never thought possible—and I wonder if the wasp has found them and adapted her specialized lifestyle to this high, cold climate with its eight months of snow and ice.

And as I sit watching the bees at the foot of the old tree on the top of the trail, who should come to rest on a piece of bark but a masarid! This wasp is much smaller and flightier than the ones I watched working the flowers at Rough and Ready. It seems to fly aimlessly about, and once or twice briefly visits a clump of phacelia just coming into bloom. So from its actions and size, I judge it to be a male masarid; it has the characteristic quick flight and high-pitched buzz.

I waited in vain for a female, but none appeared. But at Shasta Meadows, past the gate, I had the camera focused on a clump of pussy paws and I heard a masarid, and caught a glimpse of a female flying about among penstemons farther up the hillside.

*Editors' note: Elijah Davidson, an early resident of the area, discovered Oregon Caves.

They're here—so all I have to do is find their nests and just which plants they come to, and I'll have pictures and notes on them as well as their sisters who live thousands of feet lower and in a far kinder climate.

Back at the upper lake, a small bank of snow lies dripping and melting silently into the rich black leaf mold of the forest floor. Three feet from the melting snow, a tiny violet unfurls its heart-shaped leaves, and a few feet beyond that they are blooming. These seem to be the same species of tiny plant with white flowers, with blue or purple lines in the heart, that I found on Chrome Ridge two months ago.

This is one of the first hot days I've seen here. Coming across the meadow at noon it felt like the temperature might be in the 80s, but as soon as I step into the shadow of the firs, or linger near a snow bank, I reach for my jacket.

It seems the flowers in the meadow will be much later this year, and without the profusion of bloom we saw last year. But last year the bitter cherry bushes had not one fruit among the whole thicket, and this year they're going to be loaded with clusters of cherries. And so will the manzanita bushes be covered with berries. Even though the flower seeds in the meadow will be scarce, the bushes and trees will produce an abundance.

The chipmunks, who seem to be the most populous inhabitants here, will have more than enough to store away for the long winter. I notice that even the Shasta red firs have a good crop of their strange-looking cones.

But for the moment, summer dwells in the meadow, and thoughts of winter lie in the distant future.

July 24, 1974

Summer Comes to the Meadow

❀ ❀ ❀

Here at the big dead tree on the trail, the morning sun barely touches its topmost branches and we are eating our lunch, at nine a.m.!

Have come alone, Sally and I, and really started early. We were up at 3:30 a.m., and started in the dark. Parked at the west end of the trail to look at the gooseberry bushes and it was only 6:50 a.m., and in many places the sun still was behind the hill. Even the top of the meadow was in shadow when we made the climb and arrived there to eat.

Early as it is, the bees and insects are out and a pleasant, subdued buzzing can be heard from every direction. The spot where the last snow melted along the trail still is damp and green, but the last bluebells are fading and the glacier lilies are fast going to seed.

12:25 p.m.—Just below the summit of Elijah—the highest point on the trail—the blue penstemon still bloom and the masarid wasp works as fast as she can. I'd know her song anywhere, for she has a peculiar sound as she flies in and hovers a second over the flowers. She's faster and her buzz is higher pitched than any other bee or wasp I know of. And once you hear and recognize her you won't forget her, and you won't be mistaken no matter how many other insects are flying and buzzing among the flowers.

Now, in the full heat of the summer sun, it truly is summer, with the clacking of locusts, buzzing of the bees, and soaring and sailing of the parnassian butterflies. Most of the flowers have gone to seed, and only the penstemons, yellow buckwheat, and a few Indian paintbrush color the

LOWER BIGELOW LAKE - EAST SHORE

barren rocks. Here on the ridge, spring steps lightly and melts the snow long before she wanders down to the meadow and across the ponds. But also she cedes her place to summer here, weeks before the heat and dryness touch the meadow and lower trails. Summer haze lies over the hills, but a cool breeze blows off Shasta Meadows and some of the peaks still have snow in the rocky hollows of their north sides: sober reminders that cold and snow have abdicated for only a few brief months. No matter how hot the sun or dusty the trail, soon the dark clouds will gather and summer will be but a sweet memory.

August 10, 1974

Journey into Winter (Prologue)

❀ ❀ ❀

Warm and caressing, a pale sun lies gentle on the meadow this October morning. The first snow of the season has fallen, and as I look out across this, my beloved meadow, its expanse of sparkling whiteness displays a beauty almost beyond description. Not since days in the high mesa country, among the hills of home, have I seen snow such as this.

Dry and scintillating like diamond dust, it has drifted in little riffles and eddies over rocks and uneven places. It is only about six inches deep, and the seed heads of last summer's grasses and flowers make artistic patterns wherever they touch the fluffy whiteness. The brilliant red wild cherries, still on their bushes, glow like embers against the snow-laden Shasta red firs. Along the edge of the cherry thicket, the buckwheat has scattered its bright yellow petals across the virgin snow—the last poignant farewell of departed summer.

Summer has gone, and I've watched her go—and as I stand here bewitched by this unexpected winter scene, I'm not as sad at her passing as I might have been. For winter in the high country is far different from that in the lowlands. Here there is no fog or dampness or drizzle. Here the snow is as white and dry as thistledown. True, winter's wind cuts with a razor's edge, but the winter sun glows with a brilliance no lowland ever knew. If I love the gaiety of summer's happy hours, I know now I also love the silence and rare beauty of winter's inevitable snows.

7:30 a.m.—Here at the end of the road at the west end of the trail, everything is covered with three to seven inches of new, powdery snow, and the wind blows cold off old Elijah. Have just arrived—and almost didn't make it to the end of the road. Fortunately, a four-wheel drive has been here ahead of me and I followed in its tracks. Snow showed up on the road at the junction with the Buck Peak road, and the farther I came the more snow there was—and no place to turn around! I knew the four-wheel drive had to turn at the west end, so I followed and turned in its tracks.

8:00 a.m.—Have walked out to the lower lake, and at first sight it appears to be frozen over, but actually is covered with a mushy and opaque film of wet snow; but from a certain angle the pads of the water lilies can be seen beneath the surface. The snow is six to eight inches deep in this little meadow and has been drifting and blowing, as some of the trees have a white coating on the trunks facing the open space.

All around the edge of the water, the small mountain hemlocks have turned into white tepees, their branches drooping almost to the ground under the weight of snow. No wonder the ground is littered with broken branches and twigs when spring comes.

Now the sun is just touching the tops of the trees on the far side of the pond. It looks like it may be a good day, though that blue October sky is half overcast with white clouds running before the wind.

9:00 a.m.—At the big tree near my favorite spot at the edge of the meadow, we have stopped to rest. Sally is wild—the chipmunks are everywhere, scolding and scampering in the cherry thicket, in the sheltered spots on the trail and even out in the vast white expanse of the meadow. Upon tracking them I see they have been foraging among the seed heads still above the surface of the snow. Asters and the yellow Helenium daisies still seem to yield belated seeds, and the little squirrels gather them while yet the sun is warm and the wind still. They live mostly among the rocks and beneath the conical shelters of the snow-covered trees. The smaller trees, especially, make perfect shelters for the chipmunks, as their branches touch the ground and there is a very cozy, insulated dry space all around inside, under the branches.

Now the sun has just touched the meadow and the snow sparkles with a thousand, thousand diamonds across the wide expanse. A jay calls from the Shasta red firs, and I hear a red-breasted nuthatch above, on the trail.

The snow came night before last, and yesterday it must have melted a little, for every seed head and stem is decorated with tiny icicles, like the glittering tassels on a crystal chandelier.

11:00 a.m.—Have climbed to the top of Elijah to eat lunch. The wind is quiet, just a murmur among the hemlocks. The view back across the meadow is like a Christmas card. Here at the top, the snow really has drifted and piled against the bushes and rocks.

It looks like the sands of the seashore, all hummocks and dunes and wind-sculptured. Waves and ridges and tidal lines ebb and flow around the higher bushes and rock piles. In some spots I sink up to my knees, and in others the lowest rocks are exposed—such are the vagaries of the winter wind.

Chipmunks are foraging here too—their tiny tracks give them away, and they call attention to themselves by chirruping at us as we pass on the trail. Now they are the only signs of life here, where only a few short weeks ago I sat and listened to the loud clatter of the locusts as they flew over the rocks. Here, where parnassian butterflies and bumble bees flew their aimless routes in the bright, warm sun of October.

I always remember these high lands with summer sun warm across the ridges and in the hollow of the green meadow, but truly, glistening snow and crystal icicles, hoarfrost and biting wind are more a way of life than the sun and flowers of summer. Eight months out of the twelve, snow and ice dwell here—then how could I have imagined that sweet summer lingered so long? Sixteen short weeks the flowers bloomed and the insects came to them, and the birds returned and built their nests, and the dark waters of the pond warmed beneath the glow of the golden water lilies, the frogs sang their vernal song, and dragonflies sailed on silver wings. And I lay in the sweet grass of the meadow and thought summer would stay forever!

12:30 p.m.—This is to be a day of surprises and contrasts. I've been busy sketching—and suddenly my warm, bright sun has gone. I look up to the west and a great bank of grey cloud is covering the sky. The mountain ridges have turned a deep cobalt blue and the wind is picking up, blowing by fits and starts through the hemlocks. Hurriedly I pack and start down the long trail—this is no place to be caught in a stinging, swirling blizzard.

Here above the upper lake I can see the water is a dead grey, reflecting the winter sky. The meadow is white with tracings of brown and grey where the tops of the leafless willows and alders remain uncovered.

All year, in imagination, I pictured what the meadow and lake must look like when the snows of winter cover all the familiar landmarks, when the grey sky and somber firs meet on the desolate horizon. And now I've seen the coldness and loneliness of it—but still I linger. Glad enough I'll be to seek the milder climate of the lowlands when the snow comes—but for now I am fascinated by the drama of coming winter. Beside me, the seed pods of the lovely blue penstemon lie on the snow, their seeds long since dispersed by the winds of autumn. How many bees and butterflies came to the sweetness of the phlox, the daisies, the golden buckwheat? Now all the happy life of fair summer is gone, and only I remain to mourn its passing.

The clouds are lowering, the wind is picking up, and I must be on my way. The lake is cold and grey and lifeless; the meadow sleeps beneath the first snow of the season; the chipmunks have departed to their snug retreats;

and this is to be my last farewell to the meadow, the trail, the ridge, until the soft wind of spring calls forth the glacier lily, the bluebell, the buttercups, and their retinue of singing frogs, fluttering butterflies, and foraging bees.

And next spring, the bluebells will be bluer, the lilies fairer, the buttercups brighter because today I felt the chill of winter and looked upon the grey hills in their silence and desolation.

2:00 p.m.—Couldn't resist coming to the edge of the upper lake. While I have been sitting on the huge rock outcrop beside the water, the air has turned warmer, the sky is more of a leaden grey, and snow is melting and dropping off the trees.

Coming across the meadow I found two Indian paintbrush blooming, their heads barely above the snow. They looked so forlorn, like the last rose of summer pining alone on the stem; I picked them to take home so in their declining days they can be seen and appreciated.

Sal has just run off barking at a jet, and the echoes from the ridge and across the lake sound like a dozen dogs on the run.

Down by the bus, as we prepare to leave, little flakes of snow drift down—forerunners of events to come. No color lightens the day. I see a last bunch of blue elderberries drooping low among the brown and withered leaves. The valley below is cloaked in mist. The once-sunlit trees stand tall and dark and unfriendly. And so we leave them to the silence, the coming storm, and the night. The circle of the year will be two-thirds complete before we come again. And so perhaps it is with most things—a bright season of happiness, then the long dark winter of drudgery and care.

October 30, 1974

Of Snow and the Sun of July

❀ ❀ ❀

On this second week of July the sun beats down and the wind is mild here at the meadow. Just one month ago to the day and date, we were here, and snow lay white and cool over everything. Now it has retreated to the shadow of the trees and the pond is dark and cold-looking, with the edge of the receding snow still hovering on its southern rim.

Sally and I have come to the little hidden pond off the trail below the dead tree. Will make this our "headquarters" and leave the lunch and knapsack here, while we go farther up and make flower sketches. This is my favorite little hideaway, as it's hidden from the trail and we probably won't be disturbed here while we work. We love to eat lunch here, as there is water for Sal, and the view out across the Illinois Valley and to the high peaks of the Kalmiopsis Wilderness and Chrome Ridge is inspiring, no matter what the weather.

After making a sketch or two of glacier lilies and Claytonia, we went up to Elijah. No snow across the trail, but a huge drifted rampart lies along and below the north wall.

Found few flowers blooming, and doubt there will be as many as last year. The weather has turned hot, and even a few feet from the last snow banks, on this south exposure, the ground is drying. I think most of the plants won't be able to bloom before drying up in the summer heat.

The snow still lies in patches at the first gate, but all of Shasta Meadows is clear. One large drift still blocks the trail at the old log where the bluebells and glacier lilies bloom. Their blooms are as numerous as last year, but this is a sheltered spot and only in August is the heat of the summer sun felt through the deep leaf mold beneath the trees. Bumble bees work the lovely red blossoms of the Marshall's, or Applegate's gooseberry, and their loud buzzing can be heard in the bushes, even though the snow still is all about.

As I sit on a log writing this, the frogs in our little hidden pond tune up for their evening serenade. The afternoon sun strikes full on this little shelf and warms the water in the shallow pond, even while the snow banks are all around the edges and still mostly covering the dwarf alders and willows. Just a short way back toward the trail, the melting snow has made numerous little rivulets of rushing water, and there the big white marsh marigolds and the smaller yellow buttercups bloom. The water has made snow tunnels and caves, and kneeling in the icy water I'm again fascinated with that small translucent world abloom in those fairy caverns.

July 10, 1975

The Little Hidden Pond

❀ ❀ ❀

While the sun beats down and a hot wind blows across my dead, dry fields and the mud dauber sings her song of house building, I dream of a cool snow bank and a green, green meadow sprinkled with buttercups and bluebells.

It's been four days now since the last trip to the meadow and the snow at Bigelow Lakes. Took Lillian, a neighbor, this time and was so busy making flower pictures and hunting wasps on the trail I didn't write up my notes as usual.

Left all the food and extra equipment at the small hidden pond below the old dead tree. The snow bank still is there, but diminished to a patch of about ten by fifteen feet among the trees, beyond the old log I usually sit on to eat lunch and sketch. We buried our fruit and drinks in the snow while we went up to Elijah to hunt the wasps. Was hot and uncomfortable on the top along that open trail, but down by the meadow one felt almost chilly without a light jacket.

Some flowers still bloom on Elijah, and penstemon are just coming out, but will be quite scarce this year. Found very few wasps. Either they haven't all emerged yet, or they too, will be scarce. Bluebells and glacier lilies bloom all along the upper trail where the snow still remains. Marshall's gooseberry is in full bloom and, as before, the bumble bees are making the beautiful,

THE HIDDEN POND   AUGUST 30, 1976

fuschia-like blossoms their special project. The pussy paws are in bloom up
at the cleared spot beyond the gate, but they too seem not as numerous as
previously.

Down in the little meadow, as the sun turns and lights up the tiny hidden
pond, the frogs begin their tuning up. At the upper edge of the pond where
the alders are so thick, a number of flowers bloom under the protection of
the bushes. The afternoon sun strikes there and illuminates the small green
world among the tangled roots and branches. One of the flowers I hadn't
seen anywhere else is a soft-stemmed, lovely white blossom—with five petals
and tender, light-green stemless leaves growing exactly opposite each other
on the stem. This may be some type of Claytonia, but it's much taller than
any I've seen before. The lovely bluebells keep the white flowers company in
the hidden world beneath the dwarf alders, and I'm sure many other flowers
will open there as the sun warms the sodden earth.

On the opposite side of the pond, where you can see the Illinois Valley
and the Kalmiopsis Wilderness beyond, the almost level shelf is covered with
small shooting stars I believe are *Dodecatheon alpinum*. From the south
edge of the pond, the green bank has a pink tint in the sun. But most
fascinating of all, I discovered a number of strange flying insects dancing
and sailing over the little patches of open water. They never got higher than
a few inches from the surface, so to observe them properly I lay down in the
boggy grass. They are so strange in appearance that for some time I had no
idea what family they might belong to. But finally they became used to me
and flew about within range, and I think, from their shape and flying habits,
they must be some type of crane fly.

Their most striking feature, whether standing still or in motion, is the
extremely long legs marked in an unbelievable pattern of black and white
stripes! In fact, these striped legs are all you do see at first, especially as they

seem to prefer flying in a cluster that usually ends up in a tangle in the grass. But if you can ignore the black-and-white appendages and look at the bodies and wings, it suddenly dawns on you that these are just crane flies, dressed up in fancy costumes that most of their relatives wouldn't be caught dead in!

On the way back, we drove over to the other end of the trail and found the scarlet gilia in bud in all the open spaces, where the trail to Oregon Caves meets Meadow Mountain trail. A black spider wasp had filled up her tunnel in the loose soil where I saw so many wasps digging last year.

Stopped at the little lake, and no robin sang this time, but the frogs made a din, and the water lily leaves had unfurled and spread on the surface of the water. Bog orchid and mountain knotweed (American bistort) are blooming, along with myriad white marsh marigolds and yellow buttercups. Only one tiny patch of snow remains beneath the trees just before you come to the lake's edge.

Long after six p.m., we finally left. Even then the sun was high, and I would have loved to stay, as there is a full moon tonight. All too soon, the days will be short and the homeward journey will have to be started no later than 4:30 p.m. if we are to arrive home before dark.

July 23, 1975

The Impossible!

We have achieved the impossible—for here Sally and I sit halfway up the meadow while the fog lies like a white blanket in the valleys below. Rarely are the roads to this high country passable in December.

The sun and wind could be the sun and wind of April. The sky could be the sky of spring. Earlier it was a brilliant blue, but is now over-spread with the first white streamers of a coming storm. Everywhere the snow is melting and little noisy freshets splash and cascade down across the meadow to the lake.

A warm day with the illusion of spring, but without the life and song of spring. No bird flutters in the bushes, no frogs break the silence of the dark pond, no insect flies in the pale sunshine with glinting wings. Only a lone jay calls from the dark evergreens on the hill, and overhead a crow sends its raucous, mocking cry across the empty landscape.

All the leaves of summer have fallen and the grass is sodden and dead beneath the dissipating snow. As I sit here looking down to the dark waters of the lake, the air is warmer than it has been on many a day in June. But beyond those tree-covered hills, behind that rocky escarpment of Mount Elijah, the clouds of winter are building, and the frigid winds are only a range of hills away.

December 9, 1975

Fog in the Meadow

❀ ❀ ❀

On this eighth day of July, fog lies across the meadow and blots out the lake from our vantage point on the upper trail. All morning, since 7:45 a.m., it has been drizzling, as Beth (a neighbor), Sally, and I walked from the west end of the trail, up over Elijah and down into the upper part of the big meadow. And not once has the sun come out, nor the wind stopped blowing from the snow peaks to the south.

We decided to eat lunch under the old dead tree at the top of the trail, thinking the wind would be less there, but it came over the top of Elijah and swirled the fog and mist down across the lake and through the trees like a dreary day in November.

Buttercups, violets, bog orchids, and the lovely pink Indian paintbrush bloom in the lush growth of the wet places, but very few things are out on the rocky slopes. The exquisite little alpine shooting stars are sprinkled like a pink carpet among the grass bordering the little hidden pond, but a snow bank still lies among the trees at its edge. Down along the road, the penstemon are at their best, in their three or four variations of color from pink to lavender and blue. Higher up they are only budded, without showing any color at all.

In Shasta Meadows, pussy paws cover the barren soil, and I'm sure the little Cerceris will be hunting her weevils the first warm, sunny day. At the edge of the meadow, bitter cherry is just beginning to bloom, and as we came down in the afternoon a few bees explored the tiny flowers.

At the lower lake, the white buckwheat (American bistort) blooms along with the white and yellow buttercups and the lovely bluebells. The frogs sing, and two yellow water lilies are about to open their bright golden bowls to the sun. So spring is well on its way here in the high country, and after a day or two of warm sun, all our friends of summer will be on the wing. Heard many small birds in the bushes and saw some evidently just out of the nest, so the cold and drizzle hasn't dampened their enthusiasm. And unlike the persistent fog in the valleys, it hasn't really dampened our spirits either. If you love these wild places, you love them in any kind of weather under any condition. Just to be here is happiness enough: sun, clouds, rain, or snow.

July 8, 1976

The Black-and-White Crane Flies

❁ ❁ ❁

Today, Sally, Lillian, and I are back in the meadow. The sun is bright, the sky blue, and the heat in the valley beyond endurance. But here it is warm in the sun, cool in the shade, and altogether pleasant and beautiful.

Went up to Oregon Caves and had hot chocolate and a roll, bought a gift in the gift shop, then came on up, so we started up the trail rather late this time. I think it was after nine. Took the camera and all the equipment, expecting to find the wasps busy. But we didn't see any! In Shasta Meadows* all is quiet, with very few tunnel entrances showing. It rained heavily here a few days ago and that may have discouraged them—perhaps even put an end to their nesting for this season.

The pussy paws are in full bloom, and last year the little Cerceris* was out and active at the same time, but now they seem never to have been here at all. I believe we are just a bit late; the flowers are a little beyond their prime blooming period. Did see a few wasps loitering about in the sun. So again I've missed the little weevil hunter. And I so wanted to get pictures of her bringing in prey, and take notes on her methods of digging and closing the burrow.

Even the wasp colony just inside the first gate seems to have disappeared—or maybe never appeared. It may be too early for them, as the flowers there haven't started out, except for the ever-present pussypaws. They cover every bare spot with their little rosettes of dark green leaves and fuzzy blossoms.

The most interesting spot once again is the little hidden pond off the trail above the meadow. Here those strange black-and-white crane flies** dance and float over the surface of the water and entangle themselves in the grasses at the pond's edge. Caught two—one large, one small—so may have a pair. And will get them identified if I can. One thing I'm sure of: they are crane flies, but much more graceful and interesting than their common cousins.

Such an airy way they have of getting about, seeming to float on the breeze like the lightest of thistledown. As they fly, they hold their very long black-and-white-banded legs out at a graceful angle and bent backwards, so they have even more of a resemblance to a thistle sailing on its way.

---

*Shasta Meadows and the Cerceris colony: The "meadows" are two small, naturally clear, sandy areas just off Meadow Mountain Trail where you have the first glimpse of Mt. Shasta. Here, a rather extensive colony of Cerceris wasps dig their tunnels and store prey. The wasps are quite small, less than $1/4$ inch. Striped black and pale yellow, or white, they provision their nest burrows with weevils found on plants in the area (possibly taken on *Orthocarpus* species).

**Phantom crane flies—*Bittacomorpha* species: "The phantom cranefly soars slowly through the air with its legs extended. When it flies into shade, only the white leg bands are visible, and the insect seems to appear and disappear like a phantom." Also, they are an eastern species, not mentioned as being found in the west (Milne, Lorus and Margery. 1980. *The Audubon Society Field Guide to North American Insects and Spiders.* Knopf, New York. 989 p.)

But before long, they collide with each other and end up in a bundle of wings and legs among the grasses. They never seem to suffer any damage in these pile-ups, and soon disengage themselves and sail off. But they are extremely delicate, for even though I was careful, they always were injured when I caught them.

Not knowing how rare they are, I handled only the two and saved both of them for later identification. I think I should look for them especially along the edge of both lakes, for I'm sure they must be in other wet places around here. Most of the habitat seems the same, although the lakes have more water and are not as sheltered as this pond. Fascinating as they are, it will be impossible to study their life history by watching their activities— you'd practically have to wear hip boots to do that!

Perhaps I'll have some luck getting more pictures and can sketch them as they fly, so I can get someone to recognize them and tell me what they are and how they live. One always wonders when some uncommon insect like this is observed if perhaps it's a new species that no one knows anything about.

July 22, 1976

Three's Company

❀ ❀ ❀

This time just the three of us have come to the meadow—Charlotte, old Sal, and I. For at least three years, Charlotte and I have promised each other to come here and enjoy our meadow and walk the trail and do whatever we wanted without anyone else along to hurry or disturb us. Ma and other friends sometimes join us for hikes and picnics, but those are purely recreational outings, and Charlotte and I don't get any work done then.

We're sitting on the huge rock beside the big lake eating our lunch. The sun is bright and cheerful, but it has no warmth, and the September wind is cold, cold. That blue sky and the ear-ringing stillness makes any effort worthwhile—even getting up at 3:15 a.m., to be here at sunrise! Only last week, when I came alone, that sun was the sun of summer and the breeze sent the bees and butterflies about their summer business.

We have explored the north-facing hill above the edge of the lake and found many things I've missed in the years I've been coming here. Saw a lovely, waxy prince's pine in bloom; found the rocks covered with a little, creeping bramble of some kind. One had a long blossom, exactly like a raspberry flower, so I think it may be *Rubus lasiococcus*, the dwarf bramble.

Coming back to the trail, we walked diagonally across the meadow, and I walked right through a yellow jacket nest—trust me to find them! But surprisingly, none of us were stung. They evidently hadn't built up to the aggressive stage yet at this cold elevation. If that had happened on my hill at home, the little devils would have chased us clear to the house!

Now, as we climb Mt. Elijah, it's much warmer, and I hear the locusts clicking ahead of us as we wander along the rocky trail. At the junction of the two trails, we come around the north side of Elijah; the little flower garden is still in bloom. Always, that north slope fascinates me, for there the snow lingers into July, even August, and the plants have very little hot sun. Here the soil is always moist and cool. Here, the flaming paintbrush burns a full six weeks after its sisters have departed the rocky heights of Elijah at the top of the trail. The penstemon still have their blue flowers at the first coming of the snow, and the glacier lily ripens its seed in October with those of the aromatic pennyroyal.

Two years ago when I came here after the first snow, that high wall of white was under construction already. Somehow, the winds sweep the snows over the top of Elijah and lay them down in a solid barrier that may be twenty feet high by spring.

The low, weak suns of April and May hardly touch that escarpment of white. Only when the hot suns of late June and July swing around north of west do they really begin to melt that compacted mass of snow and ice. How the little plants can wait so long, when all their kind are blooming and setting seed all across the meadow and over the top of the ridge, I can't imagine. But they do, and are just as beautiful, really more so, for having waited so long.

We stay as long as possible, lying among the hard rocks and watching those white, white clouds sailing across that blue sky of September. Indeed "three is company." If only these moments of contentment and good companionship could last forever—but that is asking too much of a troubled world. Only in a long-forgotten lost paradise could all the days, of all the years, be like this.

September 20, 1976

August Lies Across the Meadow

❀ ❀ ❀

August lies hot and redolent across the big meadow today. "Loud the bumble bee makes haste, belated, thriftless, vagrant,"* in the purple heart of the asters and among the gold of helenium.

Summer has come to the high country, and the mid-day sun distills the essence of mint, lush grass, and resin from fir and hemlock into the still, hot air. The blue haze of autumn softens the outline of distant hills and the hum of bees is loud in the heat of early afternoon. Somewhere among the trees a grouse hen clucks a warning to her brood.

Where has spring gone? Only a week or two ago, the air was cool and soft with the scent of violet and trillium, and water rushed with a loud splashing down all the little canyons hidden away among the grasses of the upper meadow.

The wind sighs in the hemlocks, but I hear it moan instead among the piñon pines of the Colorado mesa country. I see the plateau in the dim haze of autumn in the high country, and if I lived here a thousand years I know these hills would never be the hills of home.

Now, as I look across the meadow sloping down to the upper lake, I see a legion of yellow helenium blossoms marching down the slope. But I shut my eyes and the sunflowers of home parade for endless miles to the shadows at the foot of Mesa Verde. I see again the Indian paintbrush burning bright among the grey sage. The Mariposa lily opens its white chalice to the brazen southwestern sun, and blue penstemon flashes beneath the rimrock like some azure gemstone of the ancient Aztecs.

The memories never die, and when hazy Autumn days lie across the waiting land and summer is ripening her harvests, then the longing for the hills of home is almost beyond enduring.

But we didn't spend the whole day dreaming of home; Sally and I came to measure the big lake, and we did. I used the tape—Sally used her nose!

Since that day in May of '76 when we took the first plant inventory of Rough and Ready, it seems we haven't done anything else when we come to our favorite wild places. Measuring the area, identifying the plants, making maps of where the rare species grow, etc., takes a lot of time, and we rarely

---

*October's Bright Blue Weather—Helen Hunt Jackson

come anymore just to hike and explore, or lie in the meadow. But The Nature Conservancy and the Forest Service both are interested in the work, so I feel it's worth my time and effort. It bothers me, though, that I haven't kept my notes up to date on our trips, and I have very few sketches for this year. But what a marvelous crash course on the plants and their families of the Siskiyous, for the real work begins after I get home with the dozens of flowers and leaves to be identified and mapped. It's a completely fascinating occupation, and I love it. And old Sal loves the exploring part of it. While I'm measuring, collecting, drawing the maps, she is cataloguing every mole, chipmunk, and mouse burrow in the area, and when we get home I think she's more exhausted than I am.

Now that the two lakes have been measured and mapped, only the big meadow and a few open spaces surrounding it need to be done. Then we can climb Lake Mountain or Elijah, or pick berries without feeling we should be doing something else.

When we left home this morning, it promised to be the hottest day of the year, and even here we had to sit in the shade of the hemlocks to eat lunch. Sal didn't mind at all; she waded in the lake most of the afternoon. The heat here is so different from that down in the valley, and I always hate going back home, for as soon as the shadows lengthen in the high places, a cool breeze springs up and the heat of the day is forgotten. But going down Low Divide we seem to run into a wall of hot air rising from the lowlands, and the lower we go the hotter it is, until by the time we reach home we're miserable and wish we had spent the night up in our lovely, cool mountain meadow.

August 16, 1977

Lake Mountain—South Peak

❀ ❀ ❀

We are sitting here just below the top of the south end of Lake Mountain, Sally and I. Far down on the valley floor I can see the road, the tawny fields of the Applegate Valley, and Low Divide where the little pond gleams in the sun. Off to the north, Walker and Old Blue and Sexton Mountain are faintly visible through the smoke and haze. Except for one high ridge between, I'm sure we could see our own little hill as well.

The air is warm, the bees are humming, and the summer sun is sweet among the fragrant hemlocks, but somehow, this last day of August has a feeling of sadness—the nostalgia of autumn, the knowing of winter's coming in a few short weeks. If asters bloom, can winter be far behind?

Coming through the meadow this morning early, it felt like the first frost will soon lie white and cold across these hills. And sitting here on the north side of the hill in the shade it is actually cold. Elderberries are beginning to take on that bluish tint they have when ripe, and all the flowers of summer are going to seed.

I remember years when the last week of August was mid-summer here with heleniums, Indian paintbrush, and buckwheat at the peak of their bloom in the meadow, and not too many weeks before, the last of the snow had melted. Every year since I discovered this high place, a snow bank has lingered on the north side of Lake Mountain. It stayed to mingle its icy whiteness with the first snows of the coming winter. But this year it has long since disappeared, and the ground is bare that for years never saw the sun of summer.

The little plants we came to see are here, and after four years of wondering what they are, now I know. Partridge foot—the little, high mountain meadow plants of the rose family that bloom in the meadows of the Hudsonian zone of the Cascades. And they bloomed all over the place this year; free of the snow as they haven't been for years, they took advantage of the sun and have a miniature forest of bloom stalks that covers the ground in reddish-brown patches. And after four years of hunting for the flowers and never seeing even a dried stalk—I missed the whole show! They've all gone to seed.

All around us the little chipmunks are running and chattering, busy with their harvest. They will have a good crop of manzanita berries and the firs are loaded with their huge cones. There really isn't too much to find right now; the berries aren't ripe and only the smaller seeds are dry enough for storage. But the little squirrels are dashing about, playing and sitting in the sun, not too serious about the work. And who can blame them if they play the happy summer days away for awhile yet?

Here at this end of Lake Mountain, the highest point has a huge pile of boulders elevated fifty feet or so above the rest of the peak. Right on the very top of the mountain, it looks as though an enormous dump truck had unloaded the largest rocks that could be found. Among the rocks are some fascinating plants whose leaves I remember, and some I've never seen before. Nothing is in bloom now, but it must be a flower garden in summer. Some of the most ancient, twisted trees I've seen in this area are growing here out of the rocks. Most are western hemlock, and their age can only be guessed. But from their vantage point I'm sure they saw the settling of the Applegate Valley, the departure of the Indians, and the building of roads into their mountain home.

As we came down across the lower meadow, the wind rustled the dry leaves of hellebore like a day in October. The sun lay golden and warm in the open spaces, bees hummed among the late asters and heleniums, and the sky was blue with flocks of white cloud. And I thought: summer is still with us; why think of cold and fog and snow to come? Remember "thirty days hath September"—and what of October's bright blue weather? So now the locusts clack their way along the trail and out across the meadow, the butterflies sail on the warm breeze, a blue grouse scolds from a fir, and today summer is weaving what will be tomorrow's sweet, poignant memories.

August 31, 1977

Lake Mountain—North Peak

❀ ❀ ❀

Again we sit on Lake Mountain, Sal and I, and look across to the valley four thousand feet below. But it's so smoky and hazy today we can barely see across to the far end of the Applegate Valley.

The September sun makes us think of summer, but the air is cool in the shade and has the feel of autumn. The soil is very dry, but everything is green and alive looking, and the little partridge foots are as bright looking as the day their snow bank melted. As I look at their forest of tiny bloom stalks, I'm already making plans to see their blossoms next year when they see the sun of spring for the first time. And I wonder how many years it will be again before they bloom as profusely as they've done this year.

Grayback stands warm in the sun while the ancient western hemlocks frame the picture of mountain peak and valley far below. I know them all now—the hills, the trees, the tiny plants growing in all the hidden places that nobody sees. They may not be the hills of home, but I've grown accustomed to them, and I know all their names and have seen them in all their moods. But again I close my eyes and see the September haze across the mesa land, I hear the golden aspens whispering among the firs of the San Juans, I know the sun lies hot and pungent over the sage of the Uncompahgre, and Mesa Verde shimmers in the heat of late summer. Yes, these hills of southern Oregon are now old, familiar friends because I know them so well, but always, across the horizon, like a double exposure on an old film, I see the hills, the trees, and the flowers of home—a picture that never seems to dull with the passing of the years.

We came today to climb the north peak, so after lunch Sal and I started across the hogback at the top and found it very hard going. Once before, I tried this on the west side, but the thick manzanita brush and rocky walls were too much. Here on the north-northeast exposure it is forested and more open, but still with those huge rocky piles and walls. Got about midway and left Sal and the knapsack at the foot of a particularly steep rock pile and started up alone. I think the old gal was really happy that she wasn't expected to climb that fortress!

The rocks are very loose and clean, with no moss or other growth on them at all. They look as though they had been dumped there yesterday. They are huge, so not inclined to move or shift around. The only danger here would be in slipping and wedging your foot in a crevice between boulders, or turning an ankle while jumping from one level to the other. But I've been doing this sort of thing since the days of climbing the rimrock and arroyos of home, so I never worry too much about the risks.

At the top of this outcrop I see that the north peak is yet some distance away, so I walk along a level place for awhile, then up over another rock pile, which I'm sure is the peak. But again I see a higher spot farther on. After several more ups and downs of this sort, at last here is the north peak—and surprise! Unbelievable! The remains of an old cabin lie at my feet. Rather, the remains of one of the early lookout towers of the Forest Service. I haven't my tape with me, but I guess it's about ten by ten feet. All that's left now are the window frames, a few boards, rusted hinges, and, a hundred feet down the hillside to the east, the wind has blown the little, peaked shingle roof. It's almost intact, with perfectly good shingles still attached.

Now I'm wondering: How in heaven's name did they get all this material up here? Not the way I just came! This confirms my suspicion that there is an old road or trail coming up the southwest side, from down along the edge of the big meadow some place. From the upper lake there appears to be a long gash, free of brush and trees, and just below the top of this ridge; I've thought for years it looked very like an old road. But I've never found where it starts up through the trees. It's probably overgrown down below, where the springs feed the big meadow, but I think it would be worth looking for, even if it is partially lost in the brush; it would be better than battling all those rock piles, where you need both hands to get anywhere at all.

Unfortunately, it was much too late in the day to do much exploring, and too, I wondered if old Sal would stay put, and I had visions of trying to get her down off that rock pile if she decided to follow. On the northeast side of the peak—which, incidentally, is also a huge rock pile, but made of smaller rocks, some almost gravel in comparison to the other piles—there appears to be a small damp place, almost like a spring, where a variety of plants are growing, some I'm sure I haven't seen before. One I did recognize—a lovely, long-stalked seed head with long white "hair"—western pasque flower. I never knew they grew here, only in the Hudsonian and Canadian zones of the high country. And a beautiful little fern grows profusely among the boulders. This looks like the same fern we saw on Rocky Top last month. What a place to explore, just after the snow melts and the sun warms those boulders.

I tried to take back four of the anemone seed heads and almost made it. Just before I reached Sal and the knapsack I slipped, threw my hand out to catch a branch—and the lovely white hair of my prize flew in all directions on the wind! Oh well, I'm sure it would have happened somewhere on the trail going down through the brush, anyhow. But they were so unusual, and how I would have loved to have them in a winter bouquet!

Now it's time to go, and Sal and I have come down off the high mountain and are sitting beside the little hidden pond, finishing the last of our lunch. The shadows are lengthening across the little pond. The lowering sun is still hot, but a mournful wind sighs in the hemlocks, and I think of the long months of winter here. We see this place in sun and pleasant weather, and the trees and meadows and hills are friendly and warm in summer's heat. It's easy to forget how harsh and cruel the mountain country can be when that bright sun has gone, frost rims the lakes, and snow is just over the wintry horizon.

September 10, 1977

The Red and Silver Helicopter

❀ ❀ ❀

Here we are at 8:45 a.m. resting on our "table rock" high in the meadow above the big lake, and already I'm thinking of lunch! The frog chorus swells loud from below, and all the snow has disappeared from the water's surface and retreated up the north side of Elijah. White patches can be seen between the trees, and that high rocky parapet below the summit is almost free of snow. Down below in the willow thicket, I see a few white islands where the sun has difficulty penetrating, but all the meadow is clear, with new green sprouts showing everywhere.

I almost changed my mind and turned back this morning on the way up. At home, the sky was clear, but when we got to Murphy I could see the mountains were covered with fog clouds. And the farther we came, the thicker they got. Finally, at the little pond, below Low Divide, I stopped as usual and let Sal out for a run, and that damn fog was as thick as the day in November when I found the little duck. But we were three-quarters of the way by that time, and I didn't want to go all the way back this late in the journey. So we started out again—and no more than six hundred feet up the road from the pond the mist began to thin, and by the time we rounded the first bend we came out into brilliant sunlight—seldom has that bright morning light been more welcome! Now, here in the meadow, the sky is a clear deep blue, but heavy fog hangs over the Illinois valley.

Made it to the top of Lake Mountain by 10:45 a.m. Old Sal is coming right along. She has a stiff hind leg, and it bothers her some, but I take it easy and rest often; and she seems eager to follow, and makes no complaint. Left her, the knapsack, and the lunch among the old hemlocks and climbed up to the top alone. Not too many years ago, she would have been right with me, rocks or no rocks. But now I won't ask her to do that, and she is content to take a nap while guarding the things I leave with her.

The snow still is five to six feet deep over the rocks, and hard climbing, but has mostly melted at the top. Nothing is blooming yet, but have found several big anemone flowers below the old lookout tower, although they are past their prime and look rather moth-eaten. They must bloom the minute the snow melts. This is *Anemone occidentalis* (western pasque flower), and a dweller of the high mountain peaks at timber line. But what is it doing here on Lake Mountain at a little under seven thousand feet? Another of the mysteries of the strange Siskiyous. This is the only place I've found them so far, but I haven't really explored that south peak, so there could be other colonies. Will have to try to see them just as they open—and I wonder who pollinates them so early in the season on this cold, wind-swept hilltop.

I sat down on the summit to finish my notes, and who should drop in for a visit but a little red and silver helicopter! I saw him coming a long way off, but didn't really pay much attention. Then he came closer and closer and began circling right overhead. I didn't dare wave as I thought he might mistake that for a distress signal. But as I watched, he set down about fifty feet away. It was a two-passenger job, and as I watched, one of the men jumped out carrying a large metal suitcase, came over to the highest point where I was sitting and said they were taking a gravity reading for the U.S. Geological Survey. I don't know who was more surprised. After all, you don't expect company at such an isolated spot. He mentioned they probably would land on Grayback sometime during the day, as they were taking readings on all the high peaks. I told him I thought I'd start saving my nickels and dimes and get myself one of those little whirly-birds, as I had to get here the hard way. As they sailed off I could just imagine taking off from my front field and ten minutes later sitting on Lake Mountain, or Rocky Top, or Grayback, and making a plant survey, writing up notes and making sketches—all before lunch! Sal was down below the rocky peak, so she, being deaf, never heard or saw the helicopter. But if she'd been with me she would have gone wild—never having seen one of those strange "hawks" up close before.

Whenever I sit here on this north peak, I marvel at the view. One has practically a 360-degree panorama—but you need a swivel neck to take it all in. Imagine the sweep of that sky when the storms come in from the coast. What an experience it must have been to sit up here in that little, rickety tower in a thunderstorm, or a late summer gale. Since the wind did blow the roof off down the mountainside, I hope it happened in winter when no one was up here.

Although there are few plants in bloom, the most interesting little new leaves are coming up. Some look familiar, but many I've never seen before. I thought that this dry, rocky southwest-facing hillside would have blooming flowers long before the plants in the meadow below budded. But the plants even on old Elijah are much more advanced. Of course, this peak is a little over six thousand four-hundred feet, and at times the wind is like ice—even on warm, sunny days.

4:00 p.m.—Now at the lower lake the frog chorus is undiminished, and if anyone were with us it would be impossible to talk without shouting to make yourself heard. The grasses and weeds are just coming up, and it's pleasant to sit among the new growth and listen to the orchestra; but in a few weeks the sedge and plants will be so tall even old Sal will be lost as she walks through them. We always seem to come to the lower lake last, then have so little time to stay. Last year, almost every time we came in the late afternoon we heard a robin singing, but today he seems to be absent, or silent. Now only the din of the frogs fills the air. Occasionally they stop all at once—and the sudden silence makes your ears ring. Then they start up, one at a time, until the whole thing builds up again. We could stay here all night to listen, but the sun is low, and with the usual reluctance we find the trail through the willows, back to the bus, and home.

June 19, 1978

Heather on Lake Mountain

❀ ❀ ❀

Here on the north peak of Lake Mountain, that huge snow bank has dwindled to a not-so-big hunk of dirty snow about four feet thick in the middle. And the tree I could walk over to on the surface of the snow and touch the top of in June towers fifteen to twenty feet above me today.

On the way up I saw so many new and unfamiliar plants all across that long, sloping, open space, but very few are yet in bloom. A low, very narrow-leaved Microseris with a large yellow flower intrigues me. It seems to be native to just this part of the mountain, and is very numerous for a Microseris.

Have come especially to find the little partridge foots in bloom. And at first I thought I'd be disappointed again, for all the plants under the hemlocks and around the top of the ridge just don't have bloom stalks. But I left Sal, the knapsack, and lunch, and explored down the north slope farther then I've gone before. This is an almost barren slope that looks to me like a glacial moraine, as it's covered with boulders, small rocks, and fine gravel. It must be almost solid rock close beneath the surface, for there are very few small trees or bushes. However, about one hundred fifty feet downhill the young hemlocks begin. And so orderly is their growth, they appear to have been planted in succession, from very tiny ones to a wall of young, vigorous trees higher than my head. As I walk among them to the edge of the belt of old trees, they are like a stairstep of evergreens, becoming taller as you go downhill. Almost without exception, these are the beautiful, grey-green mountain hemlock (*Tsuga mertensiana*), whose soft, feathery needles are like no other tree I've ever seen. The young trees especially, of about Christmas tree size, have a very soft, lacy appearance. The branches are exceptionally flexible and yielding to the touch, and unlike most evergreens, the needles are not prickly when handled. When examined, the twigs and small branches have groups of short, soft needles growing on all sides, like little clusters of stars. Once I saw these hemlocks after the first snowfall; those flexible, drooping branches bent down by the weight of the snow transformed the trees into a perfectly shaped conical spire of outstanding beauty. No other tree I know bears the weight of the heavy snows of the high country so gracefully. It seems strange to me too that the big old trees on both peaks are western hemlock (*T. heterophylla*), while *mertensiana* grows almost exclusively on the north and east slopes.

About halfway down this steep incline I call the "alpine slope," I found my little partridge foot in bloom. A small company of plants was growing out of a cleft on top of a large boulder, and almost every one had a flower stalk. The plants are low, no more than four to six inches tall, each with a beautiful little spike of cream-colored, star-like flowers. And on the downhill sheltered side of the rock, another group was in full bloom. So after four years of disappointment, at last I have seen little *Luetkea pectinata* flowers— and the wait was worthwhile! Each individual flower is very small ($^{1}/_{4}$") and actually white; but the large, rose-like centers with eighteen or twenty exerted stamens are a deep cream, and from a distance the whole stalk appears creamy yellow.

Exploring farther down the slope than I've ever been, I made another breathtaking discovery—mountain heather! A whole hillside of it growing between the small hemlocks. Slightly past its prime, the lovely, purple, urn-shaped flowers are still colorful against their tiny needle-like evergreen leaves. The plants are rather tall, twelve to fifteen inches, and as far as I could see through the young trees, they spread a bright purple carpet as though in expectation of some royal visitor. This is indeed a day of discovery, and well worth the long, hot climb through the brush.

At the top of this alpine slope, a kind of hogback runs down from the peak, and has a gentle incline for some distance to the north. Here the soil and plant life look very like those of Elijah, but there are some unfamiliar plants too, not yet in bloom. And on this barren slope where the snow has been gone for weeks, I found a number of glacier lilies just finishing their bloom—some still with their gold color tinting the fading blossoms. All up the meadow, through the trees above the hidden pond, and even on the north side of Elijah, these bright yellow erythroniums disappeared a month ago—so why are they just fading here on this dry, wind swept exposed place? These little micro-climate islands are the most fascinating part of this area, and I always experience a thrill whenever I find them.

As I make my way back just below the edge of the hogback, I see old Sal lying patiently near the knapsack where I'd told her to stay. She's just the color of the ground, and I'd never spot her if it weren't for that red harness. I'm always a little worried that she might try to follow me and get out on a rock ledge, or slip on a pile of boulders she can't negotiate anymore. In her younger days, there wasn't any place I'd climb that she couldn't go too, but now, with a heavy heart I often have to make her stay behind while I do a little more exploring—and she's not happy about it either.

On the way back, I stopped to rest beneath a gnarled, stunted, old hemlock, and looking out through its branches I can see a big clump of penstemon and scattered groups of bright red *Castilleja*, like the brilliant flames on Elijah. They're in full sun, while I'm in deep shade, and their luminescent red against that grey, rocky slope framed by the twisted branches of the old tree makes a picture of perfect composition for this hot summer day. Up the slope where the sun is warmest I hear a locust, so even here they fly and sing in spite of that ever-present cool breeze.

Sal is always glad to see me come back, and usually watches for me when I'm gone. But today I caught her asleep in the warm sun, where she had dug herself a hollow in the humus beneath the trees.

As we come back through the meadow in the hot afternoon sun, the flowers seem to be in their prime, the meadow is lush and green, the colors are at their brightest, the water still gurgles down the little hidden gullies, butterflies and bees sail about, and the birds still sing their sweet songs of April. And I tell myself I'll come again soon before the hot sun of summer scorches the delicate plants, before the seed pods form and the green grass of spring stands lifeless on the dry hillsides. But I know there will always be something at home to keep us working and busy in the heat of the low lands, while our cool meadow and the ancient hemlocks revel in the long days of summer that all too soon will turn into the dark days of coming winter.

July 28, 1978

End of the Trail

❀ ❀ ❀

Goodbye old Sal. No more will we walk the trail together. Not again in all the years to come will we be happy wanderers across the meadow. No longer will the little "Hidden Pond" slake your thirst nor cool your tired feet. Never again will I hear your cheerful bell and see you on the trail ahead of me as we trudge contentedly and wearily homeward in the late sun.

For on this bleak, rainy, November day I buried you where you lay at the edge of my field, in the lowlands beneath the little cypress tree. At last the old heart that had taken you to the peaks of Lake Mountain, to Rocky Top and across so many high ridges, failed. Do you know how you broke my heart when you left so suddenly? Do you know how empty and still and lonely those old familiar places will be without you?

It's been a long road of happy companionship and excitement since that June day in '73 when I first took you exploring with me up Knob Cone Ridge. It too was a drizzly, dark day with lowering clouds, but with a fresh wind and the smell of the sea in it. It had the feel of spring and life, and of happy discovery. How many uncounted trails we've walked in the years since! Chrome Ridge and the mad scramble after chipmunks. Briggs Valley where you waded in the beaver pond, and the field where you couldn't resist digging out mouse nests beneath the old apple trees. The little campground and the still pool you loved to play in. The sand bars along the river where you chased the waves until you were exhausted, and Charlotte and I were in hysterics over your antics. And the high country! Our beloved meadow…Mount Elijah…Lake Mountain…the warm somnambulance of "Gooseberry Hill"…Bigelow Lakes where you always sank up to your flanks in oozy mud—and came out looking like a tawny coyote with black stockings…

So many memories come crowding back—I was yours, and you were mine, and you never really accepted anyone else. I was the one you watched for when you had to be left behind. It was my word you waited to hear when we were loading the bus to go somewhere. It was me you turned to when it was time to go home and you were tired and hungry.

❀ 151 ❀

You were my constant companion when I collected maple pollen in the spring...when the call of wild geese, and flaming leaves, made me a restless gypsy in autumn...when we cut our winter's wood in all the little secret places only we knew.

Next year, how will I endure the silence and the memories when I walk the far hills and see every gopher hole you dug out, remember every log where we sat and shared our lunch? On that distant day in June, when I again go to our beloved high country, I'll see your haunting footprints in every melting snow bank. Down every dark trail and across all our happy meadows I'll hear your bell and see the red of your harness. But I dread most of all the day I stand again among the ancient hemlocks of Lake Mountain, where you waited so patiently for my return from the rocky alpine slope you were too stiff and old to explore with me.

Oh, I've seen you plodding along, slower and slower behind me on the long trail home. I've known you could no longer jump the logs nor climb the rocky ridges we used to explore in the early days. I knew we were going down the shadowy road home together for the last time. But the knowing didn't make it any easier today when I said my last goodbye—because, no matter how well prepared I may be, I've never been any good at those sad farewells.

I can only hope now that somewhere, in another time and place, when the alpine flowers beckon in some high meadow, I may see you again, young and lively, ears pricked, brown eyes shining, bouncing down that celestial trail to greet me, eager to be off exploring together as we did so many times in the past. Farewell, then, old friend, until the dawning of that glad day.

November 28, 1978

Goodbye, Lake Mountain

❀ ❀ ❀

We walked the old familiar trail today, Charlotte and I. Bluebells and glacier lilies were blooming at the edge of melting snow banks, and frogs sang loudly from the dark waters of the upper lake. But, for me, the sunlit trail, blue skies, and new-green meadow held no joy—for a tawny, bushy-tailed ghost ran before us all the way to old Elijah.

Around every bend I expected to see that red harness, to hear the pleasant sound of a tinkling bell. Across every snow bank I expected to see our frolicking companion bounding in happy abandon among her most favorite element of the high country—deep, white, cold snow.

We could see from the top of the meadow that the little hidden pond was still rimmed with ice and frozen snow. It will be many weeks yet before the alpine shooting stars tint the new grass with their rosy lavender blossoms. And from the top of the trail where the old dead tree still stands, we saw the snow, white and deep, still lying at the upper edge of the big lake. The little

MEADOW MT. TRAIL   JULY 25 '73

field above the lake where that tiniest of creeping plants (Tinker's penny) grows is brown and dead looking, even though the bright spring sun warms it at mid-morning.

Shasta Meadows are barren and lacking in blossoms yet, but soon they will be a riot of color and life. I walked down to the Cerceris colony, and a few of the early wasps were flitting about or resting in the sun. The big tree looked inviting, where we sheltered our equipment and rested from the hot sun while photographing the digging wasps, but I didn't linger—even the little black-and-yellow hunters held no interest for me today.

Elijah is eternal. The same blue skies from horizon to horizon, the warm rocks, the everlasting wind, the quiet peace which is always a part of the place. I walked down the trail a little and found the first bright ember of Indian paintbrush that will, in a few weeks, be a conflagration among the grey rocks all across the top of this lonely ridge. Stopped to see whether the rare white bleeding heart was in bloom—it was. Sat for a brief time beside my favorite dwarf cedar, and for a little while I felt better.

Here I felt at peace among friends of happier days, the plants I've come to know and love, which are as familiar as those of my own garden; the little rare flowers I've catalogued and numbered, whose habitat I've measured and mapped and plotted over the years. Here where the parnassian butterflies sail on summer days, where the locusts flitter the hot autumn days away. This clean, sun-drenched, wind-swept spot will always work its magic no matter how hurt and lonely one may be.

But soon I began listening for that old familiar bell and expecting to see those bright eyes asking to go back to the cool wetness of the little hidden pond—for rocky, hot, shadeless Mount Elijah was not my old friend's favorite spot, unless the snow lay thick and cool on the north side of the trail.

Coming back, I walked down through the meadow to our favorite little corner where the late asters grow and the little bitter cherries make a pool of lacy shade, and where the chipmunks were so numerous at the bend in the trail. From there I looked up to that long sloping cleared place on the flank of Lake Mountain; that old, overgrown road we worked so hard to find; that intriguing open space that led to the huge hemlocks at the peak; and on beyond to the ruins of the little lookout tower and the alpine slope where the mountain heather grows.

Goodbye, Lake Mountain. I won't be coming back. Your lovely pasque flowers can bloom in solitude, undisturbed by my exploring footsteps. Your tiny partridge foot and heather can bloom without fear of my trampling. The last snow bank can melt in peace throughout the long, hot summer. Your ancient hemlocks can stand in lonely majesty as they have these many decades. And when autumn comes to the high peaks, the migrating hawk will look in vain for the lone observer and her hawk-chasing friend who made your rocky ridge ring with her wild and joyous barking.

June 11, 1979

Bigelow Lakes Revisited

❀ ❀ ❀

In the summer of 1993, I went back to the lakes area to evaluate the changes in plant species and communities since those early surveys of 1973 through 1978. Bigelow Lakes was declared a Botanical Area as part of the 1989 Forest Plan for the Siskiyou National Forest; I'm told the information I provided the Forest Service about the area played an important part in their decision. The lakes, the meadows, and Mount Elijah are much the same as when I first saw them. A severe drought of seven years has taken its toll of the old hemlocks and Shasta firs, especially around the large lake. Old growth was most severely affected, but numerous, vigorous young trees are springing up among them. While there has been loss among the smaller plant species, surprisingly many have increased and produced new colonies where there were none before—notably, *Gentiana*, *Kalmia*, *Iliamna*, and *Sidalcea* (the last two, members of the hollyhock family).

Again, I stood on Mount Elijah and looked across those endless blue ridges of the Siskiyous and thought, "Indeed, Elijah is eternal."

The little hidden pond has gone back to wetland mostly, with very little open water and few of the original species of insects.

"Shasta Meadows" still has its colony of Cerceris wasps, but not in the numbers I knew in the '70s.

Many of the slopes across the valleys to the west and north are now clearcut, where there used to be dense, old, mysterious forests. The saddest part of all is the departure of the birds—especially the band-tailed pigeons, for their soft cooing is heard no more among the dense groves of Shasta red firs. We are gradually drifting into a "Silent Spring," and many bird songs are gone from these meadows and forests of the Siskiyous.

But for now, the locusts flutter on the dusty trail, the butterflies still sail among the late flowers of summer, and the wind blows cool in the meadow that holds so many memories. And the sound of a distant bark echoes back from the rocky heights of Mount Elijah.

—1993

Epilogue

Journey into Memory

Here is the story of "Journey into Memory" just as it came off the typewriter in the wilderness of the San Juan Mountains of Colorado in the summer of 1994.

Sometimes it was composed by flashlight, other times in the dim light of afternoon with a thunderstorm raging outside, and occasionally under the shade of a tree in the heat of summer. The last entries were put together as the autumn winds blew golden aspen leaves across high mountain meadows, and snow clouds gathered on the northern horizon.

Little editing has been done; the spelling is outrageous, and composition not all it should be. But it is the record of a journey dreamed of for more than forty years. May it afford my readers as much enjoyment as I've had in composing it. *

October 20, 1994

Times Leaves Its Mark

Just for old times' sake I drove into Thompson, Utah, just off the freeway. Not much there anymore—really there never was, but the passenger trains were running in the 1930s and '40s and some stopped to let passengers off to take the motor stage (bus) to Cortez, Colorado. A few times I didn't drive my car when going home from Hill Field (Air Force Base) during the war, and we always got into Thompson about four in the morning. Of course the only restaurant in the place wasn't open and the motor stage didn't leave till 5:30 or so. I remember standing on that depot platform under the single night light, watching the desert dawn come up over those barren hills with the rosy-pink Book Cliffs in the distance. Now, the rail line still runs through, and an occasional freight rumbles by. But the old yellow depot with its clicking telegraph and its green-shaded lights is gone, and a crummy coop-like shed serves the dispatcher—if there is one.

May 17-18

Mourning Dove Cove

Beautiful morning, the kind I call "alpine mornings"—clear blue sky, cold air, warm sun, and new green plants covering the slopes of glacial moraines.

As soon as the road turned south, it headed right for Lone Cone, the one solitary, snow-covered peak anchoring the north end of the San Juans.

---

*Editors' note: Mary's forty-three page "Journey into Memory" was excerpted to create this epilogue—to give the reader a sense of why Mary refers to her Colorado "hills of home" so often in the *Spirit of the Siskiyous.*

Finally, in late afternoon I arrived at the little spot in the forest where we used to picnic so long ago. It looks the same as it did in earlier years, but I remembered the trees being larger. It hasn't been logged, as there are no large stumps, but memory plays tricks—especially after fifty years!

A little dammed-up stream has created a pleasant small pond and marsh with a few islands of cattails. When I arrived, I heard a mud hen carrying on a conversation in the tulles. Later she came out for her supper, but I never saw more than just the one. The mourning doves still call, as I remembered from so long ago.

May 20

Taylor Mesa

A day or two after I began camping at my favorite spot (Mourning Dove Cove), an old fellow and his little dog stopped by to chat. He has been around Dolores since the '40s, and we soon discovered we have many acquaintances in common. So we've spent several afternoons talking about old timers, and events that have happened since I left in '45.

I left Mourning Dove Cove yesterday and started to drive up to Lizard Head Pass. But one of those mountain thunderstorms was in the making, so I decided to turn off onto a Forest Service road to Taylor Mesa and find a camping spot. I'm glad I did. I found the most beautiful alpine area. It appears to be glacial moraine and boulder fields bordered uphill by aspen and Engelmann spruce forest. The snow is still in huge drifts beneath the trees, and little rivulets are running through the meadows and over the rocks; the early flowers are blooming—bluebells, *Thlaspi*, marsh marigold, and a low buttercup I haven't seen before—and this is just the beginning.

May 31

Narrow Gauge Railroad

The eternal wind blows across the Uncompahgre Plateau as it has for eons. The plateau is an uplifted, rolling, sloping mesa much older than the rugged mountains surrounding it. It supports a variety of plant communities: Engelmann and blue spruce in the draws; quaking aspen and shrubs on the moist sites; and Gambel's oak, sage, and bunch grass across the rolling hills. The sage is the low form of *tridentata*, growing only about eighteen inches tall with much green verdure in between. Here among the low grasses, the wildflowers of the mesa lands display their colors of every hue. Blue of *Iris missouriensis*, pink of *Erigeron*, deep orange of balsam root, and the most brilliant blue-purple larkspur I've ever seen.

This is cattle country—thousands of acres of range land. The animals were brought to the high mountain meadows, as they are now, to fatten on the lush grasses for the summer, then about late September and October they were driven to the nearest rail head and shipped to market.

At the time I lived in Dolores in the 1920s and '30s, the animals, mostly sheep, were brought down from the railhead at Ridgeway on the narrow-gauge railway to Durango. It was quite an event to see those hundreds of bawling flocks going through on that little narrow-gauge line that carried mostly ore from the mines at Ophir and Rico. This was in the golden age of steam, and it was an unforgettable sight to see those little trains going through the high mountain passes—two engines in front, one helper behind—and to hear that mournful whistle echoing through those deep canyons.

Passenger and mail trains ran twice a day. In winter, a little potbellied stove at one end of the coaches provided heat. Everyone near the stove roasted; everyone at the other end froze!

In summer, the windows were all open, and the cinders that collected in your hair, clothes, seats, and luggage made traveling by train only slightly better than going by motor stage over dusty mountain roads. But it was an adventure I wouldn't have missed for all the world has to offer—and I'd gladly do it again if it were possible.

Now the mines are closed, the cattle are brought to the high country by truck, and the tourists have taken over the land.

June 7

Ammophila *of Boggy Draw*

In this tiny plant community on the edge of a small wetland called Boggy Draw I found a digger wasp, *Ammophila azteca,* busily making a tunnel in the loose, sandy mound a cactus is growing on. She was coming out every few seconds with a load of dirt, and flying a little way off and scattering it in the wind. No telltale pile of sand at *her* doorway!

It's been years since I've spent an afternoon with the digger wasps, and I'd love to see what this one brings in as prey. But—the bluebells are blooming beneath the melting snow banks, and who knows what else may be sending out new colorful blossoms in the high mountain meadows?

June 9

Four Corners Area

The hot desert wind blows across this arid land, and in the distance Shiprock shimmers in the heat of noon. For forty-five years I've dreamed of seeing that ship of the inland desert, purple sails unfurled to the restless wind. Sacred mountain of the Navahos, Shiprock can be seen for miles in this flat, desert country broken only by dry arroyos and low rimrock mesas with Mesa Verde and Sleeping Ute Mountain to the north.

Had just crossed the San Juan River, so found a road leading to the river bank and ate there. But the bank had been trashed to the point it wasn't even pleasant to look at it.

So much for the lonely, empty desert I used to know. Bottles, cans, paper, and old machinery at every turnout. I want to flee to the wild high country. But old Shiprock beckoning in the distance makes me want to stay at least for the night, just to see those brilliant colors and purple shadows creep across that ancient land of the Navahos I once knew so well.

Shiprock recalls the wildest, most exciting ride I ever had down that long, lonely road to Gallup—at midnight too!

A very good friend of mine was secretly leaving her husband to meet her lover in Gallup, and she asked me to go along so she'd have someone to talk to—and a shoulder to cry on, while her father and brother drove. In those days, the road to Gallup was no paved highway.

We left just before sunset on a stormy evening. Just as we got to the Mesa Verde cliffs, the sun came out for a brief time and painted those rimrocks the deepest vermillion this desert country can produce. Then the storm came. And truly, as the Bible states, "the lightning will be seen from the east even unto the west." And the rain came down like a waterfall. There were adobe mud flats and dips full of water. The car was a big, wooden-spoked, high-wheeled Buick, built like a tank, and went through the whole muddy mess without even spinning its wheels! But the lightning—from horizon to horizon incessantly. I believe if our lights had gone out we still could have found the road to Gallup without them. Every flash showed that straight road running like a shining ribbon over each little hill to the horizon. And old Shiprock loomed off in that sea of rain like a four-masted schooner riding a stormy sea.

How romantic—and bold! If that little, gossipy town had ever known what happened (they never knew the truth), the paper would have run a special edition! *And* if my mother had known, I'd have been under house arrest for a month!

But now the excitement and romance are gone. The old friends have passed on, and even old Shiprock, now that I know its origins, is just a pile of volcanic rocks rather than a full-masted schooner sailing an endless sea of sage and cactus.

I stayed up past eleven to enjoy the warm desert air, and hoping that something blooming might perfume the night breezes. But it seems awfully dry, even for this country, and the plants have either bloomed earlier, or decided not to flower at all this year. But the lights of a little town about five miles away came on at dusk, and I remembered how comforting it was on those long desert roads to see signs of civilization and know that you could pull up on one of those quiet streets and sleep for an hour or so, and feel perfectly safe in doing so. The Texaco star was billed as "the star that shines all night"—and it did even in those little settlements. What a relief at two o'clock in the morning, with gas running low, to see that bright star at the edge of town.

Now the star is dark, and the little towns aren't safe anymore; and those long, enchanting desert roads leading off to the horizon and the unknown are just ribbons of asphalt to get you from one place to another.

June 16

Ophir, the Old Mining Town

At Rico, just down the road from Ophir, I got to talking with the postmistress (who was born there) about the old days, and she was lamenting the changes the tourist influence has had on these small towns. She agreed that some changes were good—the better roads in winter, dependable power, more money for improvements. But she was wondering whether the price might be too high. The neighborly spirit is gone; now everyone is striving to beat friends and neighbors to the tourist dollar. Even families have been alienated, especially in rival businesses.

But the mountains are eternal. The snows still melt off the rugged peaks in clear, rushing streams, and the flowers still bloom up those steep slopes to timberline as they did so long ago when I first saw them from that little narrow-gauge train laboring up these steep passes.

June 19

Lizard Head Pass

Saw my first Colorado columbine last evening. After supper, I took a little walk up the hill from the camp, and there on the upper slopes of that long, tree-lined meadow were groups and colonies of these blue-and-white beauties! It is as big a thrill to find them as it is to walk up on a company of California lady slippers in the Siskiyous!

July 1

At the Foot of Hermosa Peak, 11,000 feet

It seems so strange to be sitting here in this lush green meadow and know that only a hundred miles or so away a devastating fire is raging through Glen Canyon, just east of Grand Junction. And sad beyond expression to hear that lives have been lost. How ironic that nine of our own Oregon people were among the casualties. Oregon, which never misses a season without a vicious fire, which came through the 96,000-acre Silver Complex fire with more than a thousand people on the fire-lines—without a serious injury or loss. Now we lose our firefighters in Colorado, a state renowned for its lush, cool climate where summer rains keep the meadows and mountains green until the first frost of autumn. For three days the borate bombers have been going over my camp, and one day there was smoke in the valleys. I feel like I'm in Oregon!

July 7

Fire on the Mesa

Deja vu—I've seen this part before. The reports of the fires I'm listening to on radio Durango could be from Evans Creek, Jones Creek, Rogue River, Walker Mountain, or almost any place in southern Oregon in the month of July. But I'm in cool Colorado where the pastures and mountain meadows stay green till frost, where mountain thunderstorms pour rain onto mesa land and mountain meadow alike, where the month without moisture is a disaster. But now it's been almost two months since our last good thunderstorm on the twenty-fifth of May.

From my camp at Mourning Dove Cove I can smell the smoke and see the brown haze on the horizon; the borate bombers are going over, and over the radio comes the order to evacuate Wildcat Canyon, just west of Durango.

I have very early memories of Wildcat Canyon. Once a year, the Elks Lodge had a celebration and reunion in Durango, and my dad always went. So my mother and I went along, as it was a two-day trip. And we went through Wildcat Canyon after dark. Row upon row of coke ovens in the bottom of the canyon cast a glow from their fires that could be seen for miles across the flat mesa land. It was always a thrill to come closer and closer to that red blaze—like approaching the portals of Hades! And I could see the silhouettes of the men working in the open doors of the ovens. Now Wildcat Canyon is ablaze in the night again, but with a terrible difference. In those days, you couldn't have set it afire with a blow torch, but year by year the fuel has built up, the storms have gone elsewhere, water has been diverted from small creeks, and one day a careless spark sets the once-wild canyon aglow again.

July 16

Durango Duck Race and Memories of Steam Trains

Came back to Alta Lakes, and as usual in the morning I listen to the news and weather on Durango's KIUP—almost as good as KAJO in Grants Pass. Well, today is the day of their famous duck race, so of course I had to listen. I was worrying about the poor ducks racing in this hot weather, and hoped the Humane Society was there to check on the welfare of the birds. But it turned out that a thousand plastic ducks are put into the river, and each is numbered and paid for by a sponsor. The finish line is a couple miles down-river, and whichever duck floats down to the finish line first wins its sponsor a thousand dollars. The little event lasted about an hour and a half and was quite exciting, as some of the ducks got hung up on rocks or caught in whirlpools and had to be rescued. It so happened that as the ducks went under the railroad bridge, the little train to Silverton came by and sounded its whistle. The well-remembered lonely sound echoing through the canyon brought back lots of memories, and I shed a few tears for the bygone days.

I always loved riding the old trains, including the "Galloping Goose," a gasoline-powered car-truck contrivance that eventually replaced the coal-burning steam engines. The Goose consisted of a bus body headed by a motorcar. The motorcar bodies were lengthened and mounted on railroad wheel-trucks. This lurching creation was worthy of Rube Goldberg.

I rode the Galloping Goose many times when working up the river in the potato fields, or helping with haying or chores on those isolated farms. The Goose went up early in the morning and came back in late afternoon; but I usually stayed until Friday, then met the Goose going into town about five.

There was no need to hurry to be along the tracks to flag it down, as I could hear it coming a good mile off.

Only once did we take a long trip on the Goose. When we came back to Dolores in June of 1936, my mother and I discovered that the little steam train from Ridgeway to Dolores had been retired, and the only way to get to our destination was to take this strange, noisy contraption called the "Goose."

But the 162-mile journey was a pleasant one and certainly one I'll never forget. There were no derailments, no accidents, not even a stray sheep in the middle of the right of way! We left Ridgeway in late afternoon, arriving at Lizard Head just before dark. There it was—this huge rock, with snow-covered skirts—the long, sloping green meadows sprinkled with their Persian carpets of flowers, with the dark, mysterious spruce forest above them.

Then the long downgrade to the Dolores River Valley. Every few miles we stopped at a lonely farmhouse to unload or take on freight. The cheery lamplight streaming out the open doorway, neighborly greetings, a little gossipy talk exchanged—all created an atmosphere of camaraderie that the modern technology and sleek efficiency of Amtrak will never duplicate.

July 30

Last Dollar Road

This morning started out bright and sunny with a few clouds over the mountains to the south. But within an hour the mountains had generated several thunderstorms that converged on the peak behind where I'm camping. Yesterday I drove up the Last Dollar road out of Telluride that eventually ends near Ridgeway on the eastside. As soon as the road tops this last ridge it drops down into the spruce forest. The spruce is lovely, dark, and mysterious, but uninteresting this time of year as everything has finished blooming and is going to seed. So I turned back and found a spot at the edge of the aspen groves with a westward view of Lizard Head, Sunshine Mountain, and Wilson Mesa—a breathtaking panoramic view of these peaks and the thirteen-thousand-foot mountains to the south.

Now there is some rain, not much thunder, and wind, and yesterday I'll swear those aspens didn't have a yellow leaf among them. But now, after the wind, the road is dotted with pale yellow leaves, and more are drifting down.

Right now it is not summer, nor is it winter, but rather that time of waiting between the seasons that could be prolonged into the middle of October's bright blue weather.

August 25

The Last of Summer's Flowers

As usual the sunflower tribe is the star of these fading summer days. From the higher elevations to the mesa lands, Nuttall's sunflower brightens the fields and roadsides. With its bright, clear yellow blossoms with a golden center, this species seems unparticular about habitat. Growing from the edge of the spruce forest at over ten thousand feet, down the river canyons and pasture lands to the sagebrush and piñon mesas, they put on the last act of summer's floral display.

September 1

Shandoka, Mountain Thunderstorm

The storm clouds materialize from nowhere and the rain pours down. A half-hour later the sun is out, but before I can get my boots on there's a crack and a flash of lightning and another storm races down from the high peaks.

Eventually the clouds will clear and the sunny days will come back for a brief time, and the quakies will mint their gold coins and scatter them on the roads and the forest floor. And the mountains will have their snowy blankets so I can get a picture of them, just as I remember these peaks from long ago. Then I'll be content (maybe) to head home to Oregon.

September 14

Halcyon Days of Gold

To walk among the quakies these autumn days is to be transported into a world of scintillating golden light, for aspen leaves are never still from that time in spring when they're the size of a coney's ear to the day when they lie in yellow drifts beneath the naked trees.

At last the aspens have conceded that summer is gone, and they are frantically turning their green to gold. The only trees in the Siskiyous that could equal that golden light would be a grove of bigleaf maples. Here at the campground I can get nothing done but wander through the aspen forest, explore the little draws, and watch ducks on the small pond.

September 25

The Old Cemetery

I visited the old cemetery on Summit Ridge today. Once this ridge above town was a lonely, windswept mesa; the silence broken only by an occasional passing farm truck and, morning and evening, the little steam train from Durango sounding its lonely whistle through Lost Canyon a quarter-mile away. Then, the fence around this little acre kept out the few stray cows or sheep that wandered by. Now, the fence keeps at bay the fancy houses and sporty cars that dot the mesa all the way to Mancos ten miles away.

Today is a typical fall day—cloudy skies, gusty wind blowing yellow poplar and willow leaves across the grassy plots of this quiet place.

All cemeteries have much the same stories to tell, but this one is different to me, for I knew the people who rest here. There was the unmarried neighbor girl who lived her entire life in this small town running the family store because she couldn't (or wouldn't) break away from a domineering father. And the dear old crippled widow who always grew a huge garden so she could share it with those of us who didn't have one. And the town ne'er-do-well who straightened up, married, and lived a commendable life to the end. Here also are the people I worked for up the river when I rode the Galloping Goose. Hardworking, honest—they had very few luxuries, and not many of the "necessities." But they raised their families, made their farms pay, and weathered the Great Depression. Many, I've heard, later sold their places and moved into town to enjoy their old age in comparative ease. Bless their hearts; they richly deserved their good fortunes.

Among others, my first-grade teacher who fostered the curiosity that made learning such a pursuit all my life. But the most poignant of all is the little headstone of the seven-year-old brother of my best friend, who drowned in the Dolores River one summer day. She was the friend I accompanied on that wild ride to Gallup that stormy night.

The train no longer disturbs the silence, and the sagebrush is mostly gone, replaced by lawns and exotic shrubs. But it still is a peaceful spot, with a view of old Sleeping Ute and Mesa Verde to the south, and the piñon- and sage-covered rim of Lost Canyon on the east, with snow-covered peaks beyond. A fitting place to end the final chapter of one's existence.

October 7